EDUCATING
the MORE ABLE
STUDENT

EDUCATING
the MORE ABLE
STUDENT

What works and why

MARTIN STEPHEN & IAN WARWICK

Los Angeles | London | New Delhi
Singapore | Washington DC

Los Angeles | London | New Delhi
Singapore | Washington DC

SAGE Publications Ltd
1 Oliver's Yard
55 City Road
London EC1Y 1SP

SAGE Publications Inc.
2455 Teller Road
Thousand Oaks, California 91320

SAGE Publications India Pvt Ltd
B 1/I 1 Mohan Cooperative Industrial Area
Mathura Road
New Delhi 110 044

SAGE Publications Asia-Pacific Pte Ltd
3 Church Street
#10-04 Samsung Hub
Singapore 049483

Editor: Marianne Lagrange
Assistant editor: Rachael Plant
Production editor: Nicola Marshall
Project manager: Jeanette Graham
Copyeditor: Sharon Cawood
Proofreader: Isabel Kirkwood
Indexer: Anne Solomito
Marketing executive: Dilhara Attygalle
Cover designer: Wendy Scott
Typeset by: C&M Digitals (P) Ltd, Chennai, India
Printed and bound by CPI Group (UK) Ltd,
Croydon, CR0 4YY

Library of Congress Control Number: 2014948708

British Library Cataloguing in Publication data

A catalogue record for this book is available from
the British Library

ISBN 978-1-4739-0794-2
ISBN 978-1-4739-0795-9 (pbk)

At SAGE we take sustainability seriously. Most of our products are printed in the UK using FSC papers and boards.
When we print overseas we ensure sustainable papers are used as measured by the Egmont grading system.
We undertake an annual audit to monitor our sustainability.

'We can (and do) argue endlessly about types of school for and methods of teaching the most able. The fact is that a single teacher stuck in the bush teaching a class of 50 under a tree with the nearest computer a hundred miles away can make a significant difference to the educational development of an able child, if the will is there.

If the will is there. In too many schools, it is not. Too many people simply do not care enough about educating our most able children, to the lasting detriment of those children and the society of which they are a member.'

(from Chapter 18 of this book)

Praise for This Book

Well-travelled, and often polemical, the authors have achieved a triumph of collaboration. The strength of this book is in their shared and uncompromising view that the most able are being ignored in the UK. They are right and they must be heard.

The well-read, left-wing reformer and the free-thinking establishment heavyweight have done their homework. Instead of getting lost in the debate about identifying the most able, they have pursued a practical path and toured the world to find out what more can, and should, be done. Instead of concluding that the solutions are complex, they have concluded that the solutions are many.

This results in a refreshing perspective and it might just be enough to stir all of us in schools to wake up, get up off our seats and do something for a change.

Professor Ralph Tabberer CB, Former Director-General of Schools in the UK

Policy makers and education leaders from around the world are beginning to realize the economic and cultural value of intellectual and creative human capital. Ian Warwick and Martin Stephen have provided a highly informative macro-view of many countries' approaches to developing giftedness and talents in young people. This book provides a superbly organized and resourceful assessment of gifted program practices and services that will save interested persons the ten thousand hours necessary to gain this kind of global perspective.

Joseph S. Renzulli, Director, The National Research Center on the Gifted and Talented, USA

A once in a generation nugget of truth that we can and must do so much more for our most able, superbly written by two contrasting writers both with unchallengeable credibility in the world of education. This skilfully-crafted book forces us to look beyond our shores only to find ourselves lacking when it comes to schooling our best and brightest. It is a provocative challenge for all educators to raise the bar. A rare blend of much needed intelligent debate with a completely practical approach for teachers to use in class. Quite simply a must read, by teachers and for teachers; a winning formula.

Graham Watts, Global Director of Education and Training, The Hawn Foundation UK; Director, Tomorrow's Learning; Affiliate Director, Institute for the Habits of Mind

Martin Stephen and Ian Warwick have produced a timely reminder of the importance of programmes that enable highly able students to achieve their full potential. By collecting a wealth of global case studies, they deliver a wake-up call to British politicians to ensure that effective provision for the highly able is seen as an issue of equity rather than elitism.

Sir Peter Lampl, Chairman of the Sutton Trust and the Education Endowment Foundation

This practical book fulfils its subtitle of 'what works and why'. The writers argue that too much (often sterile) debate has taken place about definition, identification, and genetics versus environment; whereas studies of good school/classroom practice have not been given enough attention...

The exciting message that comes through the text is the scattered but collective power of the often small but significant educational 'bonfires' that light up best practice worldwide... I commend this book to all parents, teachers, advisers and administrators, and I challenge them to audit their values and practice with regard to education.

Belle Wallace, Editor of Gifted Education International *journal and Director of TASC International*

Contents

Authors' Foreword

Charles Handy set about looking at change, wondering about how, when and why we do what we do. Inevitably it is the result of thousands of small alterations of behaviour, perception and attitudes over many years. He concluded that 'change comes from small initiatives which work, initiatives which become the fashion. We cannot wait for great visions from great people, for they are in short supply at the end of history. It is up to us to light our own small fires in the darkness.' (Handy 1994: 274) This book has attempted to locate some of those small fires which illuminate the teaching of the more able, in order to explore them and lay bare any kernel of truth that they may contain. It is likely that really interesting practice happens quite sporadically and without rational explanation. Our experience has shown that it is no more likely to occur in 'outstanding' schools than in schools facing highly challenging circumstances. It is usually sparked by teachers ducking beneath the radar of contradictory regulations and theories and focusing on meeting the complex needs of their own students.

We do not claim to have written a scientific, worldwide study. This book has no pretensions to being a truly global survey that sums up all there is to know. Rather, it is the result of two highly experienced and pragmatic educators exploring the small fires that colleagues have revealed to them over many years. We, the authors, have quite a unique experience, hopefully made more valuable because in coming at the issue of educating our most able students from different ends of the educational spectrum their shared destination is all the more interesting.

The authors come at this text from two very different starting positions. Martin Stephen has 40 years' experience both teaching at and being the headmaster of, for 27 years, three of the academically most successful independent schools in the UK. Ian Warwick taught in inner city comprehensives for 20 years before setting up London Gifted & Talented (LG&T) 10 years ago, working directly with more than 3000 schools across the world since 2003 (LG&T was a part of the groundbreaking London Challenge that transformed education across the city). This is the first time that there has been a joint publication by authors whose real world experience spans the 'great divide' between the private and the maintained sector in UK education, and the result is a work whose relevance is hopefully of interest to all schools.

This book attempts, in W.B. Yeats's phrase, to 'cast a cold eye' across some of the wishful thinking and comfortable assumptions, perhaps even gullible acceptances, casual myths and misleading stereotyping that have led educators away from exploring the process of teaching and learning in all of its real world complexity. We know from many decades of experience that teaching is messy and hard, as well as rewarding and exciting. The challenge of wrestling with obstacles and problems can be stimulating, but it can also be exhausting and confusing both for students and their teachers. The reality is that the everyday conditions of the classroom, where individual factors cannot be isolated and studied in tranquillity, where teachers are required in a moment to draw on their intuitions and experience to deal with the complex predicament they are facing and where jarring reality is guaranteed to interfere with our best laid plans, are hard and unforgiving.

Teachers need and deserve better support than they currently receive. They need fewer simplistic solutions cooked up in isolation, distorted by ideology, masquerading as silver bullets. Teaching is a complex distillation of skills, understanding, intelligence and hunches and for far too long teachers have been deskilled and undermined.

Our most able students have also been neglected. As a result the achievement agenda has become warped by affluence. If the barriers to students from disadvantaged backgrounds aren't addressed effectively then low aspirations will mean that they will slip quietly beneath the waves unnoticed. Educational progress will then never be a question of intellectual merit, but rather one of access to the most advantageous opportunities.

This raises the significant issue of why the case of the more able student has been so neglected. Why aren't the needs of these students seen as on a par with others? More able education has many unfortunate associations for colleagues in terms of elitism, giving more to those that already have, the chosen ones and the lack of focus on commitment. It also hasn't appeared to address itself to the big 'so what?' and 'why bother?' questions. How does it justify its own existence? How do we persuade our colleagues that it matters? How do we demonstrate that it has something to offer?

It is critical to start with a clear focus on equal opportunities and a commitment to meeting the needs of all students. A simple audit of current practice and provision gives schools a flying start and reminds colleagues what talent is already in the school and how they are already helping and supporting its development. It reminds colleagues why they became teachers and it reinforces their perception of learner talents (all too often easily forgotten). In many schools reaching the basic matriculation requirement is the most 'serious' issue, as this can affect outcomes from inspection or regulatory bodies, relationship with local or national funding agencies and public standing and reputation. It is interesting to note that in the course of the research for this book it became clear that this exact problem was shared by schools in the UK and schools in the USA; different cultures, differently named basic matriculation requirement – and exactly the same old problem. What is even more interesting are the different approaches countries around the world have instigated to address some of these vital questions. Hoping to address and explore all of the above issues, we started our journey with one, simple overriding question: what works well and why?

Acknowledgements

Among the many people consulted in the course of the research for this book, the authors are particularly grateful to Jeanne Allen, Sir Michael Barber, Pip Bennett, John Bray, Anne Cannizzaro, Pui-Tin Chan, Mrs Lim Lai Cheng, Laura O'Connor, Professor Peter Csermely, Tim Dracup, Quinn Duffy, The Finnish Ambassador to the UK, Professor Joan Freeman, Ms Csilla Fuszek, Maggie Gibson, Professor Gopiathan, Dr Janos Gyori, Maren Halvorsen, David Hempsall, Lesley Henderson, Nancy Herzog, Vanessa Hicks, Curtis Hisayasu, Shari Laidee, Professor David Jesson, Julie Lancour, Gerry Leversha, Dr Phil Limbert, Dr Olga Liania, Paul Miller, Paul Mortimer, Mona Mourshed, Tobi Phillips, Lynda Simons, Professor Peter J. Stollery, Mrs Zsuzsa Szilagyi, Mrs Theresa Lai, Eugene du Toit, Stephen Tommis, Sir Michael Wilshaw, Elaine Wilson, Taisir Yamin, Dr Ken Zetie.

In particular, the authors would like to thank the young people who are the reason why this book has been written, and whose talents, ability and giftedness are more inspirational than any book.

Part 1

Background

1

A Note on Our Methodology

Key points

- Too much time and energy have been devoted to identifying the most able, instead of defining how to teach them.
- Similarly, too much time and energy have been devoted to the question of whether ability is genetic or environmental in its origins.
- This book concerns itself largely with pure academic ability, as traditionally defined.
- There are dangers in using the term 'gifted and talented' to describe the most able.
- The skills versus knowledge debate is a false dichotomy.

There are three overwhelming conclusions that stand out above all others in the book that follows. The first is that provision for the education of the most able children in the UK is in a major crisis, and declining to the level where if it were a species of animal it would be deemed close to extinction. The second is that if able children are to have their potential realized, they have to spend a significant amount of their school time together with children of similar ability. The third is that too many teachers either do not recognize teaching the most able as a category of special need or are wary of it.

The brief for this project has been to analyse and scrutinize the various methods that countries from all over the world use to educate their more able children, and to pull out some of the issues so that educators are enabled to locate themselves and their own thinking within current debates around this subject. Our aim has then been to explore the class-room and school implications that each model raised, suggest ways in which this information may be useful to practitioners and offer a worldwide perspective for teachers wanting to consider their own practice. The primary task has therefore been to ensure that the level of detail and guidance is such that the approaches offered are not locked to a particular context but are flexible enough to be transferred and taken up in a variety of educational contexts, whilst maintaining coherence and integrity. We hope in this way to share what we have learnt as teachers and from teachers to highlight the challenges, outcomes and learning – both expected and unexpected – that we have seen. This has subsequently been expanded to include a brief modest proposal for educating such children in the UK, based on an amalgam of interesting practice here and overseas. In this way, specific provision anywhere in the world can be used to help all teachers to try different ideas within their own locality, for the benefit of their own more able children.

This book has benefitted from research and educational visits to China, America, Africa, Europe, Australia, the Arabian Gulf and the Far East, undertaken as part of other projects. We are also grateful to the Goethe Institute for their award of a travelling scholarship to Germany, and further visits to Australia (Adelaide), Singapore and the USA (Washington, DC, Seattle and New York) provided by sponsors. Attendance at the last five World Conferences for Gifted and Talented Children has allowed for extended conversations with many of the leading practitioners worldwide in the field.

What we have excluded from the debate

We have taken a number of executive decisions with the aim of producing a work that avoids sinking into the swamp in which so many books and articles on 'gifted and talented children' have been drowned.

First, we have largely ignored the debate over how one decides which children qualify as able or gifted and talented (G&T), and what countries have decided to call those children once identified. The naming issue is a vast distraction that keeps a small number of researchers in employment. What we are looking at is quite simple. There are far too many students who have talents and needs that are not being recognized or met in regular classrooms. A nation cannot properly educate their most able children without knowing who they are, yet there are a number of reasons for vaulting over these issues. Deciding who are and who are not 'able, gifted and talented' obsesses commentators on gifted education, often to the exclusion and detriment of all other issues. We believe, and our experience continues to indicate, that a colossal amount of time in schools is wasted on identification and naming, when it is developing provision for talents rather than selecting 'special' individuals that wins hearts and minds.

There are two reasons for practitioners to ignore the identification topic. First, it is perhaps more properly the preserve of qualified educational psychologists, a professional group with their own methodologies. Second, and perhaps more importantly, every country studied has, for better or worse, identified a cohort of children they believe more able than the average, more often than not described as 'more able or gifted and talented'. If one can cut through the jargon and the buzz-words, most of those countries have arrived at their selection through a common-sense combination of methods, usually comprising a mixture of IQ and similar tests, achievement in school-based tests, achievement in public examinations and, if one is frank, the gut instinct of a teacher.

It is quite startling to see the thinly veiled hostility shown by some academics to teacher assessment of which children are 'most able or gifted and talented'. It is as if some of the university-based academic establishment cannot allow for the fact that the actual teacher staring the relevant pupil in the whites of their eyes every day in the classroom could spot real ability or giftedness. Many articles suggest, implicitly or more rarely explicitly, that no mere teacher can be trusted to identify able children: they need a battery of tests and, even better, an army of university-based academics before any such judgement can be validated. The day may come when we can slam electrodes on a child's head and know instantly if they are 'gifted'. In the meantime, perhaps we should trust teachers to know their children. Academic measurement through tests dates back only 50 years. As it is, choosing who your most able students are by a combination of all existing methods, plus a healthy dose of teacher instinct, is untidy in academic terms but seems to work.

The second decision was to steer clear of the schism that runs like an equivalent of the Grand Canyon through all work on the able, gifted and talented, dividing, ruling and perhaps even contributing to the weakness of the cause of our most able students. That schism can be summed up as the conflict between the 'geneticists', who believe that a relatively small number of children are born gifted, and the 'environmentalists', who believe that all children are born gifted and it is their upbringing and environment that dictate the extent to which this talent is realized. Occasionally, the schism appears in a single article, as in the two comments: 'Giftedness, especially in intellectual ability, is to a large extent genetically determined' and 'Despite strong genetic influence on intellectual potential, evidence shows that children's development is also largely affected by their family lifestyle, values, goals and other environmental characteristics' (Reichenberg & Landau, in Shavinina, 2009: 873).

The current belief is to favour the view that there is no such thing as a fixed commodity of intelligence: 'both the research base and practical and moral unchangeable degrees of "giftedness" from our educational practice are incorrect, inhuman and counter-productive' (Claxton & Meadows, in Balchin et al., 2009: 3). It is interesting that the above piece mentions moral issues as needing to influence research. Doubts must be cast, surely, on any research that is committed not to finding the truth, however painful, but instead to abiding by a moral imperative. The same writers comment, perhaps more reasonably: 'Most researchers (e.g. Resnick 1999) now believe that young minds are better thought of as "developing muscles" than "fixed capacity engines"' (Claxton & Meadows, in Balchin et al., 2009: 5).

However, there is a sting in the tail in a later comment: 'The fixed pot view of ability is often associated with a restricted and rather academic view of intelligence in general' (Claxton & Meadows, in Balchin et al., 2009: 6).

It should be asked, what is so wrong with an academic view of intelligence? Clearly, the 'fixed pot' or 'developing muscle' debate is an important issue, as is the means whereby able and gifted children are identified. The advantage given to a child brought up in a home full of books, and who is read and talked to, and offered intellectual stimulation, over the child who is simply left to their own devices, cannot be underestimated. At the same time, the extreme statement of the environmentalists – 'Every child is born a Mozart' – seems just that: extreme.

> If you track their histories carefully, you find that the 'gifted and talented' have generally been lucky enough – and obsessive enough – to have the support and opportunities required. Mozart's father immersed his children in music from their infancies, carefully marketed their ability to perform and compose, opened up every opportunity to be a musician and persuaded his own employers to employ his son. Some small seed of their particular 'talent' may be there initially in the form of a mild interest or even a small aptitude, but that seed could equally have been sown by a chance event, or even by the unjustified attribution of talent by a proud parent. (Claxton & Meadows, in Balchin et al., 2009: 7)

Really? How many of the Mozart children, receiving no doubt the same stimulus from their father, equalled their sibling? True, Mozart's parents pushed and stimulated him as a musician exceptionally hard, but the problem with those who wish to prove that every child is born a Mozart is that they cannot know or show how many other parents pushed their child equally as hard, without the child taking off. It is counter-intuitive to think that all children are born with equal gifts, just as it is true that many children have their gifts and talents destroyed by lack of nurturing. Some proponents of the environmentalist school do themselves, and a rather important issue, no favours by the manner in which they approach it. In the extract above, a mere suggestion that Mozart may have had 'a small seed of talent' is offered as a fact, rather than the highly question-able, unprovable and unproven supposition that it actually is. Sometimes the academic's and the lawyer's requirement for evidence to back up a claim is a healthy safeguard, only ignored by academics at the risk of put-ting dogma before truth. We know that research on the effects of practice, notably of more than 10,000 hours, will produce expertise. But whether that practised expertise is the same as talent in terms of inspiration, cre-ativity and world acclaim is questionable.

The problem with this issue is not the answer itself: that almost cer-tainly is that gifts and talents are the result of both nature and nurture, the proportion changing in line with the current fashions or research of the day.

The problem is that too much published material takes up so much of the available space working out how to identify able children, and then asking where that ability came from. As a result, too little time is left for finding out what one should actually do to meet the special needs of those who have survived both their genetic inheritance and their early upbringing to be seen as able and gifted, and avoid them having to sit in lessons that could destroy their talent just as effectively as the wrong genes or a flawed upbringing. We have therefore chosen in this book to concern ourselves simply with how one should best deal with those who are, for whatever reason, clearly identified as able and gifted. We have also sought not to delve too deeply into the nature of intelligence itself, but concentrated rather on how to deal with it when it (clearly) manifests itself in a young person, and to focus on academic intelligence. Opinions vary on the number and type of different intelligences, but 'It is generally accepted that intelligence is not a unitary concept, but rather there are many kinds of intelligence and therefore single definitions cannot be used to explain this multifaceted phenomenon' (Renzulli & Reiss, in Heller et al., 2000: 369).

One writer lists ten human abilities: emotional; social; spiritual; somatic; visual/spatial; auditory; mathematical/symbolic; linguistic; mathematical/technical; scientific (Wallace & Maker, in Shavinina, 2009: 1127). R.J. Sternberg cites three forms of intelligence: analytical; creative; practical

(Sternberg & Davidson, 2005), whilst Joseph Renzulli (Renzulli et al., 1982) suggests two types of intelligence: 'schoolhouse giftedness' and 'creative-productive giftedness'. Others, notably Gardner (1983, 1999a; see below), have suggested many more.

The revelation that there is more to able, gifted and talented children than aptitude for traditional academic disciplines may not make academic or intellectual intelligence the most important type of intelligence, but neither does it make it unimportant. It is a special educational need that a well-educated child will have brought out in them and realized. It is an important factor in economic terms, whereby academic achievement and the strength of the research sector in particular can be crucial elements in a country's economic well-being. How the world teaches academically gifted children is a valid, relevant and important topic. In concentrating on it, we are not saying it is any more important than the seven or 14 intelligences identified by Gardner (1983). We are simply trying to say that academic intelligence, or high intellectual potential, is important.

The fourth decision was to use the fact that this text was not constituted as an article for an academic journal, or as a piece of post-graduate or post-doctoral research, to repeat opinions expressed by teachers in informal conversations, which by their nature do not allow for a full citation of who said what, when and where they said it.

There are inevitably significant problems with any terminology and there is a real danger that too tight a definition of children's abilities divides children so sharply into sheep and goats that a significant number of very able and gifted and talented children are told they are failures and this becomes a self-fulfilling prophecy. The Hungarian Genius Program and the school model offered by Joseph Renzulli et al. (1982) are only two examples of highly successful schemes predicated in part on the existence of multiple intelligences and equal merit given to both 'giftedness' and 'talent'.

However, and as with the debate between the geneticists and the environmentalists, the extremists do great damage. There is a very real danger of the term becoming one word, as in 'giftedandtalented'. Gifted children can be talented as well, and vice versa, but they are not always so. A child with high intellectual potential in mathematics requires a different service in the classroom from the outstanding artist or dancer. The danger of a blanket term is that it allows schools and teachers to believe that if they are satisfying the needs of one, they are automatically catering for the other. Some have argued that a better term for able and gifted children would be 'fast learners', but a problem with this term is that a number of gifted children are fast learners only in one or a small range of disciplines; it not unusual in a selective school to find a child in the top set, class or stream for English to be at the bottom end of the spectrum, and a very slow learner, in maths. The young people this book is about in fact answer best to an acronym first used in an Australian programme for the able, gifted and talented – the SHIP (Students with High Intellectual Potential) scheme. However, the descriptions 'more able' and 'gifted and talented' are so well established in all the available literature and publications that to try and alter them would be perverse and potentially confusing.

Finally, we have also decided not to engage with the current debate on whether 'skills' or 'knowledge' should be the key drivers in an education system for the more able. Primarily this is because the so-called argument is based on a false dichotomy. Knowledge has two aspects – knowing content/information and knowing how to do something – which can be summed up as knowing what and knowing how. Explicitly or implicitly, a significant number of teachers have a vision of a successful lesson being about the delivery by the teacher of certain facts and the successful understanding of these facts by the children. This is a valid facet of education. A grounding in core knowledge is essential for even the greatest scientific genius. But knowledge and skills go together and the all-too-frequent antithesis set up between skills and knowledge is facile and deplorable. They are not mutually exclusive alternatives. It is difficult to argue that knowledge gets in the way of reasoning because it is what we reason with. More emphasis on knowledge and facts cannot 'necessarily' be a bad idea simply because there is little doubt that knowledge builds on knowledge. The more you know, the more you are able to learn. Yet the most able can do much of the work of acquiring facts and understanding them on their own – easy to say for the experienced teacher used to seeing the most able fly, but far harder for the young teacher whose termly assessment or career-forming appraisal may well be firmly linked to the number of their students making more floor-level targets (such as 75% in the USA's Regents or a 'C' grade in the UK's GCSEs). For such a teacher, it can require real courage to recognize that the most able need not merely facts but development of their cognitive skills, that a significant amount of their work needs to be off-syllabus in the same way and for the same reason a skier goes off-piste, and that a significant amount of the work they need to do will generate more questions than answers. Education systems across the world are still geared to facts and to measurable outcomes. For the most able, it is the process that often matters more than the outcome, the journey more than the destination. It is to this journey that we now turn.

2

The Global Picture: History and Oversight

Key points

- Education of the most able suffers from being tagged as 'elitist'.
- It is held back by a belief that ability will always win or show through.
- Asian and Eastern European cultures accept more readily the existence of children more academically able than the norm.
- Schemes for the most able are sometimes in shorter supply in the undeveloped world because they are seen as a luxury.
- Schemes for the most able are vulnerable because politics dictates their survival and their funding.
- The cause of able and gifted children can be badly served by its academic arm.

Able, gifted and talented schemes and initiatives globally date primarily from post-1945, though there are examples of schemes clearly aimed at the most able that date from much earlier. The creation of grammar schools in England and the further development of *Lycées* in France and *Gymnasiums* in Germany after the Second World War are among the most extreme examples of complete educational systems being designed around high academic achievers. There is considerable difference across the world in the proportion of children deemed to be in the top cohort of ability. UK grammar schools and the Australian SHIP scheme are, or were, geared to the top 30% of ability, whilst Singapore has a scheme for the top 1% and the Hungarian Genius scheme rather joyously (albeit just a little improbably) implies that all children can be members.

A number of countries across the world operate outstanding schemes for the education of able children. Despite this, there is a strong sense that able, gifted and talented education is sometimes low down on a country's priority list, and in some countries (most notably the UK) it is an endangered species. There are a variety of reasons for this.

Why has able, gifted and talented education become an 'endangered species'?

First, education for the most able suffers from the tag of elitist, in an age when 'elite' can be a swear word. A common theme in conversations with teachers undertaken as part of this book was that resources expended on the most able were inevitably resources taken away from the broader spectrum of ability. One example of an academic statement of this concept is:

> Increasingly, the focus is moving away from the categorization of some pupils as 'gifted' (with all others implicitly therefore in the 'not gifted' category) and towards an individual focus on individual differences in developmental trajectories, recognizing that pathways to high-level achievement are enormously diverse, domain specific and incremental in nature. (Matthews, in Shavinina, 2009: 1365–6)

What one teacher described as 'fundamental egalitarianism' is a feature largely of western educational culture. One extract sums up the nervousness felt by many commentators about special provision for able students:

> What is the justification for the support of special programs for the gifted and talented? Given the low teacher salaries and high classroom sizes that plague most school systems, why should resources be expended on a select few? Such diversion of taxpayer money seems particularly objectionable in any society that adheres to egalitarian principles. Why not use the cash to help the less gifted and the less talented reach higher standards of achievement? Why shouldn't a democratic country design its educational system to make its citizens more intellectually homogenous? Why not create a nation where everybody is truly equal? (Simonton, in Shavinina, 2009: 905)

For some commentators, the undeniable value of equality of opportunity has morphed into the rather more questionable belief that all children should *only* be offered the same opportunity. Such dismissal of able, gifted and talented programmes is also made easier by the sense that to lavish such resources on able children is to bless them twice over, and that able children either need no help to achieve their potential or much less help than their weaker peers. There is also a regrettable tendency in academic circles to treat giftedness as an illness and a source of major problems. One session at a recent Biennial World Conference on Gifted and Talented Children produced a list of undesirable symptoms shown by the gifted so lengthy that it appeared such children needed treatment rather than teaching, to be sent to hospital rather than school (see below). Yet the truth is that gifted children can make life difficult for themselves, not wishing to stand out from the crowd and using their ability to measure their work and achievement so they float just above the trip wires in the system that are meant to detect underachievement. The following is clear statement of the need for special provision:

> Most classroom teachers have experienced the frustration of realizing that the work they are assigning is too easy for some of the bright students in their classrooms. Many teachers have also felt pangs of guilt as they watched these same bright students complete assignment after assignment of previously mastered review work that is not really necessary for them to complete. In many instances teachers are just too busy trying to help students who are not working up to grade level and who do not understand the work to be able to find enough time to substitute appropriate and challenging assignments for students who do understand the material and need no further review. (Renzulli et al., 1982: 188–94)

Eastern European and Asian culture seems far more ready to accept both the existence of an academic elite and the need for it to be taught as a special needs category. Yet, even in Far Eastern and Asian countries, and in China, many were newly ambivalent about their existing able, gifted and talented programmes because of the belief that hot-housing had undoubtedly given students an excellent command of basic principles and core knowledge, but at the cost of driving out creativity and imagination.

Second, for understandable reasons, countries in the two-thirds world often do not have gifted and talented (G&T) education programmes as a priority, understandably when one's concern is that large elements of the populace are not receiving even basic education. In a survey conducted by the CfBT Education Trust, where a very large number of questionnaires were sent out, 65% of respondents were from western cultures. Rather surprisingly, given their level of activity in promoting G&T schemes, Eastern Europe and the Baltic states only accounted for 10% of responses. The Middle East and South America each produced 7% of responses, the Far East 4% and Africa 2%. Too much should not be read into these figures, not least of all because a survey conducted in English will not always be accessible to some teachers in some countries, but it does convey the sense in which G&T education is a luxury for some countries with little money to spare, rather than a staple (Freeman et al., 2010).

Third, educational funding is usually provided by politicians. Where the government is firmly behind the principle of able, gifted and talented education, as in Singapore, it thrives and flourishes. In a number of western countries, one is left with the impression that there are relatively few votes in high-ability programmes. As discussed above, politicians can always comfort themselves as they withdraw provision from such programmes with the notion that the most able can use their intelligence and their ability to look after themselves, something which much research shows to be untrue.

This is essentially the political argument against the Gifted and Talented agenda. Resources are limited and should be focused on 'real kids' with real problems, who cannot cope without explicit support. All identified G&T kids tend to look a little like Harry Potter or Hermione Granger, come from middle-class supportive families and would basically succeed no matter what the school did because their parents would put all the back-up strategies into place to ensure that in the eventuality of nuclear fallout, they will still be doing pretty well: private tutoring, taking them out to see culturally interesting exhibitions and artefacts, more private tutoring and sometimes even talking to them face to face. Seemingly, no wonder they can't fail.

Except, of course, they do fail: all too frequently. Even these 'heavily supported' students often go off the rails, or misunderstand the demands being made of them or the degree of difficulty of the exam, or assume that because they might be top of their class they will automatically get the top grades they need. These students are just the tip of the iceberg. The straightforward reality is that the very children who need some of the greatest support because they are smart but disadvantaged are precisely the learners who are underachieving on an industrial scale. They are the students who don't get to go to the cultural events, don't get to hear the 'right words' spoken at home, don't have parents helicoptering in when they start to slip and slide. In short, they are the very children we need to support the most in school, or their talent will be squandered, their aspirations abandoned. A great deal of worldwide research suggests that these are the children who are not getting the support and not achieving anything like their potential, yet still governments tend to equate disadvantage with low performance.

A cynic might argue that renewed attention to the gifted and talented from government tends to follow on from a crisis. The starkest example was the money invested in G&T education in the USA in the mid- to late 1950s following the country's perceived defeat in the space race when the Soviet Russians were the first country to put a satellite, Sputnik, into orbit. Similarly, at least some of the USA's present commitment to G&T

programmes is explained by the shortage of home-grown STEM (Science, Technology, Engineering and Mathematics) specialists. In STEM occupations, 38% of doctoral employees are foreign born, whilst only 30% of college students major in STEM subjects. Comparative figures are 59% for China and 66% for Japan.

Fourth, G&T education is arguably badly served by some of its university and research arms. Partly, this is because there are very few champions of gifted and talented education in schools, and so the burden of leadership falls on academics and researchers. Winning political battles, making a cause great by taking it out to a wider public, and charismatic contributions to the media are not the first features one might associate with some university academics. Those academics have also not helped by taking up and defending fixed positions, and on occasion fighting each other more than fighting for the cause of able, gifted and talented education.

> Gifted education seems to be a fragmented, porous and contested field ... dogmatism in the field takes the form of insular or competing camps, each promoting a particular perspective and either ignoring or denigrating the others. The result has been an unsettled field. (Ambrose et al., 2012)

A further complication is that many of those who write on G&T education have never actually taught school children:

> The field of gifted education ... [consists of] ... those of us who write, conduct research, educate teachers – the chattering class of the field – and the much larger segment of the field engaged in the day-to-day practice of gifted education – teachers, administrators and policy makers – those who actually make this form of education happen. (Borland, in Ambrose et al., 2012: 13)

Much research pays scant attention to the reality of a teacher's life or the reality of a pupil's experience in school. Able, gifted and talented education has many critics and enemies, and is also divided within and sometimes against itself. It is not a recipe for a cogent and forceful justification of the need for more able programmes. We, the authors of this book, write simply as teachers with over 70 years of teaching combined behind us, with one overwhelming concern, namely to identify some of the classroom practices and techniques that draw the best out of our more able children and allow them to realize their full potential.

Global experts in gifted and talented education

There are, despite these reservations, a number of highly respected global experts in the field of gifted and talented children, some of them seminal, founding figures, and others those who have picked up or carried on the torch. A list might include the following:

Edward de Bono (born 1933) pioneered the teaching of Thinking Skills as a subject in its own right. Though not only concerned with the most able, he has been a significant influence on many of those who are and on the development of such as the Australian SHIP scheme.

Howard Earl Gardner (born 1943) is an American who was one of the pioneers of the theory of multiple intelligences in the 1980s. He identified between seven and 14 'intelligences' in a theory that has never been quite proven, but which has received much support and prompted much further thought. In his first draft proposal of seven intelligences (in *Frames of Mind*, 1983), two were typically valued in schools, the next three were usually associated with the arts and the final two were what Gardner defined as 'personal intelligences'. Though contentious, his influence has been benign in that it challenged simplistic definitions of intelligence.

Robert M. Gagné (1916–2002) wrote some of his major work in the late 1990s (see, for example, 1999), as a leader in the group that sees ability not as a static phenomenon but as something that can be developed and evolved – the 'Gagné Assumption' and 'Nine Events of Instruction'. He disputed the notion that ability can be measured simply by IQ tests and challenged, among others, the work of Piaget. One useful by-product of this type of thinking is that by discouraging classification of children simply by where they are at, and encouraging looking at where they might grow to be, a significant number of disadvantaged children at least are put into a potential pool in which they might swim as gifted and talented.

Joseph Renzulli (born 1936) has already been referred to. An American who has been influencing opinion for many years, his approach to children and to schools is holistic. He does not deny the importance of above-average intelligence in giftedness, but links it with major personality features, seeing these as the catalyst that enables giftedness to be realized. He believes in flexible, organic systems that grow out of the individual and local soul, and his whole-school programmes refreshingly demand that the pupil links in with (and is excited by) real-world problems with a clear practical application. To this element of pragmatism is added a fierce interest in creativity.

Charles Spearman (1863–1945) was an Englishman and an early pioneer, publishing in the early 1900s. An army officer for 15 years, he enrolled to study psychology at Leipzig in 1897, as Leipzig was willing to let him in without the formal qualifications required in England. He was as well known in his own time for his work in statistics, though he became Professor of Psychology at University College, London, in 1928. His theory of a general intelligence (the 'G factor') that can be subdivided into mathematical and verbal intelligence, with children deemed gifted if their measured IQ (Intelligence Quotient) is above a certain level, has been massively influential and probably still provides the definition of the most able for a majority of laymen.

Robert Sternberg (born 1949) is a contemporary American who has written about a form of multiple intelligence. He is also a critic of intelligence tests.

(Continued)

(Continued)

His theory of 'Successful Intelligence' claims that a successful person needs three different skill sets, crudely defined as analytic, creative and practical. Though highly individual, his work fits into a wider picture whereby some modern research does not deny the importance of intelligence in giftedness, but sees it almost as an inert compound made active by any one or all of environment, upbringing or personality.

Lev Vygotsky (1896–1934) was a Russian who viewed the child as being a very active participant in the development of giftedness and saw the crucial role of the teacher in unlocking it. His obsession with potential is a very helpful contribution to a tangled debate. Of particular importance to the modern debate is his concept of the 'Zone of Proximal Development' – Vygotsky's term for the range of tasks that a child can complete. It has two limits – the lower the one the child can achieve independently, and the upper what can be achieved with the help of a suitable teacher.

Questions for further thought

Why is so little attention given to these experts?

It is telling that few, if any, of the above have any real presence in the popular consciousness, and none are from the UK. It is testimony to the fact that the academic establishment concerned with G&T children has been in many cases more concerned with talking to itself than with talking to children, teachers or parents. It is also both noteworthy and regrettable that the average age of leaders in this field is so high. There are few young researchers and teachers setting the world alight with new and challenging research into the able, gifted and talented, and hence even less pressure on governments and societies in general to cater for this vital group. Too little attention has been given to the core issues of how able and gifted education justifies its existence, and far too few experts have addressed the strong charges of elitism that are all too easily levelled at the field. Highly talented but disadvantaged learners are still neglected in much of the research as are significant minorities. Teachers are not represented in the lists of experts and their experiences are devalued by many researchers. Researchers therefore have little cause to seek out these teacher experts, who are rarely reported on or referenced in the national educational media.

What are teachers doing with the models promoted by experts?

What is also becoming abundantly clear is that school providers are becoming more sophisticated in choosing and applying various models from the experts in gifted education which are appropriate to their circumstances. We believe that there is real power in the adaptive and adoptive nature of the uptake of ideas and approaches by schools. This is well illustrated by the finding that over 110 separate research authorities were cited by respondents in the CfBT worldwide survey mentioned above. Possibly because of the limited material available to practitioners of what works in a local context, there is an increasing tendency to combine approaches, selecting elements in new ways. It is a 'mix and match' approach often based on anecdotal evidence of successful programmes but it also suggests the growth of a more democratic approach that is empowering and to be welcomed. It is hoped that this book might also help teachers to locate and explore more of the approaches that can be used.

What works where and why?

The pages that follow discuss the various techniques used to nurture and teach the gifted and talented, and give details of practice in a number of countries around the world. The conclusion from a project such as this must be that there is no magic bullet. No one technique works with the gifted and talented massively more than any other. No country has a monopoly of virtue in terms of what it does and how it does it. Where countries do have a proven record of success, it is often because what they do and how they do it springs naturally out of the local or national culture, and does not necessarily transplant. Schemes for educating G&T children have many good parts, but so far no one has added the parts together to make a greater whole. One feature that showed as very common in our research was the increasing use of devolution, and a wholly or partially independent sector in education worldwide. Charter schools in the USA, city academies and free schools in the UK and the increasing number of independent schools in Singapore are typical of a trend towards local management of schools. These changes have an impact on the whole education system of a country, and not just on the way it educates its most able children, but they do in many cases have a knock-on effect on, or at least implications for, the education of the most able. Many of these effects are discussed below.

3

The Local Picture: The UK

Key points

- The 2013 UK Ofsted report (*The Most Able Students*) is of relevance to all countries interested in providing high quality teaching for its most able students, and of particular relevance to countries with a school populace of considerable economic, ethnic and racial diversity.
- The report concluded that England is letting down a high proportion of its most able children, and is more successful in recognizing problems than it is in providing answers.
- There is a clear link between underachievement on the part of the most able and their family background, social class and levels of disadvantage.
- An absence of challenge in both class work and homework was a common denominator in the failure of the most able.
- The debate about gifted children is dominated in a very damaging way in the UK by the ongoing war over grammar schools and hence academic selection.
- There is traditionally an anti-intellectual stand in UK culture, and funding for able, gifted and talented pupils in the UK was being cut drastically even before recession.
- The testing regime adopted by the UK is a contributor to the regrettable tendency to teach to the C grade, which in turn damages the most able children.

The public comments of the head of Ofsted, the UK's regulatory authority, in a 2013 headline declared, 'Brightest pupils failed by state schools, chief inspector warns'. And the text, written by Julie Henry in *The Daily Telegraph* of 26 January, stated, 'The report was disclosed after league tables showed that hundreds of secondary schools did not produce a single pupil with high enough grades in tough academic subjects to win a place at elite universities'.

At first glance, it might seem as if a report on the teaching of the most able by one regulatory authority in one European country is too parochial to be of interest in a work dedicated to examining the teaching of the most able in a global context. Yet the 2013 UK Ofsted report provides a fascinating pragmatic insight into how a developed country can still get it badly wrong when it comes to realizing the potential of its most able pupils.

A landmark report

This was a detailed report into how state schools teach their most able pupils. The findings present a discouraging picture of what it means to be one of the most able students in non-selective secondary schools in England. England is not unique in there being perhaps an inevitable tension between those who inspect and regulate schools and those who do the actual job of teaching, with both parties not fully acknowledging the needs or strengths of the other. Inevitable it may be, but it is also damaging if both sides end up fighting each other, rather than fighting the problem.

The report starts with a call to arms from Sir Michael Wilshaw, the Chief Inspector:

> Too many non-selective schools are failing to nurture scholastic excellence. While the best of these schools provide excellent opportunities, many of our most able students receive mediocre provision. They are not doing well enough because their secondary schools fail to challenge and support them sufficiently ... Many non-selective schools fail to imbue their most able students with confidence and high ambition ... The challenge is to ensure that all schools help students and families overcome cultural barriers to attending higher education. We cannot allow this to continue. I hope this report provides a catalyst for change.

The argument is sound, the need for change clear. It is perhaps unfortunate that the report makes no mention of successive governments who ought, in all fairness, to share at least some of the responsibility and hence some of the blame for the current situation. UK schools have been kicked about in a political football match that has gone on for many years. The bruises and cuts are therefore quite raw, which can produce over-sensitive and defensive reactions. It has been pointed out on many occasions that all too easily 'teachers' and 'schools' become morphed into 'all teachers/all schools'. Unsurprisingly, there is a defensive wagons-in-a-circle mentality when Ofsted say that teaching is letting students down. Teaching is a hugely personal activity. Criticism can feel like an attack on who teachers are, as much as on what they do, and yet it could be a model for the rest of the world that teachers best serve children when they do not challenge the facts but face them.

The equal opportunities agenda

As with many reports on UK education, it is necessary to disentangle a social content from an educational content. Ofsted wish to put clear blue water between the 'most able' report and any elitist agendas. It uses the 2012 Sutton Trust report (Smithers & Robinson, 2012) to establish a clear 'equal opportunities' agenda for schools working with their most able students: 'Ensuring that the brightest pupils fulfil their potential goes straight to the heart of social mobility, of basic fairness and economic efficiency.' The Sutton Trust Chairman, Sir Peter Lampl, in turn, called the Ofsted report,

> a wake-up call to ministers ... Schools must improve their provision, as Ofsted recommends. But the government should play its part too by providing funding to trial the most effective ways to enable our brightest young people to fulfil their potential.

Social messages apart, the basic findings of the report are of great concern. The 2,327 lesson observation evidence forms, from 109 inspections scrutinized separately as part of this report, show that the most able students in only about 20% of these lessons were supported well or better.

It also notes that just 100 schools, comprising 87 independent schools and 13 grammar schools (just 3% of schools with sixth forms and sixth form colleges in the UK), accounted for over a tenth (11.2%) of admissions to highly selective universities during the three-year period analysed.

Able students need opportunities

The Sutton Trust report (2012) points out that the national data show almost two-thirds (65%) of high-attaining pupils who leave primary school with UK Level 5 in both English and mathematics did not reach an A* or A grade in both these GCSE subjects in 2012 in non-selective secondary schools. This represents over 65,000 students. A quarter (27,000 students) did not reach a B Grade. In 20% of the 1,649 non-selective 11 to 18 schools, not one student in 2012 achieved the minimum of two A grades and one B grade in at least two of the facilitating A level subjects required by many of our most prestigious universities. This is a serious problem. Even allowing that UK Level 5 is a broad church, and that the most able are only a section of that group, it is still astonishing that so many students are doing so badly. To its credit, the UK has the data, even if it may not have the answers. Many other developed countries do not seem to have the data to identify that a problem exists.

Inevitably, failure to realize the potential of the most able at school leads to these same pupils failing to realize their potential after school. Recent league tables showed that almost a quarter of England's sixth forms and colleges had no pupils with the top A level grades sought by leading institutions. Perhaps inevitably, the same league tables also highlighted that some students, who achieved top marks at primary school, were not doing as well at secondary school. Ofsted believe that many are 'left to coast' in mixed-ability classes or entered too early for GCSE exams in order to gain the minimum C grades required for league tables.

The 2012 report also looked at how these students make decisions about university applications and what support they need to be successful, pointing out that 'schools must work with families more closely, particularly the families of first-generation university applicants and those eligible for free school meals, to overcome any cultural and financial obstacles to university application' (Ofsted 2013: 11). Too few of the schools worked to support their students in overcoming the cultural obstacles that stood in the way of their attending university, particularly universities away from the immediate local area. This point confirms a worldwide issue, namely that parental involvement as partners in the success of the most able is essential. As regards socially disadvantaged students, few schools used money made available for this group to support the most able in it, offering proof (as if it were needed) of the besetting sin affecting many countries in believing that the most able can look after themselves and need no special support, even those to whom life has given few other advantages.

On a general level, the report could act as a checklist for any school in the world of what not to do with the most able students, where it was found that:

- such students did not do the hard work and develop the resilience needed to perform at a high level because more challenging tasks were not regularly demanded of them; the work given to them tended to be pitched in the middle and did not extend the most able
- school leaders did not evaluate how well mixed-ability group teaching was challenging their most able students

- teachers did not challenge the most able pupils
- the curriculum and the quality of homework required improvement. Homework and the programme of extension activities for the most able students, where they existed, were not checked routinely for their impact or quality. Students said that too much homework was insufficiently challenging; it failed to interest them, extend their thinking or develop their skills.

A number of obvious answers emerge from or are recommended in the report, recommendations that have a general relevance far beyond the shores of the UK. Schools need to report to parents on whether or not their children are on track to achieve as well as they should in national tests and examinations. Students need to be tracked not just within their year, but across the years to see if they are achieving their potential, something which in turn demands extra energy and resources from schools to identify – and not to underestimate – exactly what that potential is. The publication of destination data by schools – where their pupils go – is essential, and in particular details of the proportion of pupils who go on to leading universities. In its turn, the regulatory authority – and, by implication, the regulatory authority in any and every country – must focus more closely in its inspections on the teaching and progress of the most able students, the curriculum available to them, and the information, advice and guidance provided to the most able students, as well as reporting on whether or not resources are properly used for the most able. A school's programme for its most able students should be scrutinized and reported on as a major measure of a school's success in any inspection report or findings. Or, as the Chief Inspector of Schools in England said, 'It is important that heads and inspectors focus on the progress of all children. It is a scandal that children who should be getting A* and As are not'.

Family background and underachievement amongst the most able

All this is well and good but the overwhelming relevance of the 2013 Ofsted report (*The Most Able Students*) is to highlight the most crucial issue of all, and one that is endemic to all countries. It is the link between underachievement on the part of the most able and the background of those students. The fact of underachievement is not the biggest threat to turning things around. The biggest threat is the danger of it becoming an accepted fact that a damaging background automatically leads to underachievement.

'Are the most able students from disadvantaged backgrounds as likely as the most able students from more affluent families to progress to top universities, and if not why?' Ofsted (2013) asks. The answer given by Ofsted, and by much other research, is a resounding no. We are squandering our talent on a terrifying scale. The report points out that some groups of the most able students do significantly less well than others. Students eligible for free school meals (FSM – an accepted measure of disadvantage in England), boys and white British students are not doing anywhere near as well as other groups and make less progress from their starting points at the end of Key Stage 2. Again, national data highlight that only 58% of FSM most able students in non-selective secondary schools do well enough to attain an A* to B grade in English and mathematics at GCSE. The report by the Sutton Trust (2008), *Wasted Talent?*, identified 60,000 students who, at the ages of 11, 14 or 16, were among the top fifth of academic performers in English state schools each year, but who had not subsequently entered higher education by the age of 18. The report further indicated that students known to be eligible for free school meals were 19 percentage points less likely than other school students to enter higher education by the age of 19.

The conclusion to be drawn from the 2013 Ofsted report is that England has failed to address the needs of its most able students, and more particularly failed to break the link in these pupils with a disadvantaged or poor background. It is small consolation to know that in both cases it is far from unique. The link between wasted talent and family background is not a new issue. Where the Ofsted report is least satisfactory is in suggesting what schools in the UK, and by implication other countries, do about this problem. The report argues for much greater parental involvement, and points out that the 'Pupil Premium' funding made available to English schools for more disadvantaged students tended to be spent on underachieving pupils in general, and was rarely targeted at the most able underachieving. However, much of the report is a call to arms, admitting the problem but putting statements of intent or need in place of concrete suggestions as to actual things teachers and schools can do.

Some non-selective schools in the poorer areas of Washington, DC and New York take what can appear to be a very old-fashioned route to changing their pupils' perception of themselves, awarding small prizes for the tiniest of achievements, presenting these in public and offering perks for any improved effort or sign of growing aspiration, from trips out of school to vouchers cashable in the school café. As one principal pointed out, for some of these children it is the first time they have received any reward for getting something right. The nature of the perks was irrelevant. What the children were being taught was that the more you put in, the more you get out.

What teachers need to look at is how they can help students to see themselves as learners in a very different light. If all the time their pupils believe that somehow their failures are innate and unchanging, a core set of attributes that define their very essence, they are guaranteed to give up. Instead, teachers need to look at what is in their locus of control and how their self-perception can be changed, often despite the impact of their background. A real danger is that the idea that 'poor kids under-achieve' is so familiar that it becomes accepted as a given, and that we sympathize with the under-achiever instead of challenging them and their schools on why they are underachieving. Teachers and schools need to recognize that the content of lessons, the means of delivery and all the paraphernalia of monitoring and reporting are actually secondary to the need to give self-belief to the most able, and in particular to those whose background gives them little cause for confidence. Without that crucial enabler, all else is wasted effort.

The independent/maintained school issue

Unsurprisingly, the Ofsted (2013) report found that independent school students were more than twice as likely as students in comprehensive schools or academies to be accepted into one of the 30 most highly selective universities: 48.2% of independent school students in England were accepted by these universities compared to 18% from state schools. There is a tendency in some quarters in the UK to assume that independent or selective state school = good, and comprehensive/non-selective state school = bad. Having seen and worked on both sides of this particular coin, we can confirm from first-hand experience that this is nonsense. The report does hint at support for this view, arguing that some of the brightest secondary school students in state education are being let down by teachers who fail to stretch them to get the best exam results. The belief in Ofsted is that state schools should do more for these pupils, and that they ought to be pushed, 'as they would be at independent or grammar schools'. Many state school heads in the UK could rival their independent school neighbours if they too had no pupil drawn from below the top 5% of academic ability in the country, most from prosperous, aspirational and supporting homes in which the language spoken is the language in which tuition is delivered. Of course, many independent and selective state schools benefit from putting together large numbers of the most able, who thus tend to reach critical mass, and it is easier in such schools to generate, or even simply inherit, an academically aspirational pupil culture.

The report was commissioned to investigate why many of the brightest students at non-selective maintained secondary schools or academies fail to achieve their potential compared with students who attend many of our grammar and independent schools. Despite a tendency in the UK for simplistic and partisan comment on this issue, it is a legitimate area of concern and needs to be investigated (we focus on the damage caused by the debate below). For far too long, the response to such known inequalities has been to blame the independent and grammar school sectors for creaming off the best students. It is important to point out the obvious. They don't. They may well have their unfair share of the most able but they do not have a monopoly. The report highlights that highly able students who are part of the non-selective system are not doing well. Rather, they are doing pretty badly. A majority of countries in the world do not have the seams of precious metal representing the most able gleaming conveniently on the surface, but have them buried in the ground. The selective school may collect the precious metal. Every school in the world owns land that has such metal in it.

Yet it is not that simple in other respects as well. Some selective grammar schools have been shown to have actual negative value-added for their pupils. Basic classroom management skills can atrophy in an independent or selective state school through lack of use, and the cross-fertilization that has taken place between the sectors has shown that learning goes in both directions. It is surprisingly easy to get away with teaching badly a class of bright, aspirational students, and there is weak and unchallenging teaching in all schools, across the sectors and types. Independent and selective state schools can help the general culture of teaching the most able, and they help point out one of the crucial questions in the whole area of educating the most able. Should countries be concerned with the quality of those who already achieve at high levels, or should they be concerned with those who have the ability to do so but never produce the goods? It is a crucial question that needs to be asked by anyone setting up a programme for the most able. The UK's independent and selective state schools by and large teach most able pupils who are already achieving at reasonably high levels: they have to do so to get a place in the independent school or selective state school. Where the Ofsted report performs an extremely useful function is to remind the reader of the lost army of talent among young people. During the research for this project, the principal of an outstanding US high school was asked what his worst moment had been in turning round an under-performing school. He cited the case of a boy – a first-generation immigrant – who had written proudly to his former school to say that after five years of grinding individual hard work and evening classes he had obtained a place at Harvard. The school had simply not seen the potential in him. Independent and selective state schools do many things well. Spotting raw talent is not always one of them, and for this reason alone partnership schemes, in the UK and elsewhere, may help win some battles but will not win the war.

Grammar schools and selection

One issue above all has dominated and, some would argue, poisoned the longer-term debate about educating gifted and talented children in the UK: grammar schools. The 1947 Education Act established a tri-partite system for English schools, on the same lines as was fashionable in Europe at the time, and France and Germany in particular. At the top of the tree were grammar and Direct Grant grammar schools, the former free, state schools, the latter taking a combination of fee-paying children and children paid for by the state. Grammar schools chose their pupils on an academically selective base by means of the 11+ examination, designed to test potential rather than acquired or taught knowledge. Though figures varied, grammar schools catered at most for the top 30% of the cohort. English grammar schools operated to the same philosophy as the French *Lycées* or German *Gymnasiums*, with specifically academic schools creaming off the 'top' children (as defined by traditional academic standards), and a further number – perhaps the next third – being intended to go to Technical Schools (some German versions of this type of school must rank among the best in the world, a fact not lost on local populaces who sometimes make these schools more over-subscribed than the local *Gymnasium*). Bringing up the rear in the UK were Secondary Modern Schools, offering a basic education to those who would leave school at the earliest possible opportunity to enter the employment market, largely as unskilled workers.

In terms of the custom and practice of educating the most able, the grammar schools were an extreme form of the technique usually referred to as 'pull out', in which the most able children are 'pulled out' of mainstream schooling and placed in classes or schools of their own.

The English grammar schools were an undoubted academic success. Although their critics denounce them as having been colonized by the middle classes, it is a simple fact that the grammar and direct grants schools sent more working-class children to top universities than any other English educational system, and the proportion of independent school pupils getting into the top UK universities is significantly higher now than it was in the days of grammar schools. It is a largely unrecorded and unobserved fact that the present dominance of independent school pupils in chasing the glittering prize of a top university place (up to 50% of those places go to the 7% of pupils educated in the independent sector) ironically owes much to grammar schools, which squeezed the market for fee-paying schools and forced many of them to become far more academic institutions than had hitherto been the case, and make getting their pupils a 'good' university place a priority. In the post-war period, university ceased to be a form of finishing school and a degree became a vital pre-requisite for a good job. Suddenly, the independent schools found themselves with a parent body who could no longer expect to keep their children in a life of idleness and who could, if they so chose, send their children to grammar schools free of charge. Faced with this challenge, a number of independent schools turned themselves in less than a decade into very efficient producers of academic success, and were arguably the major factor in producing the contemporary English independent schools, many of which define themselves in terms of their academic success.

However, it was not the rivalry from independent schools that did for the grammar schools. They were doomed from the outset because successive governments refused to build technical or vocational schools in any significant numbers. The result was that up to 70% of the pupil cohort were sent to what were seen as sump schools – the Secondary Moderns. Any system that seems to label 70% of children as failures is doomed to fail itself, however well it teaches the top 30%. Steps to abolish grammar schools started in the mid-1960s and were completed in 1976, although a handful of grammar schools remain today.

Other factors contributed to the downfall of the grammar schools. The 11+ exam almost certainly identified some bright children but also failed to spot others. By modern standards, the 11+ failed to recognize the existence of multiple intelligences. Results also had to be seriously fiddled to avoid girls, who did far better in the exam than boys, filling all the grammar school places.

Even now, over 30 years on, grammar schools are a hugely divisive issue. Their opponents often seem to be saying that because not everyone can benefit from an accelerated academic education then no one should be able to do so.

Above all, education in the UK has become a social and political issue, based on perceptions of privilege and disadvantage:

> In England the statistics show that the gap in educational performance between children from rich and poor backgrounds starts to be evidenced very early and continues to grow (Schwartz, 2004). Hence it is no longer

possible in education to separate ideas around the nature of giftedness from the conditions which allow it to flourish. Crudely stated, education is not a meritocracy. Gifted children from poor backgrounds who succeed are likely to be the exception rather than the rule unless the overall approach to education changes. (Woolf, in Shavinina, 2009: 1046)

Two things inimical to gifted education have taken place in England, apart from draconian cuts to funding. First, a necessary debate about disadvantage has diverted resources and thinking away from the issue of very able education, without recognizing that the two issues are integrally related. Second, the highly political nature of education in the UK and the scars left by the grammar school debate have on too many occasions let the issue of G&T children be treated as if it were a naughty wagon in *Thomas the Tank Engine*, and shunted into a siding marked 'For Grammar Schools'. If one uses as one's measure of judgement the number of young people any one English educational establishment sends to leading universities, it is clear that what was once famously referred to as the 'bog basic' English comprehensive school has failed in terms of its responsibilities to the able, gifted and talented. Yet to state this in public immediately unleashes the attack dogs of those committed to full mixed-ability comprehensive education (and there are some truly outstanding schools of this type), and usually labels the proposer a supporter of grammar schools. The sheer aggression, bitterness and dogmatism of England's equivalent to the First World War – Grammar School v. Comprehensive (unlimited rounds and no rules whatsoever) – has blocked the search for a third way, whereby English education fulfils its duty to its cleverest children, regardless of their background, which does not fight again old battles in an old war.

Teaching and testing

It is a major conclusion of this book that, counter-intuitively, it is not the children who are at the centre of successful G&T programmes, but teachers. Put simply, any gifted and talented child depends for the delivery of a programme or scheme on teachers. If the teachers are not persuaded of the importance of the group, the product never reaches the child. The cause of the gifted and talented has never been sold successfully to schools or teachers in the UK.

This leads on to the whole testing regime in the UK, which has had a seriously negative effect on the teaching of the gifted and talented. For a number of years now, the UK has pursued a policy that has seemed more concerned with weighing the pig rather than feeding it. The continued existence of schools, and teachers' jobs, may now depend on the proportion of pupils who achieve five 'C' grades or more at GCSE. As GCSE is not regarded as a particularly demanding examination, and the standard required to achieve a C or Pass grade will not set academia alight (top universities in the UK tend to expect six or more A* grades from the candidates they accept), the level to which most UK schools are expected to teach to acquire respectability is not going to demand a great deal of the most able.

To its credit, the UK Government has recognized just how stifling teaching to the C grade is for the gifted and talented, but it is a victim of its own policies. Having held out the magic C grade as the Holy Grail for so long, it is now facing the uphill task of changing the culture it has itself created. The 'Naming and Shaming' culture of Britain, whereby results are not only made public, but published in a way that invites comparison between schools, has created a climate of fear, and by labelling some schools in public as failures it may have created a self-fulfilling prophecy. It was interesting to note how horrified educational leaders in Singapore (home of one of the world's most successful school systems for all pupils, including the gifted and talented) were by the English league table obsession. Some of the most motivated educational leaders in the world see the publication of league tables as thoroughly demotivating: one such example interviewed in research for this book were leaders of the Singaporean educational system, who manage to create what is widely recognized as one of the most effective educational systems in the world without any use of league tables.

The English education system is also not immune from the school of thought that has condemned the Asian 'hothouse' style of teaching as destroying creativity and resilience. Professor Guy Claxton stated in *The Daily Telegraph* of 10 December 2010:

> [Oxford and Cambridge] are seeing a year-on-year rise in the number of young people who arrive apparently confident, with four to five As at A-level, but lacking resilience, lacking the ability to cope if they do not get great success ... these high-achieving youngsters are becoming more and more vulnerable because they are being spoon-fed more and more efficiently by their teachers to get them through their exams.

A polite view of the state of G&T education in the UK is as follows: 'Although able or gifted and talented education has a much higher profile in the United Kingdom than it did ten or 15 years ago, it is still a bit of a Cinderella in the education world' (Goodhew, 2009: ix).

A more accurate view might be that the UK is, sadly, something of a desert for the teaching of G&T children at present. There is talk of extended school days that could be used for the benefit of the gifted and talented. The government has also sought to identify the 'exceptionally able'.

Yet, on the other side of the coin, the picture is arguably worse than it has ever been. The Coalition axed the funding for regional partnerships supporting the gifted and talented in March 2011. The ten partnerships provided training for teachers and enrichment activities for pupils. The *Times Educational Supplement* of 17 June 2011 reported: 'By scrapping all funding to regional projects the government saved £20m.' Also gone is the money that supported the admirable 'Excellence in Cities' project, which has come to an end. The G&T element in National Strategies with a requirement for a Leading Teacher to be identified and trained in all schools has gone. There is no particular recognition in the state sector for teachers with an interest in the gifted and talented, no clear career path and few courses in the UK to train teachers with an interest in that field. The UK's first national initiative, NAGTY, drove itself and was driven to extinction.

In effect, the UK Government has made the clearest possible statement, by not putting its money where its mouth is, that it no longer sees education for the gifted and talented as a priority. Its lack of interest is repeated in the world at large, or at least in that part of it represented in the media. As an illustration of popular culture's vision of G&T provision, a contributor to *Woman's Hour* on BBC Radio 4 in 2011 dismissed state school programmes for the gifted and talented as 'sops' to 'entice middle-class parents into state schools and away from the independent sector'. They were not howled down. Above all, grammar schools in the UK have helped to create an environment in which it is politically correct to assert that any provision for the most able must be at the cost of the normally gifted. This is simply not true.

Questions for further thought

Why do the most able children in the UK do so badly in comparison to some other countries?

Lack of governmental support is clearly one aspect, but it might be that this seeming indifference by the state reflects a cultural attitude that feels slightly embarrassed by the whole 'more able equals elitism' agenda. If this is the case, what are the drivers that need to be employed to change attitudes? The plight of the more disadvantaged has always had multi-party support. Why has the case never been more effectively made that the very students who suffer the most from a lack of challenge in schools are almost always the most disadvantaged able students for whom school is the only likely source of challenge and advancement? Middle-class parents are accused of helicoptering in their support, but they can also be relied on to ensure that their child has all the advantages that they can muster to support them. It is far less likely that the most disadvantaged can call on similar resources, which have to be provided by their teachers. Inevitably, there are many other developed countries in similar positions that need to ask themselves the same questions.

Why does the UK independent sector perform so well?

Is it that they select children on academic ability and most of those children are from advantaged homes? It is still regrettably common to hear teachers say, we don't have any really smart kids in our school because our catchment area is the estate down the road. That statement and others like it need to be ruthlessly unpacked and analysed. It is quite probably the case that more advantaged children often blossom rapidly and demonstrate skills that schools rate highly. They may well have access to a cultural capital that puts them in good stead. But most teachers believe it is the responsibility of schools to intervene on behalf of less advantaged but equally able students to support them in their quest for top university placements or high-profile jobs. So what else does the independent sector do to benefit its most able students? What is in the DNA that seems to benefit these students? Is it ready access to subject-specific knowledge and expertise? Is it a focus on scholarship above grades? Is it a culture of assumed high expectations? What might be transferable and what strategies can we use most effectively here?

Do we assume that as regards teaching and learning one size fits all?

There is a research industry out there that perhaps seeks to justify its own existence by focusing on all the 'traits' of gifted students that require their attention and support. A casual glance at the attention put on over-excitabilities, vulnerabilities and burn-outs (part of the 'freaks and geeks' perception of ability) suggests that there are a great number of researchers professionally fretting over children that they see as being 'crippled by their ability'. Whilst it would be foolish to suggest that this is never the case, many of these anxieties are sometimes caused by over-anxiety from parents and educators on the look-out for any signs of weakness or discomfort. The fear is often about students 'burning out'. To use an analogy, the blend of fuel used for racing is tuned for the demands of different circuits – or even different weather conditions. More potent fuels give noticeably more power but that needs to be balanced against the danger of engine wear. However, it has to be acknowledged that the lack of demand made by the curriculum across much of the system is that students have far too few challenging circuits to negotiate. Put simply, the lack of ignition is a far more serious problem in UK schools than is the risk of burning out. On a daily basis, schools face students who have lowered their sights, lost commitment and ambition and acquiesced to turgid spoon feeding and easy successes. Students being constantly under-challenged and being given material they have already mastered, often caused by a rigid adherence to the basic core curriculum, has created boredom on an industrial scale (for both teachers and students). The following of a lukewarm 'set quota of knowledge', set by the faceless demands of the low-level syllabus only, has resulted in a loss of passion and a seismic disengagement that is the single biggest threat to aspiration.

Part 2

Techniques

4

Techniques and the Renzulli Approach

Key points

- The most commonly used techniques for teaching the most able are: enrichment; acceleration; compaction; pull-out schemes; projects; the internet.
- Of all academic approaches the best, most influential and most widely respected is Renzulli's 'Whole School Enrichment Programme'.
- Many countries have reported the need to modify classroom practices in order to meet the needs of more able learners – a clear recognition that they do have special needs.
- There is a need for more teachers who are able to spot high-level potential and who are trained to work towards developing it.

There are a relatively small number of techniques used worldwide to educate the gifted and talented. Many of these techniques are not mutually incompatible, and most countries use a mix-and-match approach of the following:

Enrichment is the most common technique globally. In the Tower Group worldwide survey (Freeman et al., 2010) enrichment, at 89%, is by far the most universal method of provision for gifted learners, defined as providing greater breadth for learners whether in or out of school. This essentially consists of spicing up the curriculum to include additional material that it is hoped will stimulate, stretch and generally fire up the gifted pupil. Enrichment can take place in class or out of class in extra sessions offered to selected pupils.

Extension is often linked with enrichment but implies going even deeper into learning. The gifted learner is given the opportunity to work with experts, specialists and those with a similar passion, to be in control of their own learning and to stay with their peer group whilst working with outside agencies. It is worth noting that 65% of practitioners regard differentiation as key to success, reflecting the challenge of managing classroom learning for the more able. Classroom balance between enrichment and extension is a critical issue in challenging and supporting the more able.

Acceleration is where a pupil's progress through the curriculum or school years, or both, is speeded up. In the same survey, it was found that 39.4% of the gifted were accelerated in school, with 59% reporting a more advanced curriculum and 42% reporting a faster pace. It is difficult to specify the types of acceleration but the following list, usefully summarized by Montgomery (2009), is adapted here:

- Early entry into a new phase of education – from nursery onwards.
- 'Grade skipping' – promotion above age peers by one or more years (in America it can be five).
- Subject acceleration – joining more advanced pupils for special subjects.
- Vertical grouping – classes which have wide age ranges of pupils so that younger ones can work with older ones.
- Out-of-school courses – sessions which give extra lessons in subject areas.
- Concurrent studies – e.g. a primary school child may be following a secondary school course.
- Compacting studies – the normal syllabus is completed in significantly less time, with a clustering of objectives.
- Self-directed study – which the pupils do while the rest of the class is catching up.
- Mentoring – working with an expert in the field, who may be a class teacher or an outsider.

Pull-out schemes do just that: pull children out of the mainstream and place them on specialist courses or in specialist schools. There is a broad spectrum of pull-out schemes, ranging from the use of summer schools to entirely separate schools, some of which can be subject-based. Projects whereby the able child chooses or is given a project to research on their own are sometimes combined with tertiary links, in which the mentor for the project is university-based. A number of countries favour able children's involvement in competitions or Olympiads as a means of stimulating them. Though not a technique as such, and rather more a means of delivery, internet-based schemes are on the increase, such as the IGGY (International Gateway for Gifted Youth) programme at the University of Warwick or Stanford's EPGY (Education Program for Gifted Youth).

Though not a technique either, home tuition is a traditional recourse for parents frustrated with the system's inability to cope with a gifted child. Web-based schemes make home tuition both more practicable and more attractive, as well as offering a solution to countries with large areas of remote rural land.

The old argument of acceleration versus enrichment has been shown to be simplistic and dated. The benefits sought by gifted education can be achieved through a variety of overlapping strategies. Very few responses in the Tower Group survey indicated a commitment to any one to the exclusion of all the others, and all were built on local context.

The Renzulli approach

Before looking in a little more detail at the various techniques, it is worth discussing one particular method, that pioneered by Renzulli. First, it is an amalgam of many of the techniques outlined above. Second, in the recent survey of world provision for the gifted and talented, Renzulli's theories were cited by more countries as having inspired or heavily influenced their programmes than any other single individual or source. Third, Renzulli offers a programme that seems in touch with the reality of actual schools and children. Fourth, Renzulli's work contains enough different ideas from the various warring camps of gifted education to broker a truce between them where his theories are concerned.

Renzulli's 'Schoolwide Enrichment Model' (SEM) consists of three components:

1. A strength-based student portfolio containing information about academic achievement, preferred areas of interest, learning styles and preferred modes of expression.
2. Curriculum compacting.
3. Enrichment learning and teaching.

The student portfolio is crucial, as the individual documentation of a student is crucial to every successful scheme studied in this book. There has to be a record kept of a gifted student's work and progress, not in an over-bearing, regulatory way, but simply as a health and progress check that is the equivalent mentally of the physical checks a baby undergoes, and for the same reason that the user of satellite navigation does not merely ask to be told when they have arrived, but keeps the map unscrolling in front of them so they know where they are at any given moment. The need for individual tracking, a heavy consumer of time and resources, is one reason why G&T education is often the first to go in a crisis. Though they would be the last to admit it, there is a link between schools and armies. Armies need their soldiers to do everything at the same time and in the same way, and dress them in uniform to emphasize the need for conformity and loyalty to the group as a more important asset than simple individuality. With the best will in the world, schools need children to behave *en masse*, hence assemblies, and the encouragement of competitive loyalty to one's school team, be it in football or in debating. Schools could teach industry much about building up corporate loyalty; they seek to do it with their children all the time. Renzulli's programme, and teaching the most able in general, demands a focus on the individual. When an army marches, everyone needs to turn right at the same time. A gifted child can sometimes be the tiny voice that says, 'But I need to turn left!', which is annoying and inconvenient but may well be the path to that individual child realizing their giftedness. It is frequently the measure of a good school that it can develop a personalized learning programme to accommodate the individual.

Renzulli concentrates on gifted behaviour rather than gifted individuals. He believes in a three-ringed concept of giftedness. Yes, the children have above-average ability, but equal contributors to the realization of giftedness are creativity and task commitment. The latter is edu-speak for the ability to concentrate and work hard. Renzulli believes that, 'a child's general level of ability is more or less fixed but that creativity and commitment are more dependent on the opportunities and stimuli provided ... Renzulli suggests that a talent pool of 15–20% of the school populace should be considered when looking for gifted potential' (Goodhew, 2009: 2).

There is a core of helpful common sense to much of what Renzulli says. For example, teachers knew long before psychologists proved it that a student's power of concentration was as effective as their raw intelligence in deciding the level at which they achieved. It is the flat heel versus the stiletto image. A heavy shoe brought down hard on a wooden surface will not dent it if its heel is flat, but a lighter shoe with a stiletto heel will do so. It is not so much the force and weight of the shoe that matters, rather the extent to which those are focused and concentrated on to one small space. Some years ago, a European *conservatoire* asked its staff to gauge the level of 'genius' or pure natural talent in individual students, but also asked a number of other questions of them. What emerged years later was that those students who had succeeded on the world stage had one common denominator. It was not the level of their genius. Rather, it was that all the successful ones put in at least 10,000 hours of practice a year. Renzulli recognizes what teachers know – it is not only what you've got but also your capacity to use it.

Renzulli is also interested in models of learning. 'Deductive' learning is the term used for the traditional model of learning and is sometimes referred to as 'to-be-presented knowledge'. 'Inductive' knowledge is a model which matches recent research into how people learn. Renzulli acknowledges the need for and value of deductive learning but argues that the modern workplace demands an approach to learning that is more flexible. This is 'knowledge and skill acquisition gained from investigative and creative activities' (Renzulli & Reis, in Shavinina, 2009: 1207). Inductive learning has three key features:

1. The topic or problem the student is given is personalized, meaning that students are doing the work because they want to.
2. As far as possible, students use the modus operandi of a practising professional. This immediately takes the work out of school and into, what is to many children, the far more exciting adult 'real world' – the worlds of the research lab, the business and the film studio are three examples.
3. The work the students do is always geared towards the production of a product or service intended to have an impact on a particular audience.

A crucial factor in Renzulli's approach is that knowledge is not just acquired to store away for a rainy day, but is the knowledge the student needs there and then to solve a problem – 'just-in-time' knowledge based on need-to-know and need-to-do, and which profits greatly from the mass of information now obtainable quickly from the internet. Some theories of intelligence and learning have not aged well. Renzulli's seems actually to have grown in strength through the technological revolution, despite having its origins in the 1970s.

Renzulli's model has political strengths to help it succeed in the real world. It is a whole-school programme, so avoids accusations of simply giving more riches to the already wealthy. Whilst implicitly accepting that some children are probably more naturally able than others, it places significant emphasis on the importance of environment, and on emotional intelligence and personality features such as commitment and determination. It is unique in thus giving something to both the geneticists and the environmentalists, and is a genuine synergy of nature and nurture. It carries no suggestion of pupils being selected to join its initial phase – no nasty examination that brands children as failures – and its central concept of progression through three phases in practice embraces a philosophy whereby the pupil in effect tells you how able they are, by their continuing commitment to the process. Renzulli's model walks a safe path through the political, social and politically correct minefields that have blown up so many schemes for able children.

Renzulli's programme has more than political correctness in its favour. One of the simpler facts to emerge in the course of this study carries no surprises: able children can get very bored very quickly and that boredom frequently detaches them from their studies. Renzulli's programme is an antidote to boredom. It is pupil-centred, a crucial feature. Able children know what they are interested in and glory in being allowed to pursue that interest. In many cultures, the teacher is constituted as the source of all wisdom. There are teachers whose vision of an ideal lesson is to walk into a class with 100 facts in their head, and when the lesson has finished feel assured that at least 90 of those facts have been transferred into the heads of their pupils. This is the very antithesis of a successful lesson for able pupils, at the end of which the effective teacher will expect both to have learnt things from the pupils and for a significant proportion of the good teaching and learning in the lesson to have been pupil-on-pupil. The extent to which very able children educate each other is a challenge to many teachers, who expect that they are the person who educates the children. Renzulli's system encourages the teacher to let the children off the leash, much in the manner of a nervous owner of a puppy who knows that one day they will have to let the puppy off the leash and hope they return. Bad teaching of the most able tries to keep the children under the control of the teacher. Good teaching hands at least some control over to the consumer.

Renzulli's ideas have other strengths. There is a practical, real-world element to them which children relish. His construct acknowledges the crucial importance of teachers and parents, allowing teachers to teach to their passions and interests. This in turn realizes that the content of what is delivered to able children matters less than the passion, energy and enthusiasm with which it is delivered. Good teaching of the most able children concentrates more on making the ride exciting than it does on the destination, and Renzulli's system caters for and encourages this. It allows for enrichment, acceleration, compaction and project work, making it the equivalent of a wide-spectrum antibiotic capable of attacking a range of infections.

Renzulli has also thought about and embraced the potential of computers, the web and new technology in the delivery of a programme for the gifted and talented. His ideas can carry the concept of a computer programme that is specific to the interests of the pupil and delivers suitable resources to that pupil, and is a major boost to the resources both school and teacher can bring to an able child, moving closer to giving that child their own, personal one-to-one teacher.

Of course, Renzulli's system is not perfect. It is a 'whole-school' model and the reluctance of many teachers to embrace the cause of G&T education is a potential major drawback to its implementation. It is not particularly geared to producing brilliant graduates in the STEM subjects (Science, Technology, Engineering and Mathematics), the surest route into the hearts, minds and pockets of many governments. Renzulli's ideas have been extended and elaborated since they were first launched, and are approaching a level of complexity and detail that might put off the typical deputy head whose responsibilities for G&T pupils have to compete with checking that the children who come to school on a bike all wear a helmet, and that the school lavatories are this side of respectable.

That being said, Renzulli's vision makes use of most of the recognized methods of bringing on and realizing the potential of able children, does not require the building of new schools or massive capital investment and sidesteps the highly politically charged issue of selection. It is a convincing synthesis of views on educating able children and the single programme most likely to succeed. Renzulli's achievement also lies in the fact that his theory has had a beneficial impact on the theory and practice of many people who have not adopted the whole programme that he advocates.

Many countries have reported the need to modify classroom practices in order to meet the needs of gifted learners, thus recognizing that they do have special needs. Most are educated within mainstream settings and classrooms. However, extra provision is also provided in terms of additional or extra-curricular resources, rather than as a form of differentiated instruction (e.g. structural pedagogical changes embedded in everyday teaching and learning). One great benefit of education for the gifted is spreading throughout education – personalized teaching – which raises teacher expectation for everyone. There is also a need for teachers to raise both their students' and their own aspirations. This is especially important for youngsters in cultures which do not encourage their children to aim high or those handicapped by cultural mores and language difficulties, or who have personal problems.

To provide personalized teaching that is appropriate to individual learners, teachers must be better equipped to track each student's development. For that, there will have to be more teachers in every classroom who are able to spot high-level potential and work towards developing it. What is more, provision should not only consider how it affects the gifted but also those who are excluded. High-quality education for students of high potential should not be at the expense of all the others, but a benefit for all.

Questions for further thought

What might the key barriers to top achievement be that resonate with your school?

In terms of implementing a whole-school improvement plan, an audit that looks at the key issues that impact on high-level achievement in your specific environment is the initial driver. The focus of the debate is usually on the context of home, culture or peers, with each adding its own dimension of challenge. The next issue that tends to arise is the school's perception of standards, ranging from those stipulated by the exam boards through to individual teachers who set standards within individual departments. The gaps that arise between these constructs lead to some fascinating debates about what might be happening across a school. The gap between student and teacher expectations needs to be addressed, and the causes of any disparity identified and interrogated, although that is easier said than done. Finally, issues that surround both behaviour and timetabling then need to be discussed in some detail, as the real devil is definitely here. Bringing the best out of the most able is a mindset. It is also something that can be brought crashing down by such seemingly trivial practicalities as fixed lunchtimes and transport after school.

Unsurprisingly, a significant barrier often given appears to be time, with not enough of it being allocated or being available to allocate to teaching the whole syllabus, let alone to go beyond it to foster creativity and curiosity; not enough time to embed content and concepts and get deep knowledge across; and finally too much paperwork and class administration for meaningful engagement with students. 'We need to make the cake before we make the icing' is a common and understandable attitude; what is harder to take on is that you can do both, and the key to doing so is identifying the young people you can do it with. Of course, you need to make the cake first. But does the school realize how much more quickly the cake can be made with the most able students? Trust comes into it here. The teacher has to trust the student to master much of the basic material quickly and, if needs be, on their own, freeing up huge amounts of icing time.

Another issue that commonly crops up at this point is that students' background 'levels' are too low to give them a real shot at top grades, either through not having the background knowledge or not being confident in the basic skills. Low literacy levels can also hinder this, and this too is often highlighted by schools, particularly in technical and general academic language and language acquisition.

Is lack of ambition on behalf of our students a key factor?

A barrier that defies exact definition is a school's response to its own pupils and their parents. What about the student who, in the opinion of teachers, needs to 'get a life'? The students whose course work is never quite good enough to be handed in yet? The person who will question their teacher over two marks they were deducted in their last test? Do you dismiss them by suggesting they need to chill out? Or do you ask what is prompting them to ask for more? Could it be that the problem isn't that they need to chill out, but that you are too chilled out?

Then there's the parent. Their children are perfect. If anything goes wrong, it's the teacher's or the school's fault, but never, ever the fault of their child. And? Many of the most effective schemes in the world for teaching the most able reckoned that parents who thought their children were in the most able category were subsequently proved to be correct. Parents are in contact with their children for significantly more time than teachers. They see the child fizzing round the home all evening with energies the school has failed to exhaust. They see the child who has asked for more and been refused it. Of course, there are students in danger of hypertension. Of course, there are parents who are hopelessly over-ambitious for their children. But are we sure that putting children or parents into those boxes isn't because it's easier to shut them up than to listen to them?

What helps to address the challenges identified by the audit?

It is always useful to begin to examine the significant issues through a whole-school audit of staff confidence and competence. This should focus on whether staff have the confidence to predict top grades accurately, possess the skills and knowledge to teach to top-grade level and fully understand what is required for students to achieve a top grade in their subject. In other words, do staff know what a top grade actually looks like?

Once that has been established, it is useful to gain a clearer understanding of what various departments do particularly well to help students to achieve top grades and what enables departments to make the most progress in increasing top-grade performance. Some of the issues that this tends to raise involve the use of formative assessment to meet the needs of top-grade students, how departments provide sufficient specialized support for students to achieve top grades, how they use whole-class learning to meet the needs of these students through differentiation and whether they feel they have access to sufficiently high-challenge resources and can utilize subject-specific networks to support their most able students.

Previous audits conducted have also asked departments to look at the extent to which they believe that they can provide specialized coaching for students to understand, say, the requirements of Ivy League/Oxbridge entry/interviews and provide access to out-of-class enrichment opportunities to support students to achieve Ivy League/Oxbridge entry and offer the most able students 'beyond the syllabus' activities, resources and opportunities. Schools can harbour surprising antagonism towards specialist programmes designed, for example, to help students get into top universities. Yet the moral and social justification for such programmes, as well as the educational one, is very strong. The most able will feel attracted to certain life paths, because these are those that will allow them full self-expression and fulfilment of their gifts and talents. There is nothing wrong in briefing students on what will most recommend them to Oxbridge or Ivy League universities, or on what is needed to pursue a course in research science. It is just one form of a personalized learning plan. What it can require is a fairly ruthless assessment of just how much a school's staff actually know about these specialist fields, and if the answer is not very much then to get them out to the places and people who can tell them or bring those people into school.

(Continued)

(Continued)

What would enable your colleagues to make the most progress in increasing top-grade performance?

Once the audit has been completed, it is essential to look at what staff have indicated would support them most in the top grades quest. Previous 'audit leading choices' have been exemplars of top-grade work, student booster sessions, setting or streaming guidance from examination boards and, usually most resoundingly, resource materials. Other ideas suggested at this point have been collaborative lesson planning with colleagues and clubs and enrichment classes. Both training days and subject consultant support tend to be considered far less important, with slight variations of order in some subjects.

It is both interesting, and slightly depressing, that our research suggests the major emphasis on training days in the UK at least has left a significant number of teachers unimpressed and, by implication, left the product delivered at the chalk face unimproved. Why is this? One reason might be the poor quality of some of the training supplied. Another is the sense that these days and sessions are often a 'quick fix', giving at best a momentary boost to the teacher who nevertheless soon gets dragged down again to the level of keeping their head above water. Meeting the needs of the most able is not a one-day event. It's a culture.

Often, these audits also highlight how significant teachers feel that the ability to be creative or think outside the box or be intuitive might be for top-grade students. It has often been the case that curiosity is seen to be important, but we find that schools still mainly use past papers, revision classes or testing to help students – all things that don't in themselves tend to foster curiosity. In a number of cases, creativity was accepted as a word or in a theoretical sense but not necessarily pursued as a concept. Sometimes it becomes quite clear that staff may have lowered their own expectations of what the students can or will engage with. In the most successful schools studied, almost the key ingredient was the refusal of the teachers to place any limits on how far a child could go or on how fast they got there. It is not unusual in these schools to find teachers with PhDs in their subjects acknowledging that they have themselves learnt something new from a junior pupil. The use of whole-class learning to meet the needs of top students through differentiation, and access to sufficiently high challenge problem-solving/ enquiry-based resources, are constantly raised as serious barriers. Issues such as the appropriateness of examinations, timetabling or professional development have also been commented on.

What are the subject-specific skills and behaviours that your pupils need in order to achieve top grades?

It is critical to focus in on subject-specific skills in order to get real 'buy-in' from schools. It is only then that colleagues see what is required of them on a day-to-day basis. It can be useful to supply a series of skills so that all staff can look closely at the matrix, add in additional skills and behaviours that they feel might be missing and rank which they feel might be most significant.

The following skill sets might be a useful starting point. A top student may be one who:

In English

- shows a perceptive critical faculty which enables connections and judgements to be made within and between texts
- asks questions to challenge and develop complex ideas; recognizes and accepts ambiguity
- uses an unusually wide vocabulary, with accuracy; is confident enough to experiment, both in speaking and in writing
- is passionate about reading, and open to new genres, authors and ideas
- expresses ideas succinctly, sometimes elegantly but may feel detail or support is so obvious as to be unnecessary
- identifies the main issues in debates and devises strategies quickly to deal with them, in many roles, perhaps in original ways
- is prepared to listen to and learn from others, and has the emotional intelligence to draw ideas from others and build on them without dominating discussion; understands registers instinctively and can react creatively to others' ideas to mediate and develop them.

In maths

- develops individual non-standard methods for solving problems and may skimp on explanations but be able to justify them
- sees the implications of concepts quickly, but may complicate problems by thinking of other implications or restrictions
- takes unexpected sidelines or develops short cuts, by making connections to different branches of maths and applying them creatively
- examines the strategies adopted when investigating within mathematics itself or when using maths to analyse tasks
- works quickly and may make mistakes in calculation but may also consider the elegance and efficiency of alternative lines of enquiry or procedures
- includes mathematical justifications, distinguishing between evidence and proof, and explains their solutions to problems involving a number of features or variables.

In science

- observes with insight, offering perceptive interpretations and extrapolations
- asks novel 'what if?' type questions, making links to prior knowledge but with lateral twists
- sees relationships between variables and makes perceptive explanations of hypotheses
- makes intuitive leaps in different situations, showing genuine curiosity and persistent interest in topics
- absorbs new concepts rapidly, demonstrating a great interest in the bigger questions such as the nature of the universe
- is reluctant to accept simplified explanations or to work on anything which is low level and unchallenging.

(Continued)

(Continued)

Once colleagues have had the opportunity to add in their own ideas and to tailor skills to suit their school context, the final stage is obvious. How can teachers promote those skills and behaviours in different subject areas? This issue is of course the most important. There needs to be a clear focus on what departments explicitly do to teach the skills they have agreed on. There needs to be an understanding of which tasks, activities or lessons colleagues carry out on a regular basis, starting from way down the school, that enable students to begin to develop these skills. Finally and crucially, there needs to be a sharing with one another of these approaches.

5

Acceleration and Compaction

> **Key points**
>
> - It is untrue that children on accelerated courses will fail to understand material or suffer emotionally.
> - Successfully accelerated children need a say in their course.
> - Support from, of and for families is crucial.
> - Teachers are all-important and need time and flexibility.
> - Preparatory courses are essential.
> - Acceleration saves time that frees up other resources.

Before we begin this chapter in full, it is important to understand what we mean by 'acceleration' and 'compaction'.

Acceleration involves pushing students through the standard curriculum at an accelerated rate. The purpose of acceleration is 'to move students through the curriculum at rates faster than typical or at ages younger than usual' (Colangelo & Assouline, in Shavenina, 2009: 1085).

Compaction is where the curriculum is compacted, with material deemed unnecessary for the most able or which is repetitive, taken out, so that things proceed at a faster pace. It might include students being entered early for examinations and accelerated through grade and year groups, usually to a maximum of three years.

An extreme example is where a student cuts out the last two years of schooling and goes directly to university. One such scheme, which can deal with children as young as 13 and is available at the University of Washington in Seattle, is examined in Chapter 6. Acceleration can also be subject based, in place of or alongside year/grade acceleration. In total, there are around 18 types of acceleration and compaction. A further definition of compaction is: 'clustering learning objectives, to encourage challenging teaching which provides breadth, depth and pace ... One of the guiding principles ... is that teachers need to spend less time teaching factual information and more time enabling their students to think' (Shavinina, 2009: 1399).

At school level, there are at least two objections to acceleration and compaction. One is that a student will not fully understand the material, another that acceleration damages a student's social development. In the book *A Nation Deceived: How Schools Hold Back America's Brightest Students*, (Templeton National Report on Education, 2004) there is one of the fiercest and most passionate rebuttals of that view, which suffers in extract. A comment which does not do so is:

> The literature reports generally positive effective outcomes for radically accelerated students ... Studies show high levels of self-confidence, independence, maturity and motivation in college students who have been radically accelerated compared to regular college students ... the great majority of students report that the social and emotional benefits of radical acceleration far outweigh any negative effects.

and

> The vast majority of these students progress to university and attain outstanding results. Many gain awards and scholarships. Most complete university study and attain significantly higher grade point averages than regular-age students ... Many case studies outline the career path of students who have chosen radical acceleration. A significant number complete postgraduate studies and accept offers to remain at university to lecture and to complete research. Many go on to become professors and have become leaders in their field, making impressive discoveries and truly advancing knowledge. (Miraca & Van Vliet, n.d.: 11)

The success celebrated here and below is dependent on a number of factors. A successfully accelerated student needs to have high attainment levels. Acceleration schemes are not for the faint-hearted, and there is a crucial difference between schemes that allow an able child to succeed and ones that might help to make an able child succeed. Most acceleration schemes take the child out of the atmosphere and into orbit, rather than lifting the child into the atmosphere in the first place. They deal with established and identified ability. They do not discover or create it.

Successful acceleration and compaction schemes

Every successful acceleration and compaction scheme observed in this research involved the student fully in the planning and execution of their programme. These young 'astronauts' need to be volunteers and need also to have some real control over the direction of their spaceship.

Supportive families are also crucial to success, not least of all in the need to explain to parents just as fully as to the student what is being planned and how it will roll out. In this fact might lie one of the reasons why acceleration is not embedded in many cultures. There is a greater tendency in disadvantaged families for parents to have no experience of extended education, and perhaps even no great respect for it, at least in those western cultures where education is not seen as a way out of poverty. Given the importance of parental support and encouragement, there is an extent again to which acceleration and compaction appeal to the converted, at least in the sense that they need a degree of parental goodwill and understanding of it from the outset. One should not be fooled into thinking that such schemes create the necessary goodwill. More often than not, they need to feed off it to get started and take root.

It perhaps goes without saying how crucial trained and supportive teachers are, but our research has highlighted the significant difference between top-down and bottom-up schemes. Where a country or state has decided that acceleration and compaction are a good thing, and has sought to impose them on schools, there has been a degree of lip service and some cynicism. Where the programme has come from practising teachers who were prepared to take ownership of it, and where there was one person in particular seen as being in charge of the scheme, it has worked well.

Successful schemes also contain to a high degree two elements that classroom teachers sometimes find hard to come to terms with. The first is the planning necessary for a successful scheme. For many teachers, this is not a problem of goodwill or even training but simply one of time. In conversation, the most frequently cited worry after threats to funding was lack of time or comments along the lines of 'There just aren't enough hours in the day'.

Individualization of a student's programme is a crucial factor in the success of the Renzulli model and quite possibly all successful schemes. Yet, time is money in teaching as elsewhere, and schools or countries that take teaching their most able children seriously must realize that they will have to pay for the time necessary, not just in acceleration and compaction schemes, but in enrichment and other strategies too. However, it should be noted that coverage of the normal curriculum can often be achieved in less time with gifted children, with a commensurate 'saving'. There has also been one technological innovation that has a potentially revolutionary effect on Personalized Learning Programmes. For the first time ever, a classroom teacher can carry around with them, in the form of an ipad or other tablet, the details of hundreds if not thousands of students, accessible at the tap of a screen. Previously, such records would have needed whole rooms to store them and days to find them.

The second element is flexibility, something denied teachers in more autocratic systems. Too rigid a control over what happens in the classroom can deny several of the core commandments in teaching able children. They bore easily, and boredom kills achievement. Good teaching follows their interests as much as the set syllabus, and allows for the fact that they can assimilate material far more quickly and easily than others, thus freeing up lesson time to do more interesting things. The freedom to gather flowers by the wayside in this manner requires courage and commitment from school and teachers. It is often argued that more able pupils require social and emotional support, but so do their teachers.

A further factor that has helped schemes to success is the laying on of preparatory courses to smooth the way. Many people have less of a problem with intellectual acceleration, for example with mathematicians in particular, for students who may have subject skills that have far outstripped their chronological age. It is the issue of a child's social and emotional age that most worries critics of acceleration. The reasons are obvious. Popularity, being in a social group and having friends are the very blood of life to most adolescents. Accelerate them out and you risk stranding them, gasping like a fish out of water. It is difficult enough for young adults to make the right decisions with regard to drugs, drink and sex, so how can a younger child cope if they are prematurely launched into an environment where such temptations are the norm? How is the young person kept safe from predatory adults?

Many of the answers to these valid questions are contained in the discussion of the University of Washington scheme in Chapter 6. In brief, all can be defused if sufficient preparatory time is invested in the child, a distinction drawn between a child's academic and social milieu, and plentiful support and encouragement, both social and emotional, is given. Yet this too obviously costs money. Equally, given the economic potential of highly able children, it can be argued that spending money on them is simply spending money to make money in the longer term.

Acceleration and compaction can also be rendered impractical if teachers are insufficiently qualified. Informally, a number of the schemes visited reported that schemes for the gifted and talented were held back by teachers' fear of being 'shown up'. A teacher who is not a top graduate in the subject they teach might reasonably not look forward to the moment when pupils began to ask questions beyond that teacher's subject knowledge. This neurosis is particularly evident in practicals in the sciences. Practicals are a proven way to excite and stimulate students' passion for the subject, but are all too likely by their very nature to go wrong or at least not according to plan. The teacher with a first degree in the subject may or may not have the additional knowledge in depth to sort out the problem and cope with it, but equally, if not more, important is the fact that they are more likely to have the confidence to make the effort. Furthermore, graduates are more likely to be free of 'equipment phobia' or a fear of the equipment central to the success of all practicals which familiarity removes from many graduates. Training can help significantly in calming a teacher down. Teachers in highly selective schools have become used to the possibility that some or all of their pupils might know more than they do, and that that situation is to be welcomed.

Some teachers also might need reminding that the scholar does not need to know everything but should know where to find an answer to what he or she does not know. One teacher, when faced with a question she did not know the answer to, was in the habit of telling the class to 'hang it on the hook' like a coat overnight, where she would pick it up next lesson. By the next lesson, she had inevitably researched the answer. Another excellent technique when a pupil clearly has extended knowledge is to let him or her be the teacher, and give a presentation to the whole class on the topic the following day. It is a powerful incentive as well as a useful lesson for students to be shown that the teacher is not an ambulatory Google, and that their perceived expertise is built on a great deal of research and hard slog. This also has relevance to the research suggesting that praise of the hard work that a student has put into a piece of work is more productive than praise of its perceived quality.

It is natural to focus on the children in any educational scheme or programme. What is clear from the research undertaken for this book is the counter-intuitive fact that in schemes for the most able the children come second. No scheme or programme can reach its target unless the teaching force has been enabled to deliver it. To repeat an analogy, if the pupils are the space shuttle that needs to be launched into orbit, then the massive boosters, without which the shuttle will never break free, are the teachers. Sometimes those teachers need to be reminded of simple things, such as the fact that the booster does not need to follow the shuttle into space. To extend the analogy, the teacher's job is to help the child achieve escape velocity, and shedding additional weight (the teacher) can be crucial to the process.

Acceleration and compaction depend for their success on the fact that able children can require less time to be taught the same or a greater amount than their normally able peers. They pick things up faster, often need only to go over a topic once and can be trusted to do much more of the necessary work on their own. This allows the variant of compaction which instead of skipping a year simply skips a day a week – a practice used throughout the world with the most prominent example being New Zealand's 'A-Day-a-Week' or 'One-Day School'. It is also an economic fact that teaching time on the basics can be saved and the additional resources put either into supplying enrichment for the most able or more resources for the normally able. However, the teacher whose career success depends on the number of their students who reach a bare pass grade is far less likely to take the risk of fast-laning a student. Teaching to a relatively low common denominator does not merely restrict the development of the most able students, it positively harms them.

Potential pitfalls of acceleration and contraction schemes

A notable feature of the lessons observed in the research for this book was the confidence and energy generated by teachers of G&T classes. Was it the energy and excitement of the teachers that so clearly enthused the pupils? Or was it the energy and excitement of the students that so enthused the teachers?

Does 'a rising tide lift all ships'? Some teachers of G&T groups confessed to being 'sensitized' by their work with the more able pupils. They had intellectually to be so quick on their feet, so careful to tune in to the children in the class and listen to them, that they were sure they became better all-round teachers. But the reverse scenario, that this phrase has become simply a cliché that is trotted out to calm down egalitarian qualms, must also be considered.

A weakness of some acceleration and compaction programmes is a lack of continuity. It is tempting to take a mathematically precocious 8-year-old and allow him to skip a grade or year, but unless the child in question has a special year of primary school made for them at the end of the process, or arrangements have been made with the secondary school, then the accelerated child is at best placed in the sand trap, at worst decelerated and flung into a brick wall. The same is true of schemes in school systems where the pupil moves school at age 16, into a specialist or sixth form college, and finds him- or herself back in the slow lane and deprived of the additional intellectual, emotional and social support to which they have been accustomed. Acceleration and compaction have to have their beginning and their end most carefully plotted, otherwise it becomes a big 'so what' question thrown out into the ether. It is great to speed your way through the curriculum because you can, but is the end game just to create younger graduates?

There is also a potential weakness in systems such as the UK's where early specialization can occur. Thus, a 16-year-old in the UK who suddenly opts for a career in medicine or engineering will find choice reduced if an acceleration or compaction programme has speeded them past extended mathematics or three separate sciences, just as giving up a language will make it harder for them to gain, for example, a place at a top university for English or history. In other words, an effective acceleration or compaction should still pursue a generalist programme. Acceleration and compaction must enhance a student's prospects. They have failed if they serve to restrict the available career pathways of students.

This can be rendered difficult because able children can be obsessed with a comparatively narrow range of topics. It is important for able children to exert some control over their education, but this clashes with a significant number of able children who, at the age of 13, would cheerfully choose never to go to another maths lesson in their life, or one in English.

Despite all these niggles, if the necessary hard work and resources are there:

> There is now ample evidence to show that highly gifted students who are radically accelerated do not suffer unfavourable social or emotional effect. These students do not 'burn out'; they do not lose interest in their areas of talent; and they do not suffer from large gaps in their academic or social knowledge. Rather, radical acceleration appears to offer extraordinary benefits for highly gifted children for both their intellectual development and their social and emotional health. (Miraca & Van Vliet, n.d.: 12)

The above clarion call to action contrasts with an English textbook written for teachers on how to meet the needs of G&T pupils. It cites acceleration as a valid technique, but at the same time seems to suggest that it is something to be used as a weapon of last resort, only when all else has failed. It is worth quoting in full; in the original, each question came with its own 'Yes/No' tick-box:

Acceleration Checklist
   Before accelerating a child, have you:

1. Explored all available strategies for providing for that child within his/her peer group?
2. Consulted fully with:

   o parents (such consultation should include advice on the pros and cons of acceleration and time for parents to consider this information)?
   o teachers?

(Continued)

(Continued)

   o   the child (children are rarely consulted or involved in the process)?
   o   any receiving schools or colleges? (Are they prepared to accept young pupils? Can they provide appropriate courses of study for them?)

3. Considered:

   o   the emotional/social maturity of the child?
   o   the physical maturity of the child?
   o   areas of weakness within the curriculum (e.g. presentation skills or spelling)?
   o   the friendship ties of the child?
   o   the long-term impact on the child?

(e.g. there can be a conflict at adolescence between parents and children when children want to socialize with and behave like their classmates and not their chronological age group. Is the child likely to benefit from going to university early?)

   o   drawn up a short-term plan with all concerned parties for the pupil's educational provision?
   o   made arrangements for regular review of the pupil's progress throughout his/her schooling?
   o   told parents, child and teachers of agencies that can support them if there are difficulties (e.g. NAGC or CHI)?

(Goodhew, 2009: 132)

There is much good sense in this, but also a clear negativity and an implicit disapproval of the technique, verging on fear. It suggests acceleration as the weapon of last resort – what to do if all else fails. Is the tenor of this advice to tell participants where to go *if* things go wrong, or *when* they go wrong as they inevitably will? The piece is also factually wrong. In at least two major schemes, that run by the University of Washington in Seattle and the Adelaide-based SHIP scheme, the full involvement of the child is a main priority.

Acceleration and compaction work to help get the best out of able children but cost money and time. They can also save money and time which a school can re-invest. They are not an add-on to an educational system but need to be an integral part of a system which in turn may have to bend and flex to cope with its needs. As with all school-based systems, they stand or fall on the quality and commitment of the teachers and rely heavily on parental support. They are not a magic bullet to end underachievement on the part of able but disadvantaged children, but may offer an effective strategy to assist in this long-term goal.

There is a final question which is not often asked. Acceleration to what end? Is it so that children can finish school more quickly? If it is, what do they do then? Is it so that they can finish university more quickly? What then? There are real dangers in accelerating students down the educational motorway, whilst leaving no junction from which they can join the world of work or adult life. Acceleration programmes need to be whole-life programmes, with acceleration a link or links in a chain that is strongly attached to life after full-time education ceases.

Questions for further thought

What helps students be motivated to learn?

Curiosity is at the very heart of learning. It's what drives people to want to learn more about something. Over a hundred years ago, William James pointed out two kinds of curiosity. He emphasized the biological function of curiosity as a mechanism of instinct-driven behaviour that serves in approaching new objects. The second kind of curiosity pointed out by James is scientific curiosity and meta-physical wonder with which the philosophical brain responds to an inconsistency or a gap in its knowledge. This is supported, slightly more recently, by Vygotsky's zone of proximal development theory – that we need to push students slightly out of their comfort zone for them to learn.

Once that initial spark of curiosity happens, the next step is to investigate more thoroughly. That investigation then leads to wanting to wholly understand it – to unravel the mystery of it. And, of course, that's where learning comes into action. Great lessons withhold immediate meaning. They have to be worked on. Students of all ages get too few chances to pick on ideas and texts, examine them, stick sharpened matches between their pages, interrogate them and question them about what they are for. They are difficult and puzzling over them requires engagement.

However, there are far too many lessons which begin with students being required to copy down the learning objective. Effectively, this is like starting the lesson with the words 'today's self-fulfilling prophecy is ...', and it short-circuits the intended challenge in learning. There are many different routes to excellence, but wonder is rarely inspired by a monotone announcement of what will be the result of the next hour of life.

How best to stimulate intellectual curiosity in our able students?

Enquiry and discovery are hugely significant and powerful elements of learning in any compacted or accelerated scheme. That is not to say that sometimes a clear helicopter overview of our teaching intentions across a course will go amiss. Able students often want the big picture to clarify where they are and what they have embarked upon. There is no contradiction between having a map and enjoying being on the actual ground.

(Continued)

(Continued)

Yet we also need them to like the stimulation of wrestling with unforeseen obstacles and problems, particularly if this involves anomalies that undermine comfortable assumptions. We want to stimulate their enjoyment of ambiguity, complexity and uncertainty, speculating on what isn't there, on what remains to be discovered. They need to know, and their teachers need to understand, that education is not only about finding the answers; just as exciting is finding the questions. We need to concentrate on what our subject still cannot answer and examine why things are still uncertain. It would help to design deliberate disorientation into your lessons to enable students to become defamiliarized and have to cope with and make sense of these experiences. And we need to take risks ourselves.

How do we ensure that students stay engaged?

It is sometimes easier to stretch and accelerate our more able students than it is to keep them on the journey with us. As teachers, we sometimes forget that we have become experts in our subjects. We get used to 'explaining' key concepts and the more difficult areas of our domains but we neglect to explain to our students what it is that we found emotionally engaging about our subject in the first place, why we chose to study it and what we feel it is there to explain. So it is really helpful to use personal anecdotes, stories and epiphanies in our classroom to support our students to understand why our subject is meaningful to us. That includes making it clear that there are moments where we still get excited about our subject and why that happens. It also means that we should explain to students what helped us to 'get' our subject, our own learning histories and where our sense of security and expertise comes from.

6

The Robinson Center for Young Scholars

Key points

- The Robinson Center prepares children from the age of 13 onwards to attend the University of Washington as full-time undergraduates.
- Rigorous independent scrutiny has shown high success rates and few signs of social or emotional damage.

The Robinson Center for Young Scholars, based at the University of Washington in Seattle, might seem to belong in the chapter on the USA. It has been included here for two reasons. First, as one of the most extreme examples of acceleration of able children, it follows on naturally from the previous chapter. Second, it is such a radical scheme that it deserves a chapter of its own.

Opposition to young children attending university is a deeply rooted cultural phenomenon. It was summed up by the parents of a child maths prodigy in a book published in 2012: 'We could not see any way that a frankly socially immature boy would fit in to an environment of young adults' (Thompson & Thompson, 2012: 58).

This is not the view of the University of Washington in Seattle's Robinson Center. In essence, the Robinson Center administers a programme that can see children as young as 11 become students at the University of Washington in Seattle, though more usually the youngest will be 12 or 13 years of age. There are two schemes.

The two schemes

The first scheme, the Transition School/Early Entrance Program, was started in 1977. It is a two-step programme. Entry is based on a child's grade in the US schooling system, not their age, with children normally qualifying after the US 7th or 8th Grade (usually 12 or 13 years of age). Younger children who have been admitted have grade-skipped and jumped up years. On entry, the children attend Transition School for one year, described in the Center's online prospectus as 'an intensive college preparatory program ... taught at the Robinson Center, and subsequent full-time study at the University of Washington'. In this transition year, the children will typically take one or more of the university's courses. Numbers are small (a maximum of 16, which is approximately 25% of those who apply), and a specialist, trained staff teach Maths, Science, Literature and History courses, plus some additional short courses including Ethics. Compaction is extreme, with most of the content of secondary school compressed into three academic 'quarters'. Teaching is designed both to stretch the children and, in the words of the online prospectus, 'prepare them for the rigor of the UW'. Following the Transition School year, they become 'EEPers' or Early Entry Program students at the University of Washington – regular, full-time students. The transition is not guaranteed – in 2011 one student did not move on to the university from Transition School – but this is by far the exception rather than the rule. There is a sophisticated EEP student support scheme, including a special academic advisor, the program staff, specialized activities and personalized connections to university services. There is significant peer-group support, aided by the facilities and common room of the Robinson Center. There is no further official support after the second year, but former students seemed to feel no compunction in returning to the Center to talk to staff in particular.

There is a chronic danger of 'pathologizing' gifted children as necessarily damaged by their ability. Ironically, there is a real danger to the development of very clever children by their being over-cared for by carers who are actually significantly less able than the children in their charge, and who do not recognize that many able children are actually very tough and resilient, and positively enjoy the occasional intellectual battering. The Robinson Center imposes no template on its students. It not only accepts them as they are but allows them to go where they want to go and be what they want to be. It manages to be caring but with none of the cloying, suffocating quality of care that sometimes afflicts those who see the priority of teaching as protecting children rather than preparing them.

As of winter 2011, there were 60 EEP students enrolled at the University of Washington, taking an average of 4.4 years to graduate. Results at degree level are excellent. EEP students major in more than 35 disciplines (computer science, mathematics and biology are the most popular), 46% of EEP students go on to do post-graduate research, 57% of which results in publication. Students also intern at some of the US's most prestigious companies and organizations. This has on one occasion produced a situation whereby an intern at the CIA was deemed too young by her father to start dating. Who won the argument is not recorded. EEPers have won a staggering number of scholarships and awards. As for failures, of the 352 students who have participated in the EEP, 'only 11 students who proceeded to EEP later left school altogether, and their educational status is not known' (Noble & Childers, in Shavinina, 2009: 5).

Parental involvement has emerged in the course of this study as a crucial factor in many schemes for enabling the gifted child. The EEP programme puts a different slant on this. Early on, it was recognized that some children were being driven to apply by their parents, providing an unstable foundation for the child who would have to cope with heavy demands and needed to be personally committed to success to do so. As a result, Transition School interviews were restructured so that all applicants could talk with the admissions committee without their parents present. At the same time, the Robinson Center is far from hostile to parents, seeking to involve them at all times and, if needs be, warn them that their child is likely to develop a firm mind and views of their own, rather than just being a mimic of their parents. A programme of picnics, dinners, meetings, newsletters and a parent-led Parent Support Group seem to ensure very close links and a real sense of partnership.

It is quite possible to believe that there is a major strand in English educational culture that fears failure more than it hails success. To many, the Robinson Center will appear simply too tough. Its entry procedure is highly demanding, based on test scores, interviews and days spent at the Center, and 75% of candidates are turned down. In the USA, academic attention has focused on the progress of the children accepted. One suspects that in the UK it would have concentrated on the social and emotional damage expected to be done to those who failed. When this topic was raised with staff, their response was that they did not seek to damage children, simply to find the best fit for them. They believed that if a child was not right for the programme, if it were not a fit for him or her, then they were actually protecting the child from failure. This same *rationale* runs through to the fact that at entry children have to sign a contract with the Transition School, stating that they can be dismissed for 'poor academic performance or for rendering the classroom environment emotionally unsafe for other students' (Noble & Childers, in Shavinina, 2009: 8). A brief probationary period is allowed for any offenders. The Robinson Center cannot be accused of misleading anyone, adult or child. Its mission is not to recruit students who will cope with early entry, but who will excel. It is also unequivocal in seeing as a justification behind the scheme that it attracts into the University of Washington students who might otherwise be lost to what are perceived as more prestigious Ivy League universities.

The Robinson Center benefits from its small size and clear lines of communication. Unlike so many schools, it is not answerable to a Board and hence has shown an ability to adapt and evolve. Transition School itself only came about in 1981 when it was realized that EEPers needed considerably more preparation and support than was then being given. Similarly, German was dropped in favour of more Physics when it was realized that EEPers did not have sufficient skills or knowledge to cope in this area with what was going to be asked of them.

It is a clear reason for the success of the EEP programme that the children are local and return to their parents at night. This at a stroke reduces and controls the number of 'temptations' the young people might be exposed to. In effect, the Robinson Center utilizes the most powerful and effective support agency available to a child – the family and the home the parents create. Perhaps the only weakness of the Robinson Center is that it offers no solutions to the problems of the gifted child from a dysfunctional home. There was a strong sense among the young people that the security of a strong family unit and conventionally settled home were as important as, if not more so than, the support provided by the Robinson Center. In many respects, the attitude of the young people attending the Center to the University of Washington and all the challenges and rewards it presented was indistinguishable from the attitude one might expect to find among any children to their school. The Robinson Center is a benign hothouse. It brings on talent brilliantly, but it does not create that talent, nor does it offer a cure for those whose giftedness has gone or been caused to go awry by challenging or inadequate family circumstances.

The second scheme is the University of Washington Academy for Young Scholars. Created in 2001, it allows for up to 35 academically advanced and highly motivated students who apply during their 10th Grade year and who, if accepted, join the University of Washington at 16 years of age or just below. An initial scheme saw similar students shared between high school and the university but this proved unworkable, and now the Academy students, in effect, swap two years at high school for two years at university. There is no equivalent of Transition School but there is the

'Bridge Program', which offers an acclimatization and preparation week before term starts, along with significant counselling and a variety of support from the staff at the Robinson Center. Interestingly, monitoring of the students is rigorous. In their first and second year, Academy students are required to attend regular meetings with the Robinson Centre's academic counsellor. As of autumn 2011, 338 students had entered the Academy. Again, there has been a high success rate among the 174 students who have graduated from the Academy, who have accumulated an impressive number of scholarships and awards. Nearly two-thirds of graduates sit in the top cohort for results.

A crucial element in the viability of the Academy is that it is contracted to receive funding from State sources equivalent to that which would otherwise have been expended on the student's high school years. This is important because it means the scheme is not dependent on new funding, merely a diversion of existing monies.

How successful have these schemes been?

Both these schemes seem counter-intuitive. For many people across the world, children of this age are just that: children, whose emotional and social development must be damaged by their being thrown into university life far too young to cope. Perhaps for this reason, the work of the Robinson Center has been subject to a remarkable number of academic assessments of the success of its programmes, some 15 in number. All are positive in the extreme.

The Robinson Center suggests the following as the necessary features for success of its students, most if not all applying to the EEP/TS and the Academy:

- a period of intellectual preparation
- a peer group
- a base in the parental home
- formal and informal advising
- counselling
- mentoring by teaching staff and assistants who understand gifted students and approve of and like them
- a welcoming university environment.

However, there is a clear difference between the EEPer/Transition School pupils and the Academy young people other than mere age; the latter have completed two more years of high school education.

The 'Academy Bridge Program' is the equivalent for the older students to what is on offer to the EEPers. It has four components:

- a two-day orientation camp
- a two-week 'Honours' course
- the continuing Honours course during the autumn quarter, linked to an English composition course
- a winter quarter seminar designed to help students make the most of what the university has to offer.

The Academy offers fewer events for parents than applies to the younger students but still has a welcoming reception, a parent-orientation seminar and encouragement for parents to talk to each other.

The findings of the 15 academic studies of the Center and its students can be summarized as follows:

- There is no evidence that students are harmed by early entry.
- There was no common element in EEPers who underachieved.
- Accelerants were shown to be as socially and emotionally well-adjusted as non-accelerants, and had an entirely normal friendship base.
- Such dissatisfaction as there was among EEPers was to do with relatively minor niggles such as being asked frequently if they were a genius or told they had an obligation to go on to be a renowned researcher.
- There was no evidence that EEPers missed the rites of passage of the final two years at high school.
- Acceleration increased the confidence of girls.
- A large majority of EEPers believed they were happier at university than they were or would have been at school.
- Post-graduation EEPers were doing very well professionally and socially in their lives.
- EEPers who attended Transition School were more positive about the scheme than those who had not experienced it.
- The only disturbing feature was that far more males reported 'social dissatisfaction' in their previous and past relationships, with 21 males citing the EEP as a specific and negative factor. A clear reason was the greater difficulty for a young male in forming 'romantic relationships' than for a young girl.
- It appeared that female EEPers were earning less than their male counterparts in their post-university lives. It was not clear if this was because male EEPers tended to major in the STEM subjects, which are associated with high salaries.

Given that these surveys included a period of time when Transition School was not up and running, their results are a resounding justification of the Robinson Center and the acceleration of young and able children. It is summed up by: 'early university entrants did not fit the stereotype of the socially isolated, unhappy "nerd" ... overall they revealed themselves to be well-rounded, balanced individuals on whom the EEP continued to exert a profound and overwhelmingly positive experience' (Noble & Childers, in Shavinina, 2009: 32–3).

Four additional studies examined the Academy following its inception in 2001. Overall, the Academy emerged with flying colours. This is not to claim perfection. The need for resources to support the early-entry student is clear. It is also true that early entry is not for all students. For example, some students, albeit a small minority, found the transition from being the cleverest student in high school to merely being one of a number as an EEPer too much for them. It could well be that the Robinson Center did not create this problem but simply unearthed it and dealt with it slightly sooner than might otherwise have been the case. It is also true that some parents found themselves at odds with their children as the EEP accelerated more than their intellect – but again very few families with adolescent children do not find that spreading wings cause bruises.

Early entry is often treated with great scepticism. The research undertaken on the work of the Robinson Center cannot be ignored. The traditional fear is that early entry stifles able children. It is just as true that too much school destroys others. We need to recognize that some highly able children simply 'run out of school', which has little left to offer them. It is not early entry which stifles some very able children. It is school. It is a tragedy that the UK does not have a comparable programme.

Questions for further thought

How can the ground rules for engaging with parents be established?

In any scheme that is as groundbreaking as the Robinson Center, it is essential to keep a clear family involvement to ensure that the emotional needs of the student are understood and kept to the forefront. For more able learners, parental support and encouragement at home can provide the impetus for high achievement, supplement classroom learning and help to ensure that the profile of more able education is appropriately high. Greater parental involvement in

(Continued)

(Continued)

children's educational journey will broaden provision and raise the capacity to enable more effective support for individual talents. To begin with, it is useful to distinguish between parental involvement in school life (such as attendance at parents' evenings) and parental engagement in learning, which is obviously more proactive and specialized.

The core objectives of getting parents to engage in the learning of their children are simple, although not simple to achieve. To begin the process, a few sustained conversations with a selection of parents are essential where issues regarding their involvement in their children's educational lives can become clearer. Following on from this, a series of meetings can be arranged to provide input, guidance and information on areas that parents have voiced concerns over and lack of confidence in. Some common issues can be the social and emotional aspects of learning and the importance of targeted and specific praise and encouragement, as well as strategies for increasing communication between home and school and signposting how parents can play an important part in the development of higher-order thinking.

Where parents of more able students lack social capital or language proficiency, they may be reluctant to become involved as fully in their child's education or to help them with their homework. Children's progress is accelerated by help with further reading at home and academic conversations, and it is the responsibility of educators to help all parents to help their children.

What research can help parents?

Able students sometimes have trouble connecting personal effort to achievement, seeing it as something beyond their control. Much of what they do and learn can be achieved with relatively little effort. Whilst this may seem to be a good position to occupy, it has its drawbacks. If students succeed, it can somehow be put down to luck or some other external factor. This attitude can make students feel as if effort is pointless. Praising of effort can help, but these children also need to understand the role personal responsibility plays in success. It is always useful to quote key researchers on education, especially when they summarize their positions succinctly:

> If parents want to give their children a gift, the best thing they can do is to teach their children to love challenges, be intrigued by mistakes, enjoy effort, and keep on learning. That way, their children don't have to be slaves of praise. They will have a lifelong way to build and repair their own confidence. (Dweck, 2006 in Lucas and Claxton, 2010: 38)

This Carol Dweck quotation works because of that great phrase, 'slaves of praise'. It resounds with parents on many levels. The following one by Guy Claxton from his book *Building Learning Power* illustrates well the fact that talent is important, but so is getting it wrong and maintaining task commitment and persistence.

> An issue that has to be faced is that learning capacity is as much a matter of character as it is of skill. Being able to stay calm, focused and engaged when you don't know what to do is not a matter of technical training. It requires

a self concept that has not been infected by the pernicious idea that being confused and making mistakes means you are stupid. (Claxton, 2006: 4)

Paul Tough's comments, taken from *How Children Succeed*, are useful to get across to parents the role that 'character' needs to play, which parents can see falls into their 'domain' easily:

What matters most in a child's development, research says, is not how much information we can stuff into their brain in the first few years. What matters, instead, is whether we are able to help them develop a very different set of qualities, a list that includes persistence, self-control, curiosity, conscientiousness, grit and self-confidence. (Tough, 2013: XV)

Why does parental involvement matter?

The way parents talk about their own relationship to education clearly sends a powerful message to their children. As a result, they have a huge potential to undermine the positive messages that schools might be promoting. It is not uncommon for parents to 'shift the blame' for failures past and present onto school and thereby undermine their children's relationship to school and learning. Children need to see that their parents value education. Another unhelpful approach that is also quite common is the 'empathizing too much' strategy. This tends to look like the 'I was lousy at maths too' type statements which not only can suggest that a lack of ability in a subject is inherited, but also that it is likely to be irreversible and that ability is somehow genetically fixed. Another well-meaning but damaging line that parents often take is the 'pre-empting of disappointment' one. This tends to look like the 'you'll never be a footballer/pianist/rocket scientist so get used to lower goals' line that undermines ambition. A child who might want to become an astronaut should be told that maths and science are vitally important skills and that studying these subjects will be rewarding, even in pursuit of seemingly unattainable goals and interests. They may of course even turn out to be completely attainable.

What damage can parents do if they aren't supported?

Writing in the *New York Times Sunday Review* of 21 June 2014, Judith Newman stated:

Researchers at the University of Texas at Austin and Duke University this year assessed the effect of more than 60 kinds of parental involvement on academic achievement. Across age, race, gender and socioeconomic status, most help had neither a positive or negative effect, and many kinds of parental support drove down a child's test scores and grades.

One of the biggest culprits for negative impact was 'homework help'. Effectively, parents increased their children's dependency on them. In discussions with teachers in many western countries, it becomes very clear that some parents

(Continued)

(Continued)

believe that their highly able children are delicate and fragile orchids who require special tending and they have a genuine fear of burn-out and feel that their child might be struggling when they are not getting consistent A's. It was summed up well by a teacher who commented that her students and parents (in this case in Minnesota) wanted the world 'perfectly paved'. What this looked like was a picture of students who were too passive, gave up too easily, shut down or switched off if subjects got too tricky, lacked drive, didn't want to struggle or work hard and found it difficult to problem solve. The fear of failure and of being wrong reduced the likelihood of her students taking on big challenges and this, in turn, led to narrower life choices. She believed that parents were really to blame, as they supported their children whenever she wanted to make their assignments more challenging.

What are the key messages to give to parents?

If the key elements of advice could be distilled into the emotional strategies that parents should engage with, then the following would considerably help schools. Parents can help their children to see that grappling with challenges is more important than any amount of easy success. Trying should also mean trying not to fixate on grades as a measure of worth. Parents can also ensure that their children don't see the act of trying itself as a demonstration of their stupidity or failure. They should give as much responsibility as they believe they can regarding behaviour and learning and thereby offer their children the opportunity to be trusted, whilst avoiding soft rewards that can undermine high expectations.

In terms of academic strategies, they should try not to accept their child's first responses too quickly but ask them to justify their opinions as thoroughly as they can. In turn, they should try not to over-simplify their own explanations. If, for example, a political situation being discussed is complex, parents should go into as much detail as they can to show that there are hugely ambiguous situations in the world that defy easy explanations. They should obviously try not to praise talent before effort and try not to come to the rescue of their child way before they need to.

Parents, and teachers, need to remind themselves how important it is for the most able children to be presented with questions, issues and problems to which there is no answer, and certainly no easy one. Parents also need to have reinforced to them the basic truth that a person has to experience failure and disappointment if they are to learn to cope with it.

7

Enrichment and Add-in

Key points

- Enrichment is the most common technique used to teach the most able, perhaps because it is one of the cheapest.
- It is also open to abuse and needs to be separately audited.
- Enrichment depends on the clear identification of suitable children.
- It need not but can, if wrongly handled, lead to social isolation of the student.

Enrichment can take place either within the curriculum and school day or as a 'pull-out' activity. It involves enriching the standard curriculum with material specifically designed for the most able, and adding to it. It is occasionally referred to as taking the pupil 'wider and deeper'. There is a debate over whether additional material should be academic, or simply 'novelty', as in material designed to stir and stimulate the interest of the able pupil. Traditionalists argue that exploration to a great depth and intensity of standard academic material is in itself stimulating and an antidote to boredom.

In the Tower Group world survey, the most popular techniques in use for the gifted and talented were: (1) in-class enrichment, (2) acceleration and (3) out-of-class enrichment (Freeman et al., 2010). In one sense, enrichment is not a standalone technique. It could be used to describe all the techniques and approaches described in this text, in that they all seek to 'enrich' the learning of able children. Enrichment frequently boils down to specific lesson content, and the number of ways a teacher can enrich their lessons is as variable and individual as the teachers themselves. Good enrichment is about style and underpinning philosophy more than it is about content. The lesson and other ideas below are simply intended to spark ideas about how effective enrichment can be undertaken.

Enrichment is the term and the technique most prone to abuse in the canon of teaching the most able. Because it can take so many forms, it is the term least capable of exact definition. A school can claim to have an enrichment programme which looks good in the shop window but proves to have no substance on the shelves. 'Teach First' is an outstanding UK scheme whereby top graduates teach in largely deprived schools for an experimental period of time. One very bright member of the scheme described her experiences as follows in a private note to the authors:

> As a Teach First participant in a struggling [name removed] comprehensive, I was excited by the prospect of a new Academy opening in my second year of teaching, bringing with it a commitment to tackling endemic underachievement and the behavioural issues that had dogged the school in recent years. As part of this overhaul, staff, pupils and parents were promised an 'enrichment' programme which would engage pupils in learning and provide a protected space to further their extra-curricular ambitions. Staff were initially reluctant to give up more of their time – the 'enriched' day would end two hours later than it had done previously – especially considering the particularly challenging nature of this school. Nevertheless, with promises of an annual bonus of £500 in exchange for four hours a week of their time, most teachers signed up to the programme hoping that they might finally be able to share some of their passions and interests with their pupils. What manifested, instead, was a glorified baby-sitting service.
>
> Considering the lack of achievement in the school, coupled with the pressure placed upon the new Academy to 'prove' that it had improved results, the senior leadership team introduced a programme of 'learning to learn' sessions to take place during enrichment hours instead of the expected, and promised, extensive menu of extra-curricular opportunities. If students weren't 'learning to learn' via a generic series of PowerPoint slides downloaded off the internet, they were encouraged to use the time to complete work which should have been covered in their lessons. As such, the experience became less about 'enriching' pupils' minds as holding them in a classroom, against their will, to go through an imposed, non-interactive session which was nothing more than another lesson bolted onto their already tiring day. Understandably, behaviour deteriorated – teachers weren't properly planning the sessions (because they weren't supposed to be just another lesson), untrained TAs [Teaching Assistants] were roped into managing classes of 30, and the whole morale of staff and pupils plunged into despair. What had started out as a reasonably organized and productive day habitually unravelled into chaos, fights, teacher apathy and resentment. Showing videos became a coping mechanism.

Children, particularly those from the most deprived socio-economic backgrounds, need enrichment programmes, but they deserve that these sessions are thoughtfully developed and are catered to them as individuals rather than as vehicles to achieve a C-grade government target. The talents and interests of teaching and support staff are multiple and should be harnessed to open pupils' eyes up to the world beyond the classroom. We had ballet dancers, wonderful cooks, county netball players and thespians on staff and yet all these skills were pushed aside while 'learning to learn' remained the order of the day. Enrichment programmes need to also be a way of empowering pupils to make choices about their own lives and pursuits; an opportunity for those who don't excel in Maths or English to be successful at something different and gain recognition for their efforts.

It would be easy to dismiss this as anecdotal or merely a single example, were it not for the fact that every country has similar stories. The common theme tends to be a senior management, leadership or government scheme sticking a label up marked 'Enrichment offered here' in the shop window, with bare shelves behind. As with the teacher above, these stories were told by people with a genuine passion for enrichment who were angered at what they perceived as betrayals of the cause and as abject examples of tokenism. It is easy to claim to offer enrichment. It is harder to deliver it.

This raises another issue. Too rigid a testing regime can have a detrimental effect on the teaching of the gifted and talented, particularly if the median target has been set too low – teaching to the 'C' grade' at GCSE in the UK – and partly because a culture dominated by teaching for the test encourages the teacher to stick scrupulously to what will be tested, and discourages her or him from going off-piste in a way that is crucial to effective teaching of the most able. This is the one area where an increase in the testing regime might be justified, not in the form of an exam or test but in the form of an external, objective and informed audit of any claim for an enrichment programme. For this to happen, many countries in the world would need to train their inspectorate or its equivalent to make an effective judgement of enrichment schemes. In effect, this specialist area needs its own specialists to judge it.

A cynic might also argue that enrichment is the most popular technique globally because it is the cheapest. In the example above, teachers were paid to deliver the enrichment programme. Yet a school can grandly announce to its staff that it is now requisite upon them to include enrichment activities in all their teaching, and then either not check that they do or mount an ineffective and ill thought-out programme such as that in the Teach First graduate's school. It could well be that the 'enrichment programmes' offered by a number of schools are hollow shells which do not stand up to scrutiny. Whatever their drawbacks, acceleration and compaction leave a tangible trail. Either pupils are accelerated or they are not. Either the curriculum is compacted for some students or it is not. It is far easier to claim, fraudulently, that one offers serious enrichment programmes – hence the need for programmes to be externally audited.

Enrichment has another problem which can place it in serious trouble. The issue of selection is discussed in a later chapter, but it impinges on the theory and practice of enrichment quite seriously. Teachers of able children are often warned to avoid the 'three times' approach – going over a topic once, repeating it and then doing it a third time just to check everyone has understood it. Yet, in a mixed-ability class, the three-times approach might be just what some pupils need. Similarly, it can be very hard even for a committed teacher to multi-task in front of a class of 30 or 40 pupils, and hand out work of different levels of difficulty to individual children. It is also dangerous to be seen to be giving more work to the most able, risking as it does suggesting to the child that being seen to be clever simply means you get lumbered with more work. This places enrichment firmly in the potentially toxic area of selection – toxic in the case of the UK, at any rate, which has managed to make of selection a battle lasting longer than any war in the last century. Put simply – and a fact that many teachers were willing to admit in private conversation but not to be named for – enrichment is much easier to enact in classes in which all the pupils have been selected on the basis of being in the most able group. This is not to say that enrichment is impossible in mixed-ability classes. It is to say that selective classes tend to render it easier, not so much to provide enrichment per se, but to provide it at the right level of challenge that best stimulates the most able.

This also highlights both a strength and weakness of out-of-class enrichment. The strength is that children who are prepared to put themselves forward for extra work, after school or at weekends, often have a proven commitment and have usually been identified by a nominating agency such as their school as being in the top ability band. Such out-of-school groups are thus implicitly selective without the fact being thrust in anyone's face.

A UK scheme pioneered at St Paul's School, London, between 2005 and 2011, where great care was taken by the supplying authority to find the right children, came close to foundering because of the 'out of hours' philosophy. Some children resented the Saturday morning scheme because it did seem like a punishment for being clever, others because it destroyed their chances of weekend employment, which they were dependent on for any spending money. The scheme was rescued when government funding was provided to put on the classes in normal school hours.

The issue of social isolation is not simple and is dealt with more fully in Chapter 10, which focuses on issues of selection. Both in-school and out-of-school enrichment classes can mark out a child as 'different' in a way that adolescents in particular find unacceptable. But it need not be so. Visiting a school in Australia that selected pupils from around the top 30% of the ability range to follow some 80% of the curriculum in a separate, 'pull-out' compacted stream, two things became clear. The students on the scheme relished it, with many quoting it not as a reason for their sense of isolation or being 'different' but as the cause of those feelings ceasing. For the first time in their school careers, numbers of them said that they did not feel odd or ill-at-ease in class. The scheme is living proof that enrichment can reinforce the self-esteem of able pupils rather than increase their insecurity or sense of social isolation.

Perhaps nowhere else in teaching is it as true that good practice is as varied as the individuals who teach it. The examples given below are chosen simply to illustrate some of the underlying principles that seem to be present in the most effective enrichment worldwide. A significant amount of enrichment worldwide is 'pull-out' or takes place in sessions that are additional to normal lessons, in the form of an extended day, one-day-a-week school, Saturday class or weeks out of school in the form of summer schools or other camps. These are dealt with in a separate chapter.

In-class enrichment

One example, as with a number of other cases, could not have taken place without a double lesson being timetabled, in this case 90 minutes. The topic of this history lesson was the rise of the Nazi party, and it was delivered to 15-year-olds. The teacher started the lesson in a didactic, lecturing style that would almost certainly have run counter to the principles of best teaching favoured by inspectors in that country. He also gave out notes summarizing opinions on the topic from various leading historians. The class assumed they were being spoon-fed but were well motivated to pass their examination and settled back with varying degrees of content to act like sponges. After some 15 minutes, certain of the pupils became restive. All had assumed from the early remarks of the teacher that the Nazis had burned down the Reichstag in order to blame the Communists and leap-frog into power on the back of the resulting social alarm and chaos. Yet, without announcing it as such, the teacher had started to offer the view that it was a perfectly reasonable interpretation of events to conclude that the Communists had actually burned down the Reichstag. I suspect most of that class had come into the lesson sublimely indifferent as to who or what burned down the Reichstag. Even now it was not the Reichstag that interested them, rather the intellectual challenge of an issue where there were two opposed viewpoints, each convinced they were right.

The teacher then showed contemporary and dramatic film of the Reichstag in flames. This then moved suddenly and sharply to the now famous home-video footage of 9/11 and the Twin Towers in flames. The teacher then said simply, 'Attempts to destabilize governments and countries by wanton acts of violence are not restricted to this century'. The class erupted. A number pointed out excitedly that we knew who destroyed the Twin Towers but not who destroyed the Reichstag. One pupil responded that they were not that different. Both used the destruction of totemic buildings to destabilize a country in the hope of destroying a government. The teacher then divided the class up into groups of five. For the remainder of the lesson, these groups would be constituted as an official enquiry into the Reichstag incident. Each group would prepare a five-minute report to be delivered at the next lesson. Instead of formal homework, the teacher said he wanted each group to meet over lunch, after school or over the internet to discuss further the preparation of their report, and that he expected them to give up at least 45 minutes of their time to the project or else there would be no more homework like this and in future he would set them learning from their textbook for a factual test. Noise levels in the remaining 20 minutes of the lesson as the groups discussed their report, were high but also productive.

Some of the techniques in this lesson were central to all good teaching: an excellent structure mixing different styles, a varied pace and the stimulating use of film and video footage. Yet some elements of this lesson are central to good enrichment. The teacher dared to deny conventional wisdom, and for a period of time taught in a didactic, lecturing manner that is nowadays deemed less acceptable. He did so because for the lesson to work he needed to give the students a sizeable core of factual information, and he gambled that this was the quickest way to do so and that he could retain enough of the pupils' interest and attention by a sudden change of tack half way through. He hoped that the group of very able children would spot that the viewpoint in the lecture was changing. He also recognized that able children could look at and read the notes and contemporary material he had distributed whilst listening at the same time. Other features that summed up the best principles of enrichment were the gradual take-over of the lesson by the pupils (the teacher did not say a word in the last 20 minutes, except on a few occasions to ask groups to keep the volume down), the focus on group work that recognized the ability of the pupils to learn from each other, the emphasis on argument, advocacy and being articulate, the supply of basic information that allowed the pupils to move to higher-order thinking and the sheer speed at which the factual information was provided and processed. The lesson also trusted the pupils to do the work, recognized that the natural medium to which most of the children would turn was social media and that this could be turned to advantage, and was not afraid of a competitive edge. The presentations in the next lesson, it was made clear, would be judged not just on their intrinsic merit but against each other. Two features stood out above all, features which are central to all good enrichment. First, there was an outstanding sense of this lesson being a partnership between teacher and pupils, a co-operative venture. Second, the pupils took complete ownership of the lesson and the topic.

An interesting slant is contained in a report dealing with the overall improvement of school standards, rather than just standards pertaining to the gifted and talented:

> However, we find that the vast majority of interventions made by the improving systems in our sample are 'process' in nature; and, within this area, improving systems generally spend more of their activity on improving how instruction is delivered than on changing the content of what is delivered. (Barber et al., 2010: 3)

What this means is that too many countries and schools are concerned with how to deliver material, as distinct from what that material actually is. Project work focuses on outcome and content rather than on process.

Another example hinges on the fact that a number of topics, such as the structure of the atom, are frequently deemed 'too difficult' for classes and are therefore simplified to an extent that distorts the academic truth. One simple enrichment method with 13-year-old science students was to lead the children into the greater complexities of the topic and, in the words of one teacher, 'let them enjoy a bit of the awe and wonder'. An equally accurate description of what takes place might be that the aim is to let children loose on a topic in the knowledge that they will not fully understand it. This clashes with a significant strand in modern teaching culture which states that full understanding is the goal of good education, whereas an older view states that the questions are frequently more challenging and more stimulating (or simply just more fun) than some of the answers. There are a number of dangers in teaching things to children as facts when in fact they are subject to considerable uncertainty, or teaching children only that which can be fully understood. Children taught in this way, and the adults they become, could feel very betrayed if the discovery of a Higgs-Boson particle requires most of the theory of physics to be rewritten, or a document is found that proves conclusively that Shakespeare did not write the plays attributed to him. One thing that teaching techniques for the most able could give to all teaching is a renewed faith in the open-ended question, a rediscovery of the fact that the journey to knowledge is sometimes more exciting than the destination. T.S. Eliot commented that poetry does not always have to be understood in order to communicate. Topics in teaching do not always have to be understood in order to inspire. It is not necessary that all the children fully understand whatever they are addressing by the end of the lesson. What is clear is that more able learners enjoy wrestling with the problems. These example lessons illustrate a basic law of enrichment, namely that children are often more stimulated by the challenge of enquiry than they are by the grasping of an answer. They can be more interested, not because something is there but because it is not there.

A summary of what factors constitute effective in-class enrichment would need to include:

- significant group work, allowing pupils to interact with each other and work collectively to produce an answer – able children love working with and are stimulated by the company of other able children
- encouragement to present conclusions clearly, articulately and confidently in front of an audience
- a choice of question topics to which there is either no clear answer or a number of possible answers
- the teacher as the fire beneath the pot, not the lid locking it down
- a topic- rather than subject-based approach – the more the topics are 'real-world' and based on what adults do the better.

However, what works best for the most able is often a concentrate rather than the dilute that, of necessity, in-class enrichment often is. It is easier in achievement terms, though not always in practical and administrative terms, to offer the concentrate in the form of out-of-class enrichment, as discussed in the following chapter.

Questions for further thought

How are we to set sights high for enrichment and extension tasks?

'I believe that work of excellence is transformational. Once a student sees that he or she is capable of excellence, that student is never quite the same. There is a new self-image, a new notion of possibility. There is an appetite for excellence. After students have had a taste of excellence, they're never quite satisfied with less; they're always hungry' (Berger, 2003: 8).

Often, schools will comment that they are catering to the needs of their most able students by offering them a 'free choice' in their enrichment or extension work. Sometimes this looks like a selection of ever-increasing challenges which are offered as a smorgasbord of activities. At other times, it is a completely free and open choice with no suggestions or steers given for fear of 'leading the learning'.

The problem with the former is obvious. This becomes known as differentia-tion or enrichment by punishment. Well done, you're smart. Here is some more, harder work, without explaining the reasons why a student may want to choose this. When offered a choice between being involved in a little work and another option requiring a great deal more work, some students are inclined to choose the former, even if the latter is more interesting, often because these are usually the students with a great number of other pressing demands on their time or because being bright doesn't mean you aren't sometimes lazy.

The problem with the latter is that it can be bewildering and use up great gobbets of displacement time while the students try to work out what it is that they are meant to do. It can also have the exact opposite impact of stretch and challenge with students who underestimate what they are capable of achieving and who sell themselves short.

One way around this can be to offer tasks based on a sliding scale of points. If you choose this particularly difficult activity, it's worth ten points against your term's total of homework. An easier choice may offer only one point. Then able students will often choose the harder (and more interesting) choice simply because they can see 'what is in it for them' in the longer term. They may also then go for the more audacious choice because it just interests them. Another method is to use high-quality exemplars. Rather than offering lower-level tem-plates which tend to be useful for little else but copying, show them what they need to be able to do and demonstrate how through well-chosen exemplars that set sights high and steer expectations.

How can schools cater for the enrichment needs of their students?

In any institution, there is a seemingly limited supply of expertise. Teachers get used to being only the subject teacher, with a clear idea of the syllabus and the immediate needs of their students. Many are not remotely stretched in terms

(Continued)

(Continued)

of their subject as the exam often demands so little from the students. What can happen is that their own subject passion can become ossified, effectively trapped in time. Without good subject-specific professional development, they can become out of date quite quickly. Many look to subject associations and journals to keep their expertise relevant, whilst others can drift. This in turn can lead to a reluctance to go too far from the syllabus, to offer the kind of 'off-piste' experiences that able learners can thrive on. What is always interesting is working with colleagues, undergraduates or post-graduates to support them to keep their passion alive. Another significant 'talent pool' approach across a school is to survey all staff to find out what other skills they have that may not have been utilized for years. Cantonese, film editing or stand-up comedy all have the capacity to excite, engage and transform students in enrichment classes.

8

Out-of-Class Enrichment, the Internet and Summer Schools

> **Key points**
>
> - Out-of-class enrichment allows the fruitful mixing of like with like.
> - It can be expensive, risk social isolation and be seen as a punishment.
> - Camping and trekking can play an important role.
> - Time saved can allow for the further bonus of projects.
> - The New Zealand 'One-Day School' is highly effective, as is the Swiss 'Dolphin Room'.
> - The internet offers opportunities for teaching the most able but has limitations.
> - The 'flipped classroom' may offer a solution that overcomes many limitations of internet use.
> - Summer schools work best only as the culmination of a programme.

Out-of-class enrichment

Out-of-class enrichment offers both a plus and a minus. A plus is that it can allow able children to mix freely with others who are equally gifted, in a manner that is not always possible or, in a system dead-set against selection or streaming, deemed desirable. A minus is that, by definition, any provision takes place outside of normal school hours and therefore usually demands that participating staff are paid more. As well as a financial penalty, it may carry a social one for the children. Out-of-class enrichment often takes place on Saturday mornings or after school on weekdays. In disadvantaged families, Saturday morning work may be needed to contribute to the family's income or to give the child any money at all to spend on him- or herself. Gifted young musicians, actors or sportsmen and women may well find their activity held on Saturday mornings, and it is not a fair choice to ask a boy or girl to choose between playing soccer or hockey and attending a G&T class. For many families, religious instruction is an essential add-on to a child's day. As well as taking up after-school time, the commitment required from the child and from the family may be a bridge too far when it comes to the additional demands on a gifted and talented class. After all, if these are not by their nature very demanding they are likely not to be particularly worthwhile. A very real danger of out-of-class enrichment is that it is seen not as a privilege but as a punishment for a child – 'Let yourself be selected as gifted and talented and you lose your Saturdays/after school time'. Many proponents of such enrichment seem to forget how tired a child might be at the end of the day. Nor is the use of lunchtimes the answer. In most schools, the lunch break is the focal point for clubs, societies and even team training. To take a child out of these is frequently not a kindness. Out-of-school enrichment can crash and burn on all these obstacles, though, if handled sensitively, some of the worst pitfalls can be avoided.

Able children do not just exist from the neck up. Their intellectual needs can often only be satisfied if their emotional needs are catered for – as is well recognized by the Robinson Center. It is for this reason that both the Robinson Center and the Australian SHIP scheme utilize camps as part of their programme, this and outward bound activities perhaps qualifying as a form of out-of-class enrichment.

The SHIP scheme vehemently denies that the trip to Kangaroo Island is a camp, preferring to see it as a study visit. True, the schools do undertake projects based on the trip (one such project is entitled 'Design the Perfect Holiday Resort'), but to an outsider this is pure social bonding and reinforcement of the peer group. Able students can give massive support to each other but need to know each other in order to do so. This process can be speeded up and made more tangible by enrichment in the form of sending the group off camping or trekking for a week. It is no secret what cooking one's own food, sharing chores, the sense of united purpose, the absence of home comforts, the development of self-reliance and the rest can do to and for children. The camp methodology can work extremely well in reinforcing the mutual support of an able group and their affection for each other. In the words of one commentator, 'A number of studies identified social interactions as an important factor in effective provision for gifted and talented pupils'.

An interesting variation of this idea is the practice adopted by some of the GEMS (Global Education Management System) private day schools in Dubai, whereby year groups are encouraged to come into school for a sleepover. This is not as simple as it sounds. There are obvious gender issues and concerns about adult teachers 'spending the night' with students, but these can be overcome and are not prohibitive. Whereas the camp for the most able emphasizes their distinctiveness and shared interests, the year group sleepover emphasizes inclusiveness and can help to reduce any sense of isolation on the part of the most able group.

Some of the most effective out-of-class enrichment schemes capitalize on the fact that the most able can gallop through the curriculum and thus build up a time bank. A north London school uses this time for 'Project Week' at the end of term. All normal lessons cease. A theme is decided on – for example, 'Space' – and all lessons are based on this. Physics talks about space travel, Chemistry about making rocket fuel and Biology about how a human might survive on the Moon or Mars. English looks at poems about the Sun, Moon and stars, and about being the first man on the moon. Maths does the calculations that allowed Apollo 13 to return to Earth, History explores the space race, and so on. Distinguished speakers are invited to talk and trips are mounted to the Science Museum. The combination of a break with routine, a positive assault on the academic senses and the chance to research and pursue one's own pet project makes this a heady and tremendously worthwhile experience. The drawback? This is a highly selective school. It can afford a week out of term time and 'normal' lessons for its pupils, without the risk of losing its least able their precious C grade.

One of the most highly regarded out-of-class schemes is a variation on the week-long project delivered in class time, which replaces the Project Week with one day a week throughout the year. The New Zealand 'One-Day School' was the idea of Rosemary Cathcart, and starting in Central Auckland moved across the country. Membership of One-Day School is restricted to the top 5% of the year cohort, with entry dependent primarily on cognitive tests – an attempt to ensure the scheme is populated by children with innate ability rather than those who have a high level of acquired knowledge. Participants take one day a week out of their normal school and the scheme uses classrooms not being used for normal lessons. As with so many successful schemes for the most able, learning is topic based. A wide-ranging topic is chosen for a term – 'Identity', 'Strength', 'Time' – and each week a sub-topic is followed, as in a nation's identity, strength in relationships or time travel. The key to the scheme's success is these topics, and also the division of the day into three parts, as in:

- Think, Reason, Discuss.
- Read, Write, Research.
- Make, Do, Create.

The advantages of the scheme are obvious. It allows bright children to meet and work with each other, without the social dislocation of having them do it five days a week. It makes use of existing resources in terms of classrooms and is therefore relatively inexpensive. It does not require intricate co-ordination with a child's school and its curriculum. It matches the profile of many successful schemes in that it is project and theme based, allows plentiful opportunity for both group work and individual initiative and is based on cognitive skills rather than the simple acquisition of factual knowledge.

Drawbacks are also there. The scheme depends on there being spare classroom capacity and it is not physically available to children who cannot travel to a Centre. Even on one day a week out of the mainstream, there is the capacity for children on the scheme to see themselves as 'different' or to be seen as such by the remainder of their chronological age group – though, as the Australian SHIP scheme shows, with sensitive management this need not be a problem. A major issue is cost, currently in excess of NZ$60 per week. Some fee subsidies are available but cost, however well managed, remains a significant problem for most out-of-class enrichment schemes. By being 'out of class', they are by definition an extra cost and there is a limit to the extent that staff goodwill on its own can supply the needs of a scheme. As a footnote, it was difficult not to observe worldwide, and particularly in the USA, how comparatively young staff were in the schools that offered significant out-of-hours or holiday provision, with older staff tending not to be interested because of the demands a family of one's own make on a teacher. Attempts are made to address the issue of availability by the provision of GOL, or Gifted Online, an internet programme for children who live too far away to physically attend a One Day School. Good as it is, the internet can only go so far, and in particular offers only a slight portion of the interaction with staff and other students that fires up this and so many other schemes for the most able.

An interesting 'pull-out' scheme is the 'Dolphin Room' concept, as used in the Canton of Lucerne in Switzerland. Students come out of their mainstream classroom and work on enrichment activities in a specialist, heavily-resourced room. The scheme allows able students to work in small groups with specialist teachers. As with so many schemes examined in this study, an excellent local initiative is not widely publicized, has no effective agency to promulgate and push it to a wider audience and so has little or no chance to blossom and flourish elsewhere.

Internet and web-based schemes

It is perhaps worth commenting on internet and web-based schemes for able children, seen by some as the ultimate out-of-class enrichment. They are sometimes hailed as the answer to all and any problems. Modern technology undoubtedly offers new and good opportunities for the most able, but its advantages are stressed more than some of its insurmountable weaknesses.

Strengths are clear. Internet-based programmes can offset geographical disadvantage, where children live in isolated settings or simply cannot reach a conventional tuition centre. They need not be expensive. They can bring within range of a child people and experiences they would not otherwise have available, from sight of complex experiments to talks by inspirational speakers or even lessons given by inspirational teachers. Well-planned programmes follow best practice for teaching able children, in that they are stepped and tiered in difficulty and let a child follow at his or her own pace. They can offer a wide variety of topics, far more than a conventional curriculum.

Three schemes are worthy of special mention, one of which actively seeks to overcome some of the failings of web-based learning. EPGY is the Education Program for Gifted Youth run by the University of Stanford (USA). Founded initially in the 1960s with a bias towards maths and science, EPGY is noteworthy because of its wide-spectrum, all-embracing approach. Its courses range from kindergarten to university level. They can be taken individually or on a year-round calendar, full time or part time, or simply on a course-by-course basis. Three- to five-week summer schools augment the programme. It offers OHS, or Online High School, a fully accredited and diploma-granting independent school as well, a development made possible by a donation given in 2006. EPGY offers self-directed study, as in individual work on a computer with support from an instructor, and seminars conducted in an online classroom with interaction between staff and students. In effect, EPGY offers the closest any online system can come to the dynamics of a reality classroom, and even if the student is working outside of this forum the presence of an instructor faces up the problem of the student left high and dry by an issue they cannot understand. Its use of online materials and of summer schools (see below) to augment a course is exemplary.

EPGY has not managed to solve the inclusion agenda problems. Courses can cost in excess of $700, and students need regular and timetabled access to a computer. EPGY offers a marvellous opportunity for those savvy enough to find that it exists; it still has some way to go to ensure that knowledge of it goes to all who should know it exists.

The second scheme is the University of Warwick's newly created social network site IGGY, designed for gifted students aged 13 to 18 years old from around the world. It has been created to give its members access to high-challenge educational resources and to encourage them to work with top academics and other gifted young people around the world. It was awarded a highly prestigious BETT award in 2014.

Within the online environment, IGGY members are able to create their own profiles, collaborate with others to exchange ideas, and learn about and explore international perspectives in safety. It seeks to offer a support network of academics and student mentors so that its members can access discussions and debates with intellectual peers globally and engage with stimulating content with a focus on gaming. In the IGGY context, their members gain experience, earn awards and prizes and are attributed statuses as they progress. Projects vary from short puzzles to longer-term projects requiring research, collaboration and independent study, with students suggesting new projects for study. This approach is designed to drive engagement and encourage exploration – two of the most important factors in creating digital materials for the gifted. In short, these techniques are employed to leverage a student's natural desires for competition, achievement, status, self-expression, altruism and closure.

Clearly, given its global remit it would be impossible to insist on a specific diet of content, so IGGY wants its members to be able to tailor their involvement to match their own areas of interest and personalize their learning experience. In an effort to give it some inherent structure, new developments are framed around a series of skills matrices that cover maths, science and English in the first instance. These are aimed at focusing members on some of the more global skills in these subject areas. As a concept, it is one that could be hugely beneficial for students.

A third scheme is the Khan Academy, a not-for-profit website thrust into prominence by Bill Gates, who praised it as a tool used to good effect by his own children. It has several million users worldwide and is growing. Concentrating at present on maths and elementary school pupils, but planned to develop in terms of age range and subject, the Khan Academy concept is linked to the 'flipped classroom' concept. The Khan Academy material is attractively simple. Straightforward but highly effective diagrams with a voice-over take the student through maths topics, the idea being that the student does the basic work at home and then takes it to the classroom for further discussion and the resolution of any problems – hence the link to the 'flipped classroom' concept, where normal classroom practice is to acquire basic knowledge and then take it home for elaboration and extension. In the flipped classroom, homework becomes home learning.

The Khan system clearly works very well for some children, though to date it has been seen as best suited for general usage, rather than having special relevance to the most able. At this stage in its development, it is impossible to say how much the success of the material is due to the fact that its founder is clearly a teacher of genius, whose personal imprint is firmly on the existing material, just as is his actual voice. Khan Academy has no special answer to the problem besetting all web programmes, namely that it depends on pupils owning a computer, or at least having out-of-school access to one, and having the wherewithal to access the internet.

It is possible that university-based schemes offer more to gifted students, and one of the most highly-rated is MIT's 'Open Courseware' and the 'Open Courseware Consortium' it has spawned. Other schemes worth mentioning are 'Highlights for s', a site designed specifically to stimulate interest in the STEM subjects, and the fascinating 'I labs' consortium, whose strap line is 'If you can't come to the lab ... the lab will come to you!' and which presents experience in real as distinct from actual laboratories.

Yet the limitations of internet-based schemes are significant. One is economic, as mentioned above. A computer at home or at school may be commonplace to a western child, but an impossible dream to many from the two-thirds world. Another issue is related to the fact that good teaching of the most able will ask questions they cannot answer. Good teaching responds to the pupil meeting a brick wall by teaching them how to jump over it. The loneliness of the internet is nowhere more drastic than when the child reaches an *impasse* that the keyboard and mouse cannot solve. Leaving a child stranded can have serious mental and emotional repercussions. This is one reason why Khan Academy works as well as it does – it is intended to work in harness with a teacher. The answer to students left stranded or frustrated – a human mentor or teacher who can give personalized rather than programmed help – is very difficult to lay on at all the times a student may need it, and as the demand is unpredictable such a resource can be prohibitively expensive. One advantage of the internet is that the student can use it at a time that is suitable to them. It is particularly true of any scheme that has an international dimension, therefore, that the tutor or mentor has to be available 24 hours a day, a factor that can be prohibitively expensive for the provider and impractical, undesirable or both to the mentors. It is often assumed, particularly in the popular press, that technology and the internet make the teacher redundant. This ignores the fact that what the internet does best in its current state of technology is to present problems, rather than solve them. Internet schemes do in part replace the teacher with technology, but they can also mean that the remaining humans behind the programmes cost more.

Yet the real drawback is the simplest of all. The virtual experience of learning can be as unreal as the virtual experience of combat gained from a computer game. As yet, we do not have the computer equivalent of the hands-on excitement of a practical in chemistry or biology, or a heated, face-to-face debate on a juicy moral issue. Current state-of-the-art technology cannot begin to emulate the extraordinarily dynamic twists and turns of class discussion in the most effective lessons. The traditional classroom, for all its weaknesses, is three-dimensional and technicolour. All too often, the child at the work station is in a medium that by comparison is flat and monochrome. Interestingly, the most able seem to use the web as a fact-mine, something which allows them to extract the raw material for their thinking and their opinions.

There are two weakness of the web as an aid to the gifted and talented. One is that it can provide too much information. This can play to a weakness noted by many experienced teachers of able children, namely an obsessive perfectionism. When even a simple Google search can produce thousands of possible links, it is too easy for the conscientious child to believe that a project is never finished because there is always a website they have not accessed. One school visited in the course of the research for this text makes the student sign up to a deal which *in extremis* allowed the school to raid a student's work file on the school IT system and submit draft course work as the finished product. This invasion of IT space was reserved for instances where a student identified as gifted and talented was failing to meet a course-work deadline because the work they had done on the assignment in question was 'not good enough'. This nuclear option was used, albeit infrequently, and on each occasion it had been used the work had been given the top grade. A variation on the theme of the obsessive-perfectionist is the pressure on pupils to produce simply too much factual evidence to back up their points. All too often, impressive thinking and deductive skills can simply become submerged under the mass of factual information available from the internet. This does not invalidate the web as a tool for all students, including the most able. It does suggest strongly that study skills need to implant the correct filters inside the mind of the most able, as well as in the computers that feed into those minds. A number of schools used programmes designed to filter out material and highlight the most useful available for academic research, but too few thought of spending the equivalent in staff time on helping to implant internal filters in the students.

A second problem is the fear that a room full of children gazing at a screen is testimony to a generation denied access to necessary social skills. Most successful schemes for the most able feed off and rely on collaboration, and the isolation of much internet work seems to work against this need.

To return to a topic referred to earlier, there is at least one possible solution to the problem of internet learning reducing to danger levels the social skills of children, and the loss of collaborative opportunities. In a conventional classroom, primary knowledge is acquired and, sometimes, the child sent home to polish up what they have learnt or to explore it, often through the medium of homework. In the flipped classroom, the pattern is reversed. Primary or core knowledge is acquired at home – the Khan Academy is an ideal vehicle – and then brought to the classroom to be refined and developed, including through the use of collaborative work. The concept has the advantage that it also allows the child to approach the teacher with any problems and ask for help, before a drama turns into a crisis. The flipped classroom is especially suitable for the most able students. It accepts that they can master much core knowledge on their own, but does not stop help being available when needed. It allows students to go at their own pace and allows them to collaborate with their peers. It allows the lessons to be concerned with enrichment, rather than being dominated by the need to get the staple diet down the throat of the children. For the system to work, regardless of how able the children are, the teacher needs to track data ruthlessly. A tablet lends itself to the type of spreadsheet where the various core topics or courses to be mastered by each child are background coloured as pending, under way, completed or problematic, the teacher offering a different programme to each child accordingly. The classroom becomes an environment based on the magic bullet, where individual needs are targeted, rather than on the scatter-gun approach of the conventional classroom and lesson.

Whether or not the flipped classroom is a universal panacea, a Luddite philosophy towards technology and learning for the most able cannot be justified. It seems certain that in 50 years educators will look back on our current use of technology rather as we look back on sepia-tinted photographs of children in shorts and long dresses sitting in rows whilst the teacher delivers a lecture. Computer-based programmes have all the advantages listed above as well as the drawbacks, are in highly effective use as one of a battery of techniques in a number of schemes and benefit from programmes that get better and more dynamic by the month. Yet with all this, technology is not quite yet in a position to replace or even rival the chemistry of pupil-on-pupil or teacher-on-pupil reactions. The best use of the web for the most able is as a support tool, one of the best examples being the Hungarian Genius Program discussed below. Sensible use of IT also helps make possible the extended project in its various forms, this latter being one of the few very real steps forward in educating the most able over the past 50 years.

Summer schools

Summer schools have been used for a number of years to gather young people together for a concentrated boost either to ability or their particular shared talent. Highly successful ventures for the talented such as the British National Youth Theatre and National Youth Orchestra are in effect extended summer schools for talented young people. Summer schools were a key feature in the ill-fated UK NAGTY and this experience showed both their strengths and their weaknesses. NAGTY summer schools were well organized, with stimulating and rich content. They allowed bright children to mix and meet and hence reinforce both aspirations and knowledge without entering the UK's 'forbidden world' of selective education and schools. The problems were their cost and the fact that there were never going to be enough summer schools to satisfy demand and needs.

There is far too little research on the efficacy of summer schools in general and on their long-term effect in particular. Anecdotally, the most successful seem to be those which form part of a longer-lasting course or programme, such as with the UK Open University, in which the summer schools act not as a start to study but as a reinforcement to what has gone before. The Open University pattern – distance learning with social interaction and end-of-year reinforcement through the medium of a residential summer school – is a tempting one to use in a programme for able children, the thing being that the age and maturity of many OU students allows them to cope with distance learning and its loneliness.

The summer schools mounted by the Sutton Trust were designed to introduce young people to the idea of applying to leading universities, and seem by common report to have been successful in attracting pupils from disadvantaged backgrounds. Though not specifically a scheme for the gifted and talented as conventionally defined, they might be seen as having the potential to answer a major question about summer schools, namely whether or not the experience they provide has a lasting effect. Opponents of the summer school believe that it is not enough to take a child out of their normal environment or school and give them a heightened but short experience that soon dissolves when the child returns to home or school. Supporters argue that the experience lights a fuse that can slow- or fast-burn well beyond the duration of the summer school itself. The Trust's own commissioned research states:

> Summer school attendees were more likely to engage with the university application process overall: 93% ended up applying to – and 84% registering at – university, compared to 88% and 68% respectively of unsuccessful applicants to the programme ... Summer school attendees were also considerably more likely to apply to – and end up at – leading universities than students in one of five control groups. Over three quarters (76%) of summer school attendees matched in the UCAS database went on to a leading university,

compared to 55% or less of students in the control groups who did not apply to the scheme but who had similar academic and socio-economic profiles. (Sutton Trust, n.d.: 2)

Clearly, these summer schools do work. They have one problem in terms of acting as a guide to the use of summer schools for the most able. Though the Trust is scrupulous in ascertaining that a high proportion of attendees come from disadvantaged backgrounds, it is by definition dealing with students who have achieved enough at school to persuade them that going to university is at least a possibility. The summer schools clearly turn for many a possibility into a probability and seem also to encourage students to aim significantly higher in terms of where they plan to apply to. But though this type of summer school is good at reaping a harvest, it tells us little about whether or not the summer school as a concept sows the seed in the field, puts the initial kernel of aspiration into the child, or whether it merely takes on those who are already half way there. A summer school can help a young person who has battled through a disadvantaged background and perhaps an unhelpful school. How much is it restricted to helping those who have not had aspiration killed in them by their background? Can it keep a tiny flame alight during the formative years? It could be that the summer school for the able but neglected child is like allowing a drowning man the occasional gulp of air. It does not preserve life, but rather reminds him of how good it is to have it. The summer school is likely to work for the most able only as the culmination of a much longer programme. Oasis though it might be for the able child, it does not teach them how to cross the sands to get there in the first place.

Questions for further thought

What are common attributes of more able students who lack independence and resilience?

In order to properly engage with out-of-school enrichment in whatever form it may take, students need to be both motivated to do so, as well as confident and independent. Too many learners seem to lack these skills. This can normally be seen as one of three interrelated attributes.

The first overall tendency is to shirk taking responsibilities and new opportunities for learning. This demonstrates itself as learners who are rarely subversive or irreverent in their responses and in turn just expect to be supported not

(Continued)

(Continued)

challenged. Often, they don't choose to go outside their comfort zones and are more content with exposition and stories than analysis, rarely choosing to engage with real complexity. They don't really learn a sense of confidence and adventure, rather they seem to have learned uncertainty and caution.

The second observable attribute is often that they frankly don't seem to be that interested in becoming an expert. They are seen to be reluctant to read around the subject unless specifically directed to do so, often sticking quite rigidly to the demands of the syllabus only and even questioning teachers who stray off the path. They are often content to offer generalities and opinions without feeling the need to justify or support their answers or opinions. Rather than valuing speculation or intriguing questions, they seem to be more concerned with just facts and answers and are usually more interested in their mark or result rather than any explanations or suggestions for deeper learning.

The final set of attributes can be seen in able learners who are fearful of being seen as less than smart. This tends to show itself through excessive awe being given to those students they perceive to be more successful than they are and a dismissive attitude towards those who fail. This means that they tend to allow peer pressure to overly influence them and often don't see themselves or their ideas as being particularly worthy of adult attention and interest. They are reluctant to move out of their familiar language base or to use adventurous or speculative language and show reluctance in demonstrating learning and knowledge, in case they might be wrong.

How do we counteract risk aversion?

> Children are designed to be little apprentices, and they will happily apprentice themselves to anyone they like who is doing something interesting. Even watching you struggle a bit is good learning. Teachers and parents are not omniscient or omnipotent, and it helps children grow if they can be privy to some of their elders' uncertainties: not when they are falling apart, but when they are floundering just a little. (Claxton, 2002)

Claxton points out that there has been a growing tendency for students to want everything spoon-fed and 'bite sized' – this is something that we need to counteract by encouraging them to develop their own 'chewing muscles'. We need to encourage engagement with the unknown and away from steering responses into right-answer tunnels. However, this will not be easy. The level of security that some able students seem to require, their seeming unwillingness to explore beyond the horizon and their risk aversion have been encouraged by the type of examination system that requires simple accurate retention and the corresponding attitude of dependency on their teachers as a type of ambulatory google. Sadly, it can also be encouraged by parents who are risk-averse on behalf of their children and who can seek at all costs to protect them from failure, rather than teaching them how to cope with it. So how can we counter this effectively? How do we encourage students to endure both the ambiguity and the confusion that they will inevitably face in the future?

What can help to build up children's exploring skills?

Subject-based approaches to more able education mainly stem from a view of high ability which is seen as expertise in a development stage. Successful provision can be characterized by the extent to which learners are given authentic experiences that enable them to develop as subject thinkers, through the range and reach of potential opportunities for them to engage in challenging contexts. This is good news to the extent that teachers can once again focus attention not on their own delivery of 'stuff', but on the 'stuff' of their subject itself – the reason, probably, why they became interested and excited by it in the first place.

This source of enthusiasm for the teacher should lead to an equally useful sharing of this motivation with the learners too. In outstanding settings, big ideas matter and they are not necessarily the sum of lots of little ones. As teachers, we have a tendency to believe that we can achieve significant progress by enriching and extending (both ourselves and our students). The danger in too many lessons is that the big ideas are bypassed, which denies students the opportunity to really struggle to piece things together for themselves. Questions that should be left to hang are far too frequently answered by the teacher who is fearful of a tumbleweed moment. Choices are ignored, mistakes are circumvented, often all for the sake of 'pace'.

In truth, opening our students' minds to these big ideas and challenging contexts, to their incongruities and ambiguities, often leads to more mess than mastery. Yet it is how we help them handle the mess that helps to encourage further exploration, by having the confidence ourselves to know that through the struggle and chaos solutions can be discovered; if on that messy journey we can also offer our students some inside-track informative and transformative insights on themselves as learners, so much the better.

9

The Hungarian Genius Program, Competitions and Tertiary Links

> **Key points**
>
> - The Hungarian Genius Program is a unique attempt to mobilize a whole society behind a support programme for talented children.
> - Academic competitions are one of the oldest and best ways to challenge the most able.
> - Links with universities offer outstanding opportunities for the most able.
>
> All three headings in this chapter could qualify as further out-of-class enrichment schemes.

The Hungarian Genius Program

The Hungarian Genius Program can claim to be the largest out-of-school enrichment programme in the world. As is the case with most successful schemes, it is powered by an intensity of passion on the part of those involved in it. Professor Péter Csermely is a leading figure in Hungarian education, chosen to write the first page of the brochure 'Hungarian Genius Integrated Talent Support Program', in effect the prospectus for the scheme.

> What are my dreams? If we had one thousand TalentPoints in the country in some years' time, plenty of them in the most disadvantaged regions, if Roma talents with starry eyes became teachers, doctors, and lawyers, if other countries of the European Union were standing in line to get the Hungarian model of talent support, I think this ship would be navigated to port (Csermely, 2011: n.p.).

Professor Csermely believes in networks – people or web-based – as being inherently more efficient than conventional hierarchical systems, and the Hungarian Genius Program is based on interlocking networks which 'make the flow, the distribution and use of information efficient' (Csermely, 2011: n.p.).

At the core of the programme is a comment on the 'zoomerang' returned as part of the CfBT survey of world provision for the gifted and talented (see Freeman et al., 2010), a copy of which is held by the authors: 'We believe every member of society is talented in a way.'

This is a three-year programme launched in June 2009 as part of Hungary's National Talent Programme, itself launched in 2008 and springing in turn from the 2006 National Talent Support Council. Its initial focus was on adults and the need to train people to deliver teaching and create a network for learning. Underpinning the whole idea is the existence of an effective network for delivery, suggesting the Hungarians have learnt two crucial lessons: never roll out a scheme without first ensuring you have the means to deliver it (a self-evident truth that seems on occasion not to have occurred to various UK governments) and get your teachers on side before you seek to achieve anything in education. At the same time, the scheme recognizes that it is not only teachers who can recognize and nurture talent, and that for success it is the wider community that has to be persuaded of the importance of finding and nurturing talent, not just the schools and teachers that serve those communities.

There is, of course, a further core issue to the scheme: the recognition that talent among young people exists everywhere and that it is worth discovering and growing. It is to be wondered if this could take root in the UK, where there is a strong and vocal lobby seemingly determined to offer all children only the same, identical opportunities.

So-called 'TalentPoints' are the nodes of the network, talent-supporting groups or communities founded by educational institutions, the church and/or civil institutions. Membership is voluntary, and TalentPoints have four main tasks:

- talent identification
- talent development
- talent counselling
- dissemination of best practice.

By spring 2011, there were 400 TalentPoints established or planned throughout Hungary. The Hungarian Genius portal provides access to all the Program offers, but also to any resources that will aid the talented. It includes an interactive map of institutions that support talent. It is noteworthy that the scheme uses 'talent' as a generic term, comprising high ability as well as many other skills. There are numerous fields of talent support, such as intellectual talents, arts, sports and craftwork. In its literature, the Program highlights, for example, a brilliant folk dancer.

Talent Days, often organized by local communities, held 500 events in 2011, involving 50,000 people. In part, these are professional meetings for adult helpers, who have available to them 10–30-hour training courses in over 80 subjects, but talented young people are encouraged to 'introduce themselves' at these events.

Talent Support Councils can be geographical or domain-specific. They comprise representatives from education, local business and government. They bring together TalentPoints with a view to:

- organizing forums for talent support activists
- influencing wider policy and decision making in talent support
- organizing Talent Days and conferences, and participating in them
- organizing discussions for individual TalentPoints and Talent Workshops, and promoting initiatives suggested by talented youths themselves.

The 'Friends of Talent Club' is an organization for all those who support talents and talented activity. Talent loans are available, and have been used for such things as to buy a violinist a decent instrument, to fund an athlete's first world event and to pay fees for tuition overseas.

The Hungarian Genius Portal website (http://geniuszportal.hu/) plays a dominant role in the Program. It allows easy communication between all levels and sectors of the network. Information and news (conferences, courses, Talent Days, etc.) are posted, but even more significant is the Interactive Talent Map, where best practice is shared and TalentPoints inside and outside of Hungary are listed.

The Hungarian Genius Program is funded by the EU, and the latest available figures for costs and numbers (March 2011) are given below:

Total Budget:	€2.4m
Registered TalentPoints:	400+
Number Pending:	60
Talent Days:	50
Hungarian Talent Support Councils:	20
Background Studies Written:	21
Books Written:	20
Training Programmes:	86

Number of Courses Taught: 526
Number of Trainees: 9,529
Visitors to geniuszportal.hu: 26,000+
Total Number of Expected Participants: 20,000

The Talent Bridges Program began in 2012 as a response to the perceived need to bridge gaps in the TalentPoint network, encouraging the area of social responsibility in students and increasing media coverage. This is the official comment. Unofficially and off the record, some of those involved believe that the Program's main weakness is its need to work more closely with students. By its own admission, there was too much of a sense of competition between various branches of the Program, and a need to strengthen bonds between members and co-operation among the various branches of the Program.

The Hungarian Program is unashamedly nationalistic and driven by economic reality (www.geniuszportal.hu):

> We have defined three major goals in the field of science education: to identify, to support, and to develop gifted people. The present period of economic crisis does not facilitate the achievement of these goals: countries that are more fortunate and wealthier than Hungary can lure our talent away, and thus deprive Hungary of the intellectual capital that these people represent.

The Hungarian Genius Program is mirrored only by the Swiss 'Netzwerk Begabungsfoerderung' scheme, in German-speaking Cantons, and discussed in a later chapter. The Swiss scheme is smaller and lacks the evangelical fervour of the Hungarian Program, which unashamedly seeks to reach out to the whole of Europe and beyond. As with so many schemes worldwide, the Hungarian Program owes much to the passionate conviction of a number of individuals.

This in turn raises the issue of whether or not such schemes can transfer or move to other cultures or countries. On the surface, the Hungarian scheme lacks some of the cultural specifics that make it nearly impossible to transfer, say, the Singaporean or South Korean systems to the west, but it does nevertheless have local elements that allow it to flourish in its own culture. Hungary has a proud history and tradition of cultivating talent, and appears to have both a national will and a government that is willing to support talent without fearing accusations of elitism.

Yet it is a little difficult to see a nationwide network such as this translating to the UK. It would require the equivalent of regular sessions in which the local Rotary Club sat down with the local university and the church to plan events to nurture and develop academic and other talents. One of the major achievements of the Hungarian Genius Program is its recognition that the duty to educate our children is not simply the job of 'education-alists' but also a wider social responsibility shared by all those with influence and resources.

A further element that seems embedded in Hungarian educational culture is love of competition. This may account for the smoke signals that on occasion emanate from the scheme that there is too much competition between the various sectors of the network, but it also accounts for the Hungarian National Secondary Schools Competition, involving 20 subjects, 30,000 students and 700 institutions. Competitions – local, national and international – are universally admired in all countries that recognize the most able as having special needs.

The Hungarian Genius Program makes outstanding use of networks, existing adult agencies and the internet. It recognizes the multi-faceted nature of talent and is willing to look for it regardless of ethnicity or background. It is too young a scheme to be objectively judged in terms of its outcomes, but it is a wonderful breath of fresh air in the world of educating the most able, a world which is too often beset by self-doubt, internal bickering and grudging governments. If it has a problem, it might lie in the fact that its concentration on the adults who deliver the Program has tended to be rather more visible than its impact on able children.

Competitions

Competitions for the most able are usually recognized as beneficial, and can be local, national or international: 'many of these competitions are cost-effective, inexpensive ways to develop talent ... We believe that competitions should be much more widely used internationally' (Campbell et al., in Heller et al., 2000: 535).

Academic competitions were first pioneered by Soviet Russia. Its Academic Olympic programme started in maths in Leningrad as early as 1934. Pole position in Europe is nowadays held by Germany. It has 20+ nationwide competitions and dozens more at local level. Nationwide, over 100,000 students participate individually or in groups in a wide range of disciplines.

The USA is also a committed participant in Olympiads. Participants in US Olympiads have been very successful at gaining places at leading universities, and 229 Olympians produced 2,921 publications. Early research showed that Olympians produced 12.8 publications per person as distinct from a 1.9 average in the group of 800 gifted males.

Among the advantages of Olympiad-style competitions are the following:

- They allow like minds to mix and compete with other like minds, without taking the owners of those minds out of mainstream school.
- The competitive element acts as a spur and a challenge to the most able.
- Both the travel and the competitive element make Olympiads exciting to young people in a similar way to sports players being enthusiastic about an away fixture.
- A relatively small number of highly subject-aspirational teachers and lecturers are needed to organize competitions, which can benefit a disproportionate number of students.
- Questions can be devised specifically to challenge and stimulate the most able.
- They allow students to rank themselves on a national or international scale.
- They sell well to students because participation in them is seen as a valuable addition to an application to a top university.
- They are either zero or low cost to the attendee, and are colour blind in respect of the influence of race, colour, creed or religion on their attendees or outcome. Put bluntly, they are very politically correct across the whole spectrum of political views.

Their only weakness is more of a limitation than a failing: they only really adapt to the testing of maths and science, rather than to the arts. Despite this, they represent one of the most painless and effective ways society has created to satisfy some of the needs of the most able.

Tertiary links

Something of a poor relation in global terms, a tertiary link usually means an able student choosing a project which they then progress with the help of a mentor from the local university. Such schemes can work exceptionally well in individual cases, but they depend for their success on rather too much luck – the luck of there being a university near enough to offer support, the luck of there being a university willing to release its staff for such a project and the luck of there being a mentor who is a specialist in the field a student wishes to study. Such schemes also suffer from the fact that few universities have the staff or resources to make such support the rule rather than the exception. Harsh economic facts rule here also. Universities have long faced a publish-or-die situation for their staff, to which now in many countries is added savage funding cuts. Many universities do not find themselves able to offer their own undergraduates sufficient contact time, never mind students who have yet to join them.

There is a further category of tertiary link which could have wide implications for the most able, but is only being nibbled at worldwide. Such schemes have the student completing not just the work necessary to qualify to enter university, but also work to excuse them the first year of undergraduate study. There are significant advantages for both the student and the university. The student is excused the expense of a year at university and also avoids one of the pitfalls that affects a number of the most able. In the UK, for example, the most able students, particularly in maths and science, will have been enriched to avoid boredom and to provide stretch and stimulus by studying several topics more commonly found in a first-year undergraduate course. The stereotype is the student who suffers burn-out at university. A more common trait is of failure of the burners to light up at university. The able student finds themselves covering work they have already done at school, becomes bored and fails to acquire the work habit they will need for subsequent years.

The advantage for the university is that, for some students at least, it will mean the university does not have to lay on a remedial first year, which is both expensive for the institution and often some way outside its skills set. It also means that it can set out its stall to attract the brightest and the best and, in an era dominated by access issues, offer a great deal in terms of the actual cost of a degree to poor and/or disadvantaged students.

Schemes such as this appear easier to mount in the American-style of university, where a generalist course marks the start of a degree prior to the choice of the 'major' – in effect, where the first stages of a degree course are perceived as being easier than their counterparts. In practice, this need not be so. Maths is one example. The modules already exist at A level, in Pure Maths 1 and Pure Maths 2, that many top university departments would have liked their undergraduates to have done. The problem is that either, for cultural and social reasons, more students opt to do the Statistics module, or they do not have maths teachers qualified to deliver Pure Maths. A straightforward answer would be for schools to join together in clusters and, with sensible use of compacting for the most able, adopt a variation of the New Zealand A-Day-a-Week School, in which all members of the scheme attend one of the cluster schools on a Friday to have their university modules delivered to them.

There is a significant roadblock in the way of any progress on a scheme such as this. It is the tendency to set the median for the performance and achievement of school pupils in the middle of the spectrum of ability and motivation. It is a sad reality that many teachers have never taught classes of only the most able students and have no comprehension of just how far and how fast such pupils can go if no limits are put on them. These teachers fret that too much will be demanded of young minds, that children will be pushed over some undefined edge – the 'cloying care' brand of teaching referred to in an earlier chapter. Children can of course be pushed too far and too fast, but only if the necessary selection and monitoring procedures are not in place. There is an equal if not greater danger in holding back the most able and attaching a ball and chain to their ankle so they do not outpace the teacher or embarrass the class by their brilliance. The Robinson Center in Seattle has proved beyond any reasonable doubt that children as young as 13 can cheerfully master advanced university courses.

Such schemes as there are for students to build up course credits that can be cashed in at university tend to be in partnership with newer universities, who are perhaps more willing to contemplate the radical and innovatory, and who in some cases are hungrier in their recruiting than some of their more established counterparts.

Two facts argue strongly for more global attention to schemes such as this. The first is that it is far cheaper to educate young people at school than it is at university. A second is the unpalatable fact that many of the most able simply grow out of conventional schooling one or two years ahead of their peers. A sensible society would change the nature of the school to fit the child, rather than expecting the child to fit the school. A new and exciting development in world educational systems should be the hybrid sixth form – a seamless garment linking the most able students with leading universities.

Questions for further thought

What is the impact of cultural influences on schools?

Although it is important to recognize that schools are not the only determinant of a learner's progress and that societal, cultural and personal factors all impact on how they will progress at school, schools need to address the many factors they have the power to control. Head teachers and senior leaders must have the courage and conviction to tackle challenging and controversial cultural factors and to facilitate open debate and understanding. The idea of using the community as curriculum can be a powerful counter to closed or insular environments.

(Continued)

(Continued)

National and international competitions can reveal talents that are exceptional not only in a small community, and can therefore open that community's eyes to the talent within. It is important that schools take responsibility for developing their learners' long-term aspirations beyond, as well as within, the community.

> We need to create an educational system that sees equality as an essential requirement of effective more able education provision. Where all educators hold high expectations towards their culturally diverse students. Where schools celebrate the diversity which is their strength. Where there is a requirement to be completely committed to breaking down the barriers that prevent individuals from realising their potential. Where high levels of challenge are the right of all students. (Warwick & Matthews, in Balchin et al., 2009: 272)

What barriers can communities create?

Communities exert huge power, and like all power it can be used for negative as well as positive ends. It is essential for schools to feel confident enough to challenge the community where necessary to counter the negative effects of insularity and lack of ambition, values conflict and disinterest. In some communities, it must be recognized that more able students can actually be held back, consciously or unconsciously, as success can be seen as a threat to the continued existence of that community. If a child goes off to a top university, is it likely that they will return?

The 'Anna Karenina' principle describes any endeavour in which a deficiency in just a single factor dooms it to failure. Derived from Tolstoy's book which begins, 'Happy families are all alike; every unhappy family is unhappy in its own way', it posits that a successful endeavour is one where every possible deficiency has been avoided. If you are unfortunate enough to have lived in a community damaged by poverty and worklessness for several generations, then in fact your 'cultural unhappiness' may start to look depressingly similar. To take just a single illustrative example which is relevant to this book, how does community influence language development? Home and school contexts represent different cultures, subcultures or both and influence language acquisition in noticeable ways. By the age of 3, children raised by professional parents have heard 13 million words spoken and those with parents on welfare have heard just 10 million (Hart & Risley, 2003).

Hart and Risley (2003: 193) went on to speculate that these categories may be 'important for the language-based analytic and symbolic competencies upon which advanced education and a global economy depend'. Children absorb language not just in dedicated 'vocabulary-building' moments generated in schools, but in every moment. It is therefore no surprise that vocabulary deficits can be handed down through generations.

Owens, in *Language Development: An Introduction*, found that maternal race, education and socioeconomic class influence parent–child interactions in the early linguistic environment. When speaking to their infants, middle-class mothers 'incorporate language goals more frequently in their play with their infants', and, in turn, their infants produce twice as many vocalizations as lower-class infants (2012: 130–5).

Children from different cultural environments may be learning to use language differently, according to Beverly Otto (2006: 64–8), and may therefore experience difficulty in participating in the language environment in classrooms.

Our cultural background is always there, formative and significant, and it is this that can all too easily be responsible for imposing a ceiling on ambition and achievement. There are always examples of children that we have taught who have almost miraculously transcended quite traumatic early childhood experiences. What is quite depressing is how few make that journey.

What can schools do to better engage with communities?

In outstanding schools, parental and community engagement often enhances and extends learning substantially beyond the taught curriculum. Many schools might use this additional capacity in order to offset the effects of socio-economic disadvantage in other parts of the school community. Regular, frequent engagement by parents within the school is likely to lead to a greater understanding of the needs of that school and experience shows that this may become a tipping point, beyond which whole-school more-able provision becomes substantially easier to deliver. Does the school ensure the curriculum teaches that every culture interprets its history and learning through certain grand narratives and that these, in turn, contribute to the identities of individuals? Does it teach that most people have a range of affiliations, loyalties and sense of belonging?

Using specific activities to demonstrate the impact of and potential for parental and community engagement in the school for more able education can also be a powerful motivator. Consider how the school can develop confidence in the community to involve itself and enhance more able provision, whilst recognizing that in disadvantaged communities some families are more isolated than others. Engage parents, teachers and learners in a three-way dialogue around aspirations, the role of the school, responsibilities for educating, access to opportunities, challenge and support. Discuss how the school can translate current community involvement into greater engagement. Consider the ideas of 'community as curriculum' and 'school as community' and the extent to which these might overlap. Explore how further engagement between the school and the community can be of benefit for more able provision. Treat your community as a resource to be nurtured, fed and involved, just as you do your pupils. If the most able children are the flower, their community and family are the roots; one doesn't grow without the other.

10

Specialist Schools and the Issue of Selection

Key points

- UK independent schools are academically some of the most successful in the world, and show good practice as regards teachers, aspirations, use of post-graduates and the avoidance of boredom.
- Post-graduate students are a neglected teaching resource for the most able in the UK.
- The Teach First scheme has great unused potential for teaching the most able.
- Some specialist schools offer an unacceptably bleak learning environment.
- Some others, such as the Dutch Leonardo schools, fall foul of the access agenda.
- The most able are advantaged by being educated together.
- Even in successful all-ability schools the needs of the most able are not always met.
- 'Vertical' grouping of the most able (by ability rather than age) can be beneficial.

Specialist schools for the most able are the extreme variant of the 'pull-out' technique, whereby able children are taken out of the mainstream and attend schools specializing in the gifted. For most Europeans, specialist schools mean the English grammar schools, French *Lycées* and German *Gymnasiums*. Although they do not always like to admit it, leading UK independent schools are among the most specialist and selective in the world, with the top 10 or 20 recruiting from little below the top 5% of academic ability in the cohort. Eastern European countries have a tradition of specialist schools for the most able, as does Singapore and a number of other countries. Yet, for all the strength of many individual schools, specialist schools are increasingly unfashionable in the state-funded arena and are arguably more in retreat than ever before in their history.

The famous French *Lycée* system has evolved, with the all-ability Collège acting as a middle school and the *Lycée* taking over at the age of 15 for three years. There are now three types of *Lycée* – General, Technical or Vocational – which UK observers might be forgiven for translating into Grammar, Technical and Secondary Modern schools. The trend that has largely gone unnoticed in the UK is for 20% of pupils in France to be in 'private' schools. These cannot be compared directly with UK private schools, in that 90% of them are religious schools and provided they teach the national curriculum the State pays for teachers' salaries, meaning far cheaper fees than in the UK. What is interesting in terms of educating the most able is that in a recent survey by the French newspaper *Le Figaro* in 2012 only six of the top 20 highest-achieving *Lycées* were in the State sector. The magazine *L'Etudiant*, in a comparable league table, reduced this to five.

If the growth of independent schools in Singapore is a conscious policy, and the newly independent Raffles Institution one of the academic flagship schools of the world, then it has to be asked if a world trend in educating the most able is not linked to the provision of some form of independence for schools. Outstanding though many of these schools are, the presence of fee paying as a criterion for entry leads inevitably to accusations of a negative elitism, in which access to education for able children is more a function of parents' income than the ability of their child. This directs criticism at the wrong target. Aspirational middle-class and immigrant parents will seek to colonize academically successful schools, and little can stop that happening. The trick is not to close the academically successful schools or impose a quota of disadvantaged children on them, but to make academic aspiration a feature of the culture of communities and ethnicities where it does not exist. Where there is great disparity in a system between schools that are high achieving and those that are low achieving, it cannot make sense to start a cure by dismantling the high achievers.

Independent schools in the UK

UK independent schools have been at the heart of such a fierce political debate for so long that a major area where they might be useful to Education UK plc has often been overlooked. Precisely because the very top independent schools have such an academically selective entry, they have evolved (sometimes unconsciously) a whole range of techniques for teaching and dealing with the most able. It might be useful to sidestep what some regard as the politics of envy and replace it with emulation. What can we learn about educating the most able from the most successful UK independent schools?

It is first necessary to establish their credentials. Figures here are from the Independent Schools Council Annual Census for 2012. In the UK, at GCSE, just 6.5% of entries come from independent schools yet their pupils gain 26.0% of the A* grades. A third of students getting AAA or better at A level come from independent schools. When the UK brought in the new A* grade at A level, St Paul's School gained proportionately more of the new grades than any other school in England, with over 50% of grades in that year being gained at A* by its pupils. Four independent schools – Eton, Westminster, St Paul's Boys and St Paul's Girls – and state-funded Hills Road Sixth Form College in Cambridge, together sent 946 pupils to Oxford and Cambridge between 2007 and 2009. By contrast, 2,000 lower-performing schools combined sent a total of 927 students to the two elite universities, gaining less than 6% of available places (Sutton Trust, 2011: 19).

Before the experience of these schools is mined for what it can teach us, certain caveats have to be sounded. The majority of UK independent schools are significantly less selective than the old grammar schools and many are not selective on academic ability at all. Independent school pupils are just as capable of disrupting a lesson as any other child. However, the ABC of the issues that, if dealt with well, are a common denominator in virtually all good schools – Attendance, Behaviour and Curriculum – are significantly easier to get right in most independent schools than they are in non-selective state schools. One problem with academic input into the education of able children is that many of those who write about it are the product of independent, grammar or selective schools, and have a vision that does not always adapt to a school where, say, over half the pupils can claim free school meals.

All this being said, it is simply not true that the most selective schools in the UK can simply sit back and watch whilst able young people achieve top grades. It is one of the curses afflicting the education of the most able that some people believe ability alone is the guarantee of its own success. The myth is perpetuated further by the undoubted fact that some children triumph against all the odds to achieve academically at the highest level. To assume that all children can do this is to count only those who survived the loss of the 'Titanic' and ignore those who died. Though we are right not to always treat able pupils as 'fragile and delicate flowers', 'geeks' or children 'crippled by their ability', that same ability is not simply a brute force of nature that will fight its way through any environment. It can be prone to self-doubt and hung up on a fear of being 'different'. Like a rare (as distinct from fragile) plant, it sometimes needs special food. UK independent schools can get things seriously wrong when it comes to educating the most able. Some of them get some things right, particularly with regard to nurturing that particular flower. The techniques and approaches listed below can also be found in the highest achieving state schools in the UK. They will not be news to the staff of Tiffin Boys' and Girls' Grammar Schools, Henrietta Barnett School, the Invicta Grammar School, the Oratory School, the Cardinal Vaughan School, Thomas Telford, Hills Road Sixth Form College and Hampden Gurney Primary School, and a host of others. What the independent school experience can do is to highlight and focus on techniques used to teach the most able, something harder to do in a state sector where the most able are inevitably in the minority. So what do the most academically successful UK independent and maintained schools do with and for the most able that helps to produce their stunning results?

Factors for success

Teachers are at the core of their strategy. It is not that independent schools pay their teachers more, though some do. The real key to their success is to appoint a teacher not as a social worker or as an administrator, but as an impassioned evangelist for their subject. Top independent schools attract graduates to teach because they let the graduate teach the subject they love to students who are expected to love it as much as the teacher. The traditional academic disciplines remain a freeway that leads directly to the heart of many able children. In top academic independent schools, every teacher has a good degree in the subject they teach (a feature of teacher recruitment in many educationally successful countries) and many have PhDs. Not only does this equip the teacher with a level of knowledge that both commands the respect of the most able and allows answers to at least some of their questions, but it also has a crucial knock-on effect on the teaching of science in particular. As has been discussed earlier, practical work remains the most exciting and challenging way to teach science, to both the most able and the normally gifted. It has stayed so despite increasing restrictions on what can be done. Experiments carried out by science teachers 30 years ago would now cause a Health and Safety consultant to spontaneously combust, which in itself is unsafe. Yet it is not

Health and Safety that threatens the practical lesson. By their very nature, practicals are a voyage of discovery, and a voyage where things will go wrong or do the unexpected. It is almost a litany in many great schools that the certainty that a good degree-level knowledge gives is an essential part of the confidence to undertake a practical lesson.

A further element in these schools' success is aspiration – not the academic aspiration of the pupils, vital though this is, but the aspiration of the staff, where anything less than an A grade is seen as a failure. In popular culture, this qualifies as a 'downer' or depressant that greatly increases stress levels and typifies the hot-house culture. One is tempted to point out that the hot-house is there because it makes things grow. Rather than acting as a depressant, the A* aspiration is a stimulant and a challenge. This is the only exception to the rule that the teacher of a class of very able students does not necessarily have to know more about a subject than the pupils. A science teacher taking a practical needs to know more than it is reasonable for his or her pupils to know, namely what has gone wrong and what it is necessary to do to put it right.

This points to another truth known to a number of academically successful schools. Able children like challenge and are often spurred on by the fear of failure rather than put off by it. Children like risk: it is a major factor in many forms of their experimentation. Able children need to be offered challenge, risk and even the prospect of failure in class. Schools have become so obsessed with protecting children that they have sometimes failed to teach them how to cope or take risks, like the proud parent who has banished so much dirt from the home that the child loses its ability to build up its natural resistance.

Independent schools have also latched on to the UK's, and possibly the world's, greatest hidden resource, a force akin to the ghost army summoned by Aragorn to defeat the forces of Mordor in Tolkien's *The Lord of the Rings*. Post-graduate students and post-doctoral research fellows are by definition very skilled in their subject. Research is frequently a lonely business and always badly paid, and the man or woman in their mid- to late 20s is quite likely to be looking to settle down and in a position to welcome additional income. Some leading selective independent schools recruit such people as teachers. There is a reasonable income, job security, the chance to teach the beloved subject and like minds, both among the staff and the pupils. A variation on this that could impact greatly on the opportunities non-selective state schools offer their most able is for one school or a cluster of them to pay a post-graduate to come for one day or even one morning or afternoon a week to teach a class of the most able in a given year group or to bring teachers up to speed with the latest ideas or research. This can be done without threatening the success of any current research. This suggestion needs to be viewed alongside the fact that in 2009 one of the largest south London comprehensive schools started the summer term without a single graduate scientist on the staff for the following September, and the fact that post-graduates are a world-wide species, though largely untouched for teaching purposes outside the university itself.

A potential problem here is one that the UK's admirable 'Teach First' scheme has invented for itself. It recruits graduates from top universities to teach in state schools for a two-year trial period. The problem is that the agenda seems social and political as much as educational, in that the expectation is that graduates will teach in tough, inner-city environments. Teach First's publicity, taken here from its website (www.teachfirst.org.uk), constantly emphasizes the 'challenging' nature of the schools recruits will be sent to, as in 'Since its founding in 2002, Teach First has placed over 2,520 teachers in schools in challenging circumstances to work with students to raise their achievement, access and aspirations'.

And it is clearly stated that Teach First is not about helping the most able, but rather the disadvantaged, who will, of course, consist of some highly able students but for whom the scheme is clearly not designed: 'Teach First is a charity that recruits exceptional graduates looking to make an impact in the classroom of schools in challenging circumstances and who have a desire to address the inequalities in education in the long-term.'

The problem here is not with the stated aim but rather with a wasted opportunity. A number of graduates who might wish to teach their subject are deterred by the fact that the 'challenging' school will give them relatively little opportunity to use the full range of their knowledge. If the independent sector can teach the world anything, it is that in a system that looks after its most able there is room for the teacher whose agenda is more to do with their subject than with the admirable task of putting the world to rights. Post-graduates and post-doctoral researchers offer the raw material to make just that happen. There is also an inherent paradox in Teach First. The graduates can also offer a simple example to students about what is possible, but a great number have also come through the independent sector so their story is not necessarily so appropriate.

Independent school practice can also be informative on the nature of teaching, as well as on the nature of the teacher. Strenuous efforts to improve UK state education have largely followed a path to creating 'good' schools outlined in the Barber et al. McKinsey (2010a) report already referred to, in that they comprise a massive imposition of central control – the establishment of a compulsory National Curriculum, teacher appraisal, inspection and publication of results, to name a few. An almost inevitable consequence of this mentality is a move to judge teachers by process as much as by outcome. An inspector now comes to a lesson with what is, in effect, an advance definition of a good lesson, measured by ticks in a box. There is, even more worryingly, also a data-driven perception of a good or outstanding lesson. This approach is an anathema to some outstanding teaching. By what an inspector would deem totally 'the wrong route', many teachers teach the skills that let students sail through the exam. Eccentricity should not become the rule, simply because freedom to deviate from the prescribed pattern is open to abuse and can become a charter for the teacher who is simply too idle to obey the rules. Yet the most able frequently need a light touch from their teacher. As any skier knows, it is dangerous to go off-piste but also exhilarating. UK independent schools can teach the mainstream that the most able need to go off-piste at times, and that sometimes an outstanding lesson needs to tick just one box, not all of them. As a bonus, the occasional chance to cease the route march and gather flowers by the wayside is as exhilarating for the teacher as it is for the student.

Independent schools that cater best for the most able in the UK are also aware of a number of other truths that are revealed when the mass of one's pupils are in the top 5% of the ability band. One truth is that such young people get bored very quickly and that boredom is death to academic achievement. The avoidance of boredom can be addressed by various classroom strategies including judicious use of acceleration, compaction, setting and streaming, enriched or additional material covered in class, and out-of-class activities, such as project work, participation in Olympiads, local and national competitions, access to online learning and a host of educational visits. Perhaps because the founding fathers of UK independent schools were the big boarding schools, which have contributed a significant amount to the overarching culture of all independent schools, extra- or co-curricular activities at the leading schools for the most able occupy a high priority. The historical reason is that the boarding school with pupils in its care 24/7 understands more than most what the Devil finds for idle hands to do. The pupil-management imperative has evolved into something with a specifically educational advantage, in that a pupil who is enthused by their sport, art, music, drama, debating or whatever has a fuse lit that burns on and into the classroom.

A sense of fulfilment outside of the classroom and an absence of boredom fuel academic success inside it. The most able of our children do not live in a bubble or exist only from the neck up. Independent school experience illustrates that the most able are not egg-heads, freaks or anoraks, but normal young men and women who happen to have extra ability that, whilst it might need extra provision, also leaves them with the same needs and desires as the normally gifted.

This is perhaps a cue to refer to the other famous European series of selective schools for the most able, the German *Gymnasiums*, if only because the *Gymnasiums* seemed least interested in extra-curricular activities. Understanding the German secondary education system is not straightforward. The local state, rather than Federal government, dictates educational provision. A post-war system that was in effect a variant of the Grammar/Technical/Secondary Modern model has been complicated by the existence nowadays of five types of school: the *Gymnasium*; the *Realschule*; the *Hauptschule*; the *Gesamtschule*; and the *Förderschule*. German educational development has been complicated by unification and soured both by a grammar versus comprehensive debate and a battle over the extraordinary system whereby lessons can start at 7.30am and finish by lunch, without the school even serving lunch. Yet, despite the fog and smoke of educational battle, the *Gymnasium* is still the best and preferred route to passing the *Abitur*, the qualifying exam for university. The *Gymnasiums* are a convincing argument in favour of all schools, be they selective or not, supporting extra-curricular activities. There was no doubting the ability either of the students or the staff at one Berlin *Gymnasium*, yet it was, not untypically, a cold place. There appeared to be no social meeting area for the students, who sat on bare concrete floors outside the classrooms. The teachers unlocked each room (these were not laboratories) to let the children in and locked each room at the end of the lesson. 'Herr Professor' clearly saw the job as turning up and teaching, with no reference to pastoral care or extra-curricular involvement. The children dispersed at 1.00pm. If they were lucky enough to have a sports or other club near them, and good enough to get in, the odds were that they would not be mixing with a majority of their colleagues from school in out-of-school hours, thus denying them the chance to augment, cement and expand the easiest friendships to make – those at school with one's peer group.

An effective school for the most able must surely regard the pastoral involvement of teachers and the provision of extra-curricular activities as crucial. The alternative is a concrete jungle which freezes out as many children as it enables. Like the Spartan method of birth control, leaving children out on a hillside overnight, what the stripped-down selective school provides is an environment where those who survive are the toughest, rather than the most able. Some South Korean high schools (see below) seem to take this a stage further.

There are other lessons to be learnt from the UK's selective independent schools, though the majority owe as much to common sense as to any

'Eureka!' moment. The UK's leading independent schools do not share the contemporary backlash against homework. Many remain obsessed with making their pupils read, a traditional practice endorsed in the PISA 2009 Results: Executive Summary, which states, 'In all countries, students who enjoy reading the most perform significantly better than students who enjoy reading the least' (2010: 12).

Poland goes one stage further in placing an emphasis on classic texts in its reading lists for students. This is in contrast to the UK. What price the classics in the UK, and a philosophy which seems to think that children demand books that lead into their world, not books that take them out of it? We patronize children by assuming they can only be interested in what they know and are familiar with. Thomas Gradgrind in Charles Dickens' *Hard Times* had his way with children as much by telling them what they should not look at as by suggesting what they should.

The same PISA report suggests why UK independent schools sit at the top of world rankings, without once mentioning wealth, privilege or elitism:

> Results from PISA suggest that, across OECD countries, schools and countries where students work in a climate characterized by high performance expectations and the readiness to reward effort, good teacher–student relations and high teacher morale tend to achieve better results. (2010: 12)

The fact that this lesson applies equally to a top UK independent school and to a non-selective KIPP school in New York, the latter with an entry of massively disadvantaged children, shows that the comprehensive system can work for the mass of children. This does not automatically mean that it works as well for the most able. The question defenders of the UK comprehensive school have to answer is why it has so often failed to generate 'high performance aspirations', as highlighted in the most recent (2013) Ofsted survey on more able students.

Pull-out schools outside the UK

Various countries offer specialist, 'pull-out' schools of one type or another. Some of these fall outside the scope of this text, in that their agenda is primarily social, rather than catering for the needs of the most able. One example is Turkey's Inanc Foundation, which takes very poor children from all over the country for high-level boarding education. Somewhere on the cusp is Brazil's Embraer High School, which takes only very poor children and offers them an engineering speciality. Founded by a Brazilian aircraft manufacturer, it is a day school which provides meals and transport. Another half-way house is the 'Children's Palace', and there are many of these 'palaces' across China. These are purportedly non-selective and provide high-level out-of-school education for young people prepared to make the considerable commitment required.

India has a growing number of JNV (Jawahar Navodaya Vidyalaya) boarding schools for able boys and girls from poor rural districts. There were roughly 593 JNV schools across India as of 2010. Russia has a series of language schools that teach all subjects in a foreign language. The problem with this apparently good idea is that it requires two teachers for the price of one – for example, a Russian citizen who can teach maths and speak English to the same level of competence. Heads who have struggled to appoint a teacher who is proficient in two languages, never mind another language and another subject, are unlikely to be killed in the rush to man the barricades in defence of this approach.

The Fazekas Mihály Gimnázium (in Budapest) has an international reputation for mathematics, part of a Hungarian model whereby bright young mathematicians are sent to specialist schools in big cities. A distinguished UK maths teacher reports in a private note to the authors:

> [the students] are able to interact together in a way which is most stimulating for able youngsters who otherwise might not find anyone like them. A significant gesture of the teaching is problem-solving; they are asked to tackle really hard problems individually, then discuss them with their peers, and finally to present their solutions in front of the whole class, enabling criticism and cross-fertilisation. Apparently there are dormitories at Fazekas and some students live in digs and go home at weekends, so it is possible to attend the school even if your family live out in the countryside.

Soviet Russia led the way at one time in specialist schools. It is reported that many of these face serious financial difficulties, and also declining standards because of the need to accept fee-paying students on the basis of their ability to pay, rather than their ability.

The South Korean system educates students in high school for their last three years, at 15–18 years of age. Daewon Foreign Language High School and the Minjok Leadership Academy are the highest performing schools, with staggering success rates. However, the success rate of these highly selective schools has to be seen alongside bitter debate over the South Korean system, discussed in a later chapter.

The first Leonardo schools in the Netherlands were started in 2007, and again are on the cusp. Should they be seen as separate, pull-out schools or as an extreme variant of pull-out within the child's existing school? Though housed within an existing 'host', our experience suggests that the children see themselves as attending a separate school. The Leonardo model is for a separate mixed-age class of gifted learners within a normal school. The Leonardo schools share a principle with the Adelaide-based SHIP scheme, in that they are a school-within-a-school, with the children joining in with the mainstream for some activities. They are private schools that receive state funding and also funding from private companies. Hybrid schools, independent but also part-funded by the state, are a clear way forward for the education of gifted pupils. There are currently 42 Leonardo schools (primary) and eight colleges (senior), with the aim being 120 schools and 60 colleges.

One commentator described the genesis and philosophy of the Leonardo schools as follows, and in so doing summed up a point of view central to many people's beliefs about G&T education. The originator of the Leonardo model is one Jan Hendrikx, a former teacher and primary school principal who spent some 12 years of his career working with gifted children in mainstream settings:

> He became convinced that teachers faced great difficulty in meeting the needs of their gifted learners in a mixed ability environment. Despite their best efforts to provide enrichment and faster pacing, many gifted pupils were insufficiently challenged and motivated.

> The Dutch education inspectorate estimates that almost one-third of their students with an IQ of 130 or above are underachieving relative to their potential. This rises to six in ten for those with an IQ of 145 and above. Hendrikx points out the tremendous waste of human potential that this represents, and the loss to the Netherlands in terms of wasted human capital. (Gifted Phoenix, 2011: n.p.)

Students are nominated by the host school and must have IQs of over 130. They receive lessons from native speakers in English from age 4 and Spanish from age 8. The curriculum is non-standard and deals with special areas of interest such as ICT, science, learning to learn and even starting your own business. Dutch and maths lessons are set to the student's individual level and there is great emphasis on art, philosophy and culture, as well as music lessons and mental exercises. 'Leonardo time' is provided for students to pursue their own interests and sport is part of the curriculum. In an interesting contrast with South Korean high schools, the willingness to countenance sport goes along with similar encouragement of art, music and drama. This is also true of the Fazekas Mihály Gimnázium. Close, two-way links are developed with outside organizations such as universities and businesses and significant parental involvement is invited and encouraged. There is also a 15-day training course for teachers an honourable exception in the global spectrum.

As with many such projects, Leonardo schools fall foul of the access agenda. The Dutch Government is willing to spend an average of €5k on each pupil a year. The cost of a Leonardo education is not less than €7k a year. Parents can be asked to pay between €1k and €3k a year towards their child's education. There is also political controversy about the schools.

A growing trend is for specialist schools for the most able to be set up in partnership with a university or even a business, as with DLR in Germany. ASMAS (Australian Science and Maths School) is a good example. Purpose-built for 15–18-year-olds on the campus of Flinders University, Adelaide, Australia, it offers:

- a whole curriculum delivered through science and maths
- a focus on meta-cognitive learning styles
- interaction with university and industry
- students setting their own learning target.

A comparable example is the University of California at Los Angeles (UCLA) Laboratory School. Set on campus, it has a fourfold purpose:

- to train teachers
- research
- to be at the cutting edge of educational innovation
- to provide outreach to teachers.

Students are taught in multi-age groups spanning two years, and the teachers move with the children in two-year 'loops'. Staffing is very generous.

It is one of the functions of and justifications for specialist schools to point out techniques that might not be identified within the constraints of mainstream teaching. One such, and a growing trend worldwide, is to recognize chronological age as a potential strait-jacket that simply restrains and holds back ability. The argument traditionally used for keeping children within their age range is that intellectual development must be matched by the corresponding speed of emotional development. What special schools, and other innovations detailed elsewhere in this book, show is that knowledge and intellectual capacity can far outrun emotional development, and that in fast-laning the former one simply needs to keep the latter at a slower pace. Children are not one-size-fits-all. The intellectual part of the brain and that part which deals with emotional and social maturity are not one single locked cabinet but two distinct vehicles that can be moved at different speeds. Very often, schemes for the most able unthinkingly operate these within year groups, rather than creating 'vertical' groups united not by the age of the pupils but by their ability.

Do pull-out schools work well? Yes, for those who attend them, but the more they multiply, the more they are likely to be accused of sucking strength out of the mainstream.

The issue of selection

Several books could be written on the issue of whether or not it is educationally, morally or social justifiable to select children to attend schools reserved for the most able. It is a debate that has come near to tearing the heart out of British education, and it can also be a particularly sterile debate. This is because it is akin to a force of nature that academically aspirational parents will seek out schools where their child will meet children, and parents, with similar aspirations. State entry into unashamedly selective schools is not available only through an exam, such as the UK 11+, or by buying into independent education. Many aspirational families simply move house into the catchment area of a successful state school, thereby colonizing a school. The case for and against grammar schools will be examined later, along with whether selective schools should exist. There is little to be gained by asking if selective schools, by drawing off talented individuals, damage the education of the middle and lower tier of ability, or if selective schools similarly siphon off the best teachers and so damage the mainstream. Similarly, it is fairly pointless asking if it is fair or justifiable that well over two-thirds of entrants to Oxford and Cambridge come from the 7% of pupils educated in the independent sector. All are good questions which need to be addressed. However, the most useful question to ask, solely in the interests of the most able, is this: do the most able children benefit from being educated together?

The answer is unequivocally yes. Selective schools are not the only way to achieve this, though they may be the easiest.

There is little doubt that very able young people together reach a critical mass as a result of their interactions, egg each other on in a wholly positive way and, as an economist might say, make the take-off into self-sustained growth. It is this latter event which sometimes mitigates against widespread acceptance of the needs of teaching the most able on the part of teachers. The stereotypical lesson has the teacher as leader, the children as recipients. Conversely, many of the most successful lessons for the most able leave the teacher behind at an early stage, with the students learning from each other. This might explain why so many teachers of the most able describe themselves as the least able person in the room.

It has been commented on in the USA and in the UK that the most common reaction to standard high school fare from the most able students is boredom, often on an industrial scale. Boredom is an issue that advocates of the all-ability school have yet to answer satisfactorily: 'One of the common reactions of gifted students in the US to public schools is boredom' (Gallagher, in Heller et al., 2000: 688). It is hard to remain keen and enthusiastic if you are continuing to repeat things already learned. Disengagement is just as serious an issue for the most able as the physical absence from school that cripples attainment. It is far harder for the truly able to disengage in a class of similar ability, and no fun at all. Supporters of non-selective education in the UK have been very vocal and successful in getting their message across in the media. But there is evidence that able children do better in a selective environment:

> Although the gifted youngsters in this study were quite young there did seem to be an advantage in grouping them together, allowing the teacher to press on to more challenging and complex materials and topics with these students. (Gallagher, in Heller et al., 2000: 688)

A UK view is provided below:

> Demands posed by mixed ability teaching presented a number of challenges to progress. The G & T pupils felt their progress was slowed by the presence of their less able compeers who required and received more teacher input. The needs of less able pupils were prioritised. (Brooks, 2010: 5)

These comments go to the heart of the issue. Much comment on all-ability teaching concentrates on the advantages for the less able in being educated with the most able. Yet an equal issue is the extent to which the most able are held back and disadvantaged by only being able to proceed at the pace of the slowest.

The cause of the most able is badly served by the fact that in general parlance the case for educating the most able together is seen as synonymous with selective education and selective schools. The two need not be the same. To educate the most able with each other for the majority of the curriculum does not require them to be in a separate school, as the

Australian SHIP scheme shows, or even the Leonardo schools. Streaming and setting in maths, but also in science and perhaps even in modern languages, can allow pupils the benefits of like mixing with like, without completely dragging the most able out of the mainstream. Motorways manage a slow lane, a cruising lane and a fast or overtaking lane. There is no theoretical reason why a school cannot do the same. Properly handled, out-of-school enrichment can achieve much at relatively little cost, as the New Zealand One-Day School has shown. Bringing able children together need not be at the cost of having them only mix with like minds.

Questions for further thought

What can independent and state school partnerships achieve?

First, they can help define what a teacher of the most able looks like. Teaching the most able requires some different skills and techniques from those required for teaching the normally gifted, and teachers in some independent and selective state schools have of necessity to acquire some of these techniques and practise them over extended periods. They have become used to focusing very clearly on the core question of what outstanding teaching for high-ability students looks like and they can offer up some of their insights for exploration.

A second area is concerned with raising the sights and aspiring to a place at a top university. Independent and selective state schools are sometimes criticized for their 'obsession' with places at top universities. It is essential that this does not convert into the school mocking the aspirations of a most able student. Where only a small proportion of the pupil body is in the most able category, and resources are tight, high aspiration to a leading academic institution becomes simply a minority interest and a central part of neither the student nor the school's culture. Visiting a leading independent or selective state school can act as a cold shower or wake-up call. The reality across many state schools is that more able education is often all too vulnerable when resources and teachers are stretched. It is seen as dependent on political whim and is viewed by many as less significant than other student needs. In addition, it has probably not done itself many favours by failing to clarify what it actually looks like in subject-specific areas. It is certainly true that academics have not supported it well. It still has an elitist stigma, and unless it steps up to address the disadvantaged agenda far more effectively it may always be too easily side-stepped. Whatever the independent and selective state might fall prey to, it is not this, and from that different culture low aspiration for students can be more easily challenged.

A third area is the sharing of interesting and transferable practice, both in the classroom and across schools. This, of course, applies across the board and to all sectors, and the Australian experience is the strongest possible argument for schools forming clusters in order to share good practice in teaching the most able. An advantage of the cluster is that an independent or selective state school can take its place as a member of the cluster and not necessarily demand to be seen as the leader.

One crucial area of good practice, and a fourth key technique, is the monitoring of success in programmes for teaching the most able. There is testing fatigue across the teaching profession, which has led to the frequent accusation that the UK and the USA spend far too much time weighing the pig rather than feeding it. This is unfortunate in that the only good programme for the most able is the one that continually asks itself how well it is doing. There are relatively simple ways of doing this, from the predictor tests in common use in many schools to comparisons of the progress of the most able students with that of other students in the school, and nationally, and to what extent this reflects an ambitious vision for students. It is essential that teachers can identify specific ways in which teaching and learning for their most able students have improved as a result of the work they have done. There are too many assumptions that simply because a school has a scheme, it means the scheme is working well.

What is the problem with mixed-ability teaching?

There are many arguments against the use of ability grouping summed up in the book *Keeping Track: How Schools Structure Inequality* (Oakes & Goodland, 2012). Teachers' expectations for students tend to be shaped by initial groupings, confining students to rigid tracks and leading teachers to devote fewer resources to low-achieving students. Concerns about ability grouping focus on the inequalities that can inadvertently arise when organizing students by ability, as this can result in students from disadvantaged backgrounds being under-represented, which in turn can be seen as a force of societal polarization. Inequality is therefore perpetuated by trapping poor and minority students in low-level groups. These are social arguments that have some legitimacy and force. What they aren't though is an academic argument about the benefits or constraints of attainment grouping in terms of progress and with all students in mind. They don't attempt to answer critical questions about who might benefit from it most and who might be harmed. They also don't acknowledge the clear tendency for students to seek out like-minded peers, even if the more able are needed in the regular classroom to act as role models for other students. Although there might not be anything wrong with serving as a positive role model, it could be argued that it is a little questionable for adults to view a student's function as that of role model to others, possibly at the expense of their own progress. If educators are to make informed decisions based on findings about ability grouping, they must study the original research and be sure that the questions they are asking are the same ones posed by researchers.

There is a tendency for teachers to teach to the average level. Differentiation strategies can be hugely effective as long as the spread of ability isn't too wide. When it is, more able students get frustrated by being with very low-ability peers as work tends to be more structured and repetitive. These students already get it and want to engage in more interactive strategic and analytic activities. The same context can also be intimidating for the less able, who may not respond well to the more high-challenge competitive environment that bright students need and which can make them feel inadequate. Bright, average and slow youngsters profit from grouping programmes that critically adjust the curriculum to the aptitude

(Continued)

(Continued)

level of the groups. Without that adjustment, there is little impact on schools and they might as well lump all students together in one class, which research suggests may help average and struggling children, albeit at the expense of top performance.

Are our top students getting short shrift?

Streaming or tracking is essentially attainment grouping (more normally and inaccurately called ability grouping, even though the recognition of potential is rarely used). The key distinguishing factor has to be what then happens in the classroom. Is the curriculum the same or enriched? If so, is it differentiated and, if so, is it through greater depth or pace?

In a brilliantly argued chapter in *Bad Education* (Baines et al., 2012: 37–57), a book which sets out to examine myths that have surrounded teaching and learning, Ed Baines takes on a research-based analysis of all the significant studies done on ability grouping over the last few decades.

Some of that research has, for a number of years, sought to help answer questions about grouping, with researchers applying new techniques of research review to this subject. As an example, two prominent sets of reviews – the meta-analyses of James Kulik and Chen-Lin Kulik (e.g. Kulik, 1992) of the University of Michigan and the best-evidence synthesis of Robert Slavin (1990) of Johns Hopkins University – have attempted to pull together all the available information. Kulik and Kulik's meta-analysis reported little effect of ability grouping on achievement when there was little variation in instructional experience. However, when the classroom experience was varied by ability grouping the effects were markedly in favour of ability grouping, particularly for high-ability students, whilst low-ability students do much worse and actually fare better in mixed-ability classrooms. When students are streamed in mixed-age classes, Slavin reports markedly in favour of this form of ability grouping, concluding that those in high-ability sets made greater progress and that high-ability groups benefit from an enriched or accelerated curriculum. Programmes of enrichment and acceleration, which usually involve the greatest amount of curricular adjustment, have the largest effects on student learning. In typical evaluation studies, talented students from accelerated classes outperform non-accelerates of the same age and IQ by almost one full year on achievement tests. Talented students from enriched classes outperform initially equivalent students from conventional classes by four to five months on grade-equivalent scales.

In both the meta-analyses and the best-evidence synthesis, some forms of grouping were found to improve the academic performance of more able children, and it is likely that the real benefits were greater than could be shown by the method of measurement due to the glass ceiling impact of standardized testing on the highest achievement. It is important to note that learners benefit from an appropriately high level of challenge and skill, particularly when the problems and concepts are perceived by students to be interesting and necessary (see Csikszentmihalyi et al., 1990). In his conclusion, Baines conclusively states that 'the more able pupils benefit from ability grouping, while the less able are disadvantaged by this approach' (Baines et al., 2012: 42-3).

There we have it, in a single sentence. Whatever we choose to do next will at least be clear. Ability grouping isn't an evil; indeed most estimates now are that more than 60% of all primary schools are doing it. Teachers who use grouping argue that it has become indispensable, helping them to cope with a bewildering mix of strengths and weaknesses and widely varying levels of ability and achievement. The horns of this dilemma are quite stark though. It's the equity versus excellence agenda written large.

11

Teacher Training, Resources and the Cluster Approach

Key points

- The quality and commitment of teachers dictate the success of schemes for teaching the most able.
- A significant number of teachers either confess to no interest in teaching the most able or are worried they will be shown up by very able students.
- There is a chronic shortage of teacher-training courses for teachers of the most able.
- There is a need to recruit top graduates who are allowed to specialize in teaching the most able.
- Cluster groups of schools are central to effective provision for the most able.

One of the starkest features to emerge from this study is the crucial and overwhelming importance of the teacher in the success of any scheme for the most able. Time after time, successful schemes were those driven by passionate and committed individual teachers, and time after time when lip service or no service at all was paid to the cause of the most able it was because teachers were clearly not convinced of its worth. The teacher is crucial to the success of any approach, meaning that resources must be devoted to external and in-house training for teachers in approaches to the most able. Gifted and talented programmes simply do not exist unless there are teachers who believe in them and are willing and able to carry them out.

It is extraordinary that an age which in general has recognized the need for specialist training to complete specialist tasks has not seen this need when it comes to teaching the most able. Put at its bluntest, clever children need to be taught differently:

The 'effective' teacher shows higher levels of flexibility and greater acceptance of their pupils. The positions of student-teacher are, in comparison to traditional instruction, often exchanged. The teachers find themselves in the role of fellow-student in a course, which is partially organized by the students themselves (Grotz, 1990, p. 17). (Heller, in Balchin et al., 2009: 63)

The case for training is rendered even more urgent by other factors, all of which work against the cause of the most able. Privately, many head teachers will state that too many of their staff are either not especially interested in G&T teaching or untrained in it. Some may even be a little frightened that they will be 'shown up' in classroom interactions. This is enhanced by the disgraceful lack of any meaningful support for a teacher who wishes to keep up academically with their subject, brush up their knowledge and keep up with the latest developments in their subject. It is symbolized by the fact that in the UK a teacher will be lucky at Inspection to have their lesson observed by an Inspector with a degree in the subject that is being taught in the lesson.

It is also remarkable how little teaching of the gifted and talented features in most teacher-training courses. This reflects both a general lack of interest, in the UK at least, and also the fact that gifted and talented is not marked as a way-station on any recognized promotional or career path in UK education. An interesting variation on the Old Grey Whistle Test, in educational terms, is to walk into a large, city centre, flagship branch of Waterstone's, go to the Education section and see how many books there are on the shelves on a given topic. Gifted education rarely features. Our two leading academic institutions, the University of Cambridge and the University of Oxford, are not praised for the clever students they attract, but criticized for the poor ones they do not. The role models we parade in front of our pupils are not Watson, Crick or Curie, but rock stars, soccer players and industrialists, some of whom seem to bully their way to the top. What glittering prize awaits those who support the cause of the most able?

Resources available to the teacher who is determined to swim against the tide of apathy that typifies gifted and talented in too many schools are thin indeed. NAGTY is gone, as are other government-sponsored resources. Warwick's International Gateway for Gifted Youth is building but not yet fully built. London Gifted & Talented offers some excellent online material, including a library of resources for teachers, and there are a few other sources – but these lose much of their value if they are simply downloaded and flung at a student who is simply told to get on with it.

Worldwide, the Hong Kong Academy offers advice, help and resources for teachers in the manner NAGTY perhaps should have done. The UCLA

Laboratory School offers teacher training and teacher outreach, and some other sources are available to the teacher who has a lot of patience. Institutions which offer help to teachers of the most able do not usually have the resources to buy a place on a Google front page. The University of Nijmegen (Netherlands) is one of very few to offer a post-graduate course in teaching the most able; the course has 14 modules, each of 40 hours, and 200 teachers have thus far received diplomas. However, these are small fires in the darkness: 'Without exception however, there is a need for training of teachers globally which in turn will prepare them to recognize and meet the needs of children from all cultures who exhibit gifted attributes' (Baldwin et al., in Heller et al., 2000: 876).

Every institution offering teacher-training courses in the UK should be required to offer modules and a potential for specialization in teaching the gifted and talented. Schools should not only be required to have a policy for the gifted and talented but also a programme and a dedicated co-ordinator. Increasingly important, with the decline of LAs and the growth of 'independent', stand-alone academies and free schools, schools should be required to form clusters where resources for teaching the most able and good practice are regularly shared.

The government has been extraordinarily fickle in its attitude to teachers and teaching of the gifted and talented. Its reaction to the most radical proposal – allow graduates to specialize in teaching the most able and not be required to teach other ability bands – would be akin to the Synod's reaction to a proposal to abolish God. However, most people in the UK have had experience of being taught by a brilliant individual who is inspirational for the most able and yet unable to lower their sights to even understand the mindset of those for whom their subject is difficult. Why do we assume that the same secondary teacher can expect to teach equally well at all levels of ability? Every leading school has a teacher renowned for their ability with the Oxbridge maths class, but who is the kiss of death to less able classes. They will also have the opposite, in the teacher who specializes in scraping a C grade at GCSE for those to whom this is the equivalent of climbing the intellectual Eiger without oxygen. The cry that often arises is, 'You're taking the best teachers away from the least able!' What does 'best' teacher mean? In terms of qualifications and success with the most able? Some of the 'best' teachers love teaching the also-rans and detest teaching the most able. We would not drive a Formula 1 car across the Sahara or a Land Rover at a Grand Prix. Why do we expect the secondary teacher to be a generalist, 'all-terrain' vehicle?

The problem for government in allowing such a specialization is dual – first, the fear that the influx of top graduates this would bring into teaching would cost too much, and second the fear of killer accusations of 'elitism'. Even if all the proposals above prove impossible, one thing must happen if there is to be any hope for the gifted and talented in the UK: the UK must set up at the very least a national online facility, modelled on the London Gifted & Talented scheme, where it is easy for teachers to access resources and teaching material, and exchange interesting practice.

Clusters

Even if they were to have the will – and there is at least a suspicion that many schools worldwide do not – mounting proper activity for the most able students from the resources of an individual school can be extremely difficult. Most often, this is because priorities are driven by simple funding mathematics: the more students there are in a group, the more funding will be found for them. Gifted children can comprise the top 30% of a cohort in academic ability, but are more normally classified as representing the top 10 to 15% of a cohort. In other words, 85% of pupils are not in the most able or gifted category, and so a mixed-ability school that puts significant resources in the way of G&T places itself at the wrong end of the firing range with a large bullseye painted on its chest marked 'elitism'. It would be wrong to blame such schools too harshly. An elite school such as St Paul's in London does not put significant money and staffing into Oxbridge preparation because it believes such lessons are simply a good thing. In the reverse of the pressure affecting many schools, it does so because it knows half its pupils will apply to those universities. Schools need to be market economies if they are to stay funded. One answer is for schools to form themselves into clusters for the teaching of the most able. The advantages are clear. The costs of a G&T co-ordinator are spread out among five or ten schools, as is the cost of specialist teachers who can spend a day or even just a morning or afternoon in an individual school. Economies of scale start to apply: 65 students on a single coach to hear a lecture at the local university costs far less per head than might a smaller group, given the oddity of school travel in that there is usually either a minibus (and the 15 pupils who can be crammed into it) or a coach (taking 65 or so) and nothing in between. Clusters mean larger groupings of the most able, which in turn are a huge benefit to them socially, academically and emotionally, also giving the cluster more power to attract inspirational speakers. It is not only student talent that can be pooled across clusters but teachers too, with the cluster having a far wider talent pool of staff to draw on than might be the case with go-it-alone schools. Within a well-run cluster, such as those in the LG&T networks, there is no reason why local schools seen as elitist, such as grammar schools and good independent schools, cannot be used by the cluster, with some of their staff and resources voluntarily giving back to the wider community.

The role of the teacher cannot be emphasized strongly enough in the delivery and effectiveness of any scheme for the most able. Much has been made in this study, and will be made in the following chapters, of the social reinforcement that occurs when students of like ability are educated with each other. There are far fewer studies acknowledging the equivalent process with teachers, yet the process is equally important. Gifted and talented may not offer a significant position in the hierarchy of a school, or command respect in the culture of the school or the wider culture it serves. It is usually under-resourced, is hardly glanced at in teacher-training courses and can attract negativity. This makes it all the more important that teachers with an interest in teaching the most able work in a structure where they can meet others who share their passion, share good practice and brainstorm new ideas.

Questions for further thought

What is the problem teachers have in talking about more able education?

What are the 'issues' that teachers tend to have about the more able in schools? How can they be raised straight away and then 'checked in' before the training journey so that the baggage doesn't slow down discussions about improving teaching and learning? In short, how can teachers engage with the hearts and minds agenda?

It is automatically assumed that if you are dealing with students who are disadvantaged or have special requirements, then of course their needs should be met. It would be grossly unfair not to do so. And yet the needs of the most able are frequently ignored, as if somehow their needs are tangibly different. There still arises that faint whiff of elitism, the robbing of Peter to pay Paul syndrome and the 'Matthew' effect (to those that have, more shall be given). The perception is also that they have a Dementor-like capacity to suck the finances out of the system and away from the genuinely needy, so how can we counter our colleagues' hesitations, reservations, discriminations and accusations?

What useful practical advice comes from practitioners?

Having travelled to many schools across many nations, we have pulled together advice from teachers who have run schemes for the more able. From their own experience, they have suggested some clear pointers for other schools that are setting up programmes.

In terms of school-wide procedures, the key is to be inclusive of all groups within the school community with clearly agreed identification procedures, knowing who your pupils are and what you actually want and need to do with and for them. Set up as many opportunities as you can to celebrate all talent and achievement across your school, whilst ensuring that the impacts of any interventions are monitored and evaluated from the start. As much as is possible, differentiate your curriculum with high-level challenge for the gifted using as many strategies of compaction, acceleration and enrichment as might be appropriate for your school. Work closely with leadership teams and governors within your school. Classroom strategies should develop authentic problem-solving materials to enhance subject-specialized challenges as the engine room of an effective programme. Try to participate in real-world competitions that help to provide opportunities for any student to shine, keep the momentum going and don't be hung up on doing it the same way it's always been done.

Forming partnerships beyond school in networks with like-minded schools is essential but don't let your partnerships become simply a comfort zone and include at least some schools who might challenge the way you've done things. Some schools have an almost unconscious belief that they need to provide everything a child needs, but by looking outside of themselves they can improve access to good facilities and get volunteers from outside school. In addition, seek subject expertise from beyond your school and bring in graduates and researchers to help you keep your staff up to date. Utilize the internet to find specifically designed online multimedia resources and act as a filter and quality-assurance agency for your students. Get parents involved to support your work – and they can't or won't do that unless you specifically explain what it is you're trying to do, how you plan to do it and why. This is the key to building good communication networks with all your key stakeholders as neglecting public opinion is a dangerous option.

Involving pupils by asking them what they want and think they need, and asking them if they think that what they're getting is working and how they think it could be improved, will benefit your programme in many ways. The two most important benefits are that students will feel closer to the programme and you will have authentic voices to use whenever anyone asks why you are embarking on a particular course of action. In the same way, ongoing continuous teacher development and involvement at all levels is an effective strategy. Good high-ability schemes are owned and driven by teachers, not by top-down management orders. Try and work it so that involvement in programmes for the most able is woven into a possible career plan and has some element of progression in it for teachers, rather than being a one-off cul-de-sac.

What six strategies work to engage teachers regarding the more able?

What gives teaching geared to the top its point and purpose is that setting up both policy and provision for more able students is a great lens to look through for *all* students. It's also a way of really looking closely to see if your school *is* actually differentiating effectively. Colleagues who worry that it's yet another special group that requires so much more work are also off track. The problem is that many teachers are *not* looking at how the needs of their most able students are being met. Instead, they are looking at some mythical middle ground and aiming materials at that, in the hope somehow that the top and bottom can access the resources and, in terms of the more able, create their own stretch and

(Continued)

(Continued)

challenge. This effectively means differentiation by outcome which simply means no differentiation at all, as it merely requires that teacher and students turn up.

It is important to frame the more able agenda as an 'access to high challenge' initiative for *all* students as this means that your senior leaders will be far more prepared to engage with it as part of their wider teaching and learning ambitions. And without their clear support you are in danger of being sidelined in terms of what is actually happening in your school. If your role is reduced to that of a gatekeeper of an elusive more able register, then your influence and impact will be pretty minimal. With clear support, you are far more likely to have impact, to meet the governors and to be called into management meetings to add your voice to key dialogues. The 'low threshold high challenge' agenda is for all students and is a pretty good rallying call across most schools.

Talking to small groups of more able students about what they enjoy, which lessons stretch and challenge them, and where they see their aspirations taking them means that you can appeal to colleagues in a far more specific and personal way. Ideally, speak to parents too, so that you have a pretty clear idea of what their concerns might be. This helps to clarify and adjust your strategies, and it also serves as a useful source of evidence to inform some of your school's own observations and enquiries. A useful balancing voice can be generated by interviewing interested colleagues about how they are raising expectations and achievement. By doing this, it triangulates your evidence as well as personalizing your top-end agenda and that in itself gets colleagues to engage. Teachers respond brilliantly to individual cases, far more than they do to imposed causes.

Try to start from what your school needs, how it sees itself and then ally more able education to that. It is far simpler to look at the stated key objectives of your school and then effectively write the more able agenda into these. It might be choosing to become a 'Thinking School', developing assessment for learning or trying to create more independent learners. Your job then becomes 'How can what I do with the more able help the school to achieve these objectives?' This normally has quite a profound double impact. It embeds top-end differentiation at the heart of what your school is actually doing, and it means that many activities that happen outside of your immediate influence become part of your impact.

By keeping your policy simple and sustainable (preferably by stating a couple of key 'manifesto' beliefs), it means that colleagues see that what matters to the more able also matters to them too. This is your school's vision for what it wants to achieve in working with your most able students and it won't then be seen as 'yet more' to deal with. This will include your definition of what 'most able' means in the context of your school and each department, but with a flexible and inclusive 'talent pool' or 'revolving door' approach to identification. Start with a clear focus on equal opportunities and meeting the needs of *all* students. If you do this, then many colleagues' concerns are immediately side-stepped and your focus can be more quickly moved on to provision, which is a far more fertile territory in most schools. Teachers will instinctively engage with something that they can really put their hearts into and which makes a difference to the lives of their students – rather than having endless squabbles over who should or should not be on the register, which is genuinely pointless.

Finally, done well, it reinforces teachers' perception of learner talents that are all too easily forgotten. It can restore the pride in achievement that teachers rightly feel. It's time to stop politicians standing in the shadows and spitting at the sunlight, and recognize that a simple focus on the talents of our students can help to restore some pride and professionalism. The teaching of the most able needs to be simplified. It is nothing more or less than giving numbers of our children what they need from their teachers.

12

Disadvantage, Gender and Ability as an Illness

Key points

- Gender issues affect the most able boys and girls, albeit in different ways and at different times.
- Disadvantage dominates educational debate to the exclusion of issues relating to the most able.
- There is no evidence to confirm the 'geeks and freaks' popular vision of the most able, who are frequently entirely normal other than in their ability.
- School leadership is crucial to successful schemes.

Inevitably, in a work of this nature there arises a rag-bag of issues that for one reason or another do not merit a chapter or section of their own, but are nevertheless important, either to flag as worthy of further study or simply to note as work in progress.

Gender

Gender differences are inevitably a feature in some research into the gifted and talented. There is no research to suggest that boys are inherently more gifted than girls, but significant research to show that boys are twice as likely to be seen as gifted than girls:

> There is a stable ratio of two boys to every girl when parents identify their children as gifted … Many studies have shown that in most cultures, families

encourage boys more than girls to be independent, self-reliant, and able to assume responsibility, and that this alters their approach to both school and work. (Reichenberg & Landau, in Shavinina, 2009: 876)

In a remarkable cross-cultural figure, in China 69.5% of children identified as gifted by their parents were boys, 30.5% girls, whilst for a comparable UK study the figures were 64.3% of boys and 35.7% of girls (Reichenberg & Landau, in Shavinina, 2009: 876). One explanation that has been suggested is that boys have more behaviour problems and are more demanding, fitting in better with the stereotypical image parents have of a gifted child. Really? There is widespread evidence that girls' self-esteem, and hence their achievement, takes a plunge in adolescence. Girls are also seen to suffer, both the most able and the normally gifted, due to the 'romance culture', whereby their status is achieved by their relationship with males. Boys have their own problems, including serious damage done by 'redshirting' (holding back gifted boys from starting school, often so they perform better at sport). What emerges from reading the various studies is that gifted boys and girls have an outstanding ability to sabotage their own prospects, and self-destruct. It is no surprise to realize that teachers are often the only real antidote to this. It is a surprise to see how few commentators have used their findings on gender as a reason to justify single-sex education.

There is too much research to be quoted here that suggests unconscious discrimination in class against girls. Boys who call out are more likely to get the teacher's attention, whilst girls are told to put their hands up and are given less demanding work. There are serious issues here, particularly for the cause of all-girl and single-sex education, but to a surprising extent the co-educational lobby has had it all its own way. At the heart of this is one of those untested assumptions that unconsciously underpin many people's thinking, namely that it is 'natural' and hence the best way to do things to educate boys and girls together. It is similar to the assumption that intelligence is its own best friend and that you need to do so much less for the gifted because of all they can do for themselves. All are untrue, of course, but so are flying saucers and yet enough people believe in them. So with all-girl education, western culture has an all-pervading assumption that co-education is nature's way of doing things. The case for co-education is not a done deal and needs to be re-opened, in particular in the case of the most able.

The issue is confused by some of the data affecting boys, in that whilst it may be easier for boys to be recognized as able by teachers and parents, boys also have a remarkable tendency to take themselves off the radar screen that detects ability. A 1993 study found nine times more male than female underachievers. It is suggested that:

> Underachievement may be a way in which gifted boys define their masculinity. When talented boys are held back and denied gifted education, they often become bored, difficult children. While females aspire to leadership positions in their schools, young men often detach, fearing the stigma of participating in girl-led and girl-dominated groups. (Colangelo & Davis, 2003: 493–4)

It is known that girls can take less challenging courses, and so show up less well in assessments based on the difficulty of the course. All in all, a reasonable conclusion might be that the most able boys and the most able girls have a developed capacity to self-destruct – they just do it in different ways and perhaps at different times.

This latter point emerges with the issue of the 'double dip' detected in boys in the UK in the final year of primary (Year 6) and sometimes again when they transfer to secondary school, in Years 7 and 8. Reasons offered for the decline in the final year of primary include:

- the absence of any new learning: the final year can concentrate just on consolidation and bringing the weakest up to scratch, with nothing to challenge or stimulate the most able
- 'revision then rounders': prior to SATS (the national test taken by all English children) there is a concentration on revision and practice papers, followed by a 'jam-packed social calendar of events celebrating the end of KS2 ... Little opportunity for cognitive challenge was apparent either pre- or post-SATS' ('Challenge of Secondary Transfer', Brooks, 2010)
- the domination of the curriculum by core subjects and a narrow focus even within these: 'they've gone from ... knowing everything well to knowing everything completely parrot fashion ... too much revision' ('Challenge of Secondary Transfer', Brooks, 2010)
- weak subject knowledge on the part of the teacher.

At secondary level, problems include:

- repetition of work done at primary school
- crises over homework
- increased bad behaviour
- negative peer pressure
- failure to identify the gifted and talented
- cruising in Year 8
- increasing criticism of teachers.

The study from which this is drawn notes that G&T pupils are very sensitive indeed to the nuances of teacher/pupil relationships.

Such material as there is suggests that ages 11–14 form a tunnel for both boys and girls which most enter but from which some do not emerge.

It is interesting to record the findings of a 2007 survey. Groups under-represented in the high-attaining group in the UK were:

- boys
- pupils eligible for free school meals
- pupils with an identified special need
- pupils born in the summer
- black Caribbean pupils
- black African pupils
- mixed-race pupils.

Chinese children were the most highly represented in the high-attaining group (DfES, 2007: 13–16).

Disadvantage

If gender occupies paragraphs in the ultimate handbook on the gifted and talented, then disadvantage occupies chapters:

> In England the statistics show that the gap in educational performance between children from rich and poor backgrounds starts to be evidenced very early and continues to grow … Hence it is no longer possible in education to separate ideas around the nature of giftedness from the conditions which allow it to flourish. Crudely stated, education is not a meritocracy. Gifted children from poor backgrounds who succeed are likely to be the exception rather than the rule unless the overall approach to education changes. (Woolf, in Shavinina, 2009: 1046)

In both the UK and the USA, the gifted agenda has, to a significant extent, been taken away from the general issue of how to educate the most able, and turned into the debate on how to ensure that the most able among the disadvantaged are identified and brought on to their full potential. Valid though this aim is, it has drawn attention away from the fact that once schools know who the most able are, they do not have a very good track record in dealing with them. At times, schools seem to be putting huge efforts into identifying the raw material and drawing it out of the ground, even though, having found it, they do not have the refineries to process it. The irony remains that the best vehicle the UK has ever had for sending able poor children to leading universities was the grammar school, howled down most loudly by those who attended one, for elitism. Wheels come full circle. Change may be in the wind when one of the most left-wing newspapers traditionally opposed to grammar schools prints an article (*The Independent*, 21 May 2010) suggesting they are the only way forward (or should it be backwards?) to address the issue of ability and disadvantage.

Gifted and talented as freaks

Some of the available literature seems to support a view of the most able children as suffering from an illness rather than being in possession of a gift, an issue referred to earlier. There is a cultural stereotype of the most able child as an 'anorak' or 'geek', terms which in part have replaced the older 'swot'. The character Brains in *Thunderbirds* is an example of the stereotype as an adult creeping into children's culture. The 'geek or freak' stereotype is encouraged by the media. One recent instance was a young boy who was clearly very gifted indeed at mathematics and was made the subject of a documentary, *The Growing Pains of a Teenage Genius*. This was followed by a discussion on Channel 5's *The Wright Stuff* entitled 'Can Clever Be a Curse?' The media seem to want it to be so, and the coverage in this case acknowledged that the boy in question suffered from Asperger's Syndrome but did not do enough to separate out the problems caused by Asperger's from those caused by giftedness (see Thompson & Thompson, 2012).

At the recent World Conference for Gifted and Talented Children, one presentation consisted largely of a list of the dysfunctional 'types' that the most able could become. There is some fact to back up the urban myths. The most able have a remarkable talent for self-sabotage. The gifted child whose talents are not recognized and who becomes bored can be a dangerously explosive commodity. Twenty years ago, the head of a comprehensive school serving one of Manchester's most deprived areas commented drily that all the children she knew who dealt in drugs, as distinct from merely using them, were in the top third of the ability band. Among male adolescents in particular, it is frequently not cool to work hard, and the able child who finds him- or herself having to choose between working at their ability or having friends is truly between the devil and the deep blue sea, and likely to drown in whichever he or she chooses.

Yet, in practice, it appears that, if properly handled, the most able do not have to have problems and may even be less prone to them than the normally gifted: 'Freeman (2000) suggested that the gifted appear to be emotionally stronger than other children, with lower levels of anxiety, higher productivity, and higher motivation' (Reichenberg & Landau, in Shavinina, 2009: 880).

What does emerge from research is the damage that can be done to a child who is wrongly labelled as gifted, often by their own family, and simply pushed too hard. The situation of a normally gifted child in an environment for the most able, where the normally gifted child cannot live up to what is being demanded of them, is cruel, summed up by the off-the-record comment of a senior teacher in one of the UK's top five academic schools: '[name of school removed] is heaven for the bright, but hell if you're not.'

Wrongly labelling children has done great damage to the cause of the most able and is a dangerous element within any educational system on two grounds, in addition to any damage done to the child. First, the child who suffocates or drowns by being wrongly identified is always quoted as the rule and not the exception by opponents of special provision for the most able. Second, because most disasters are caused by over-aspirational parents who are unrealistic both in their assessment of their child and in their hopes for their future academic achievement, it gives fuel to the all-too-easy dismissal of a parent who actually has a gifted child as simply being 'pushy middle class'.

Another commonly held view is that gifted students 'prefer a quiet learning environment, and prefer to learn alone rather than with peers' (French & Shore, in Balchin et al., 2009: 176). One broadcaster, CNN's Sanjay Gupta, stated, 'In the popular imagination, the genius is a loner' (French & Shore, in Balchin et al., 2009: 176).

If teachers are asked, they make it clear that the most able delight in group work, whilst their teachers also believe it to be essential. What emerges from a study of the research is that the gifted child who feels isolated within the peer group understandably prefers to work alone (or not to be seen working at all), but the gifted child who is well supported at home and school has no such qualms:

> We found no studies indicating that co-operative learning had a deleterious effect on gifted children's academic or social outcomes. Especially in homogenous groups, co-operative learning can serve some needs of gifted children in mainstream classrooms. (Balchin et al., 2009: 178)

It is a growing urban myth that genius is odd, which may be a contributor to why photo editors always choose a picture of Einstein with his hair at its most wild. A child does not have to look or act in a bizarre manner to be gifted.

Leadership

The leadership of a school's head or principal has a large element of the intangible to it, and research academics gravitate towards what can be most easily measured or proven. It is extremely difficult to measure whether staff trust their head or whether heads will go the extra mile, which G&T programmes frequently require of them. In addition, few of the academics writing research papers have worked in schools and felt at first hand the power a principal can exert. Frequently, this goes beyond any formal management structure, and the issue is confused in the UK at least by what has been a fashion for flat management structures where the head is not seen as a leader of the pack, but rather as a first among equals and chair of the Senior Leadership Team. The truth is that the head and her teachers account for over half of a school's success:

> Nearly 60% of a school's impact on student achievement is attributable to principal and teacher effectiveness. These are the most important in-school factors driving success, with principals accounting for 25% and teachers 33% of a school's total impact on achievement ... Nobody has cracked this yet – nobody knows how to ensure we develop and select the best [leaders]. (Barber et al., 2010b: 5)

What applies to schools in general applies to the most able in particular. Any scheme for gifted and talented is going nowhere in a school unless it has the support of the principal. It is an interesting comment on the status of gifted and talented education, at least in the UK, that a leadership or headship course that gives any form of priority or status to the teaching of the gifted and talented is impossible to find.

Questions for further thought

Who are the children that high-ability programmes tend to miss?

Measures put into place in many countries worldwide to support students 'at risk' or 'hard to reach' or 'severely disadvantaged' tend not to focus much attention on the more able. It's as if these groups are regarded as somehow mutually exclusive. A recent national UK study (Warwick, in Montgomery, 2009: 219–65) found that there are a number of common factors that impact on students who have high potential but are identified as being at risk of underachievement. They tend to:

- have an incomplete prior attainment history
- achieve relatively less well in written work
- have achievements seen to be outside the regular school curriculum (for instance, culturally specific gifts and talents)

- come from families whose needs and aspirations do not match the offer from the school and for whom there are cultural or other resistances to participation.

Some of the key features that arise are that these students:

- tend to have more gaps in their academic vocabulary and handle certain features of writing less confidently
- have less grasp of idiomatic speech or take things more literally than intended
- lack 'cultural capital'
- haven't been exposed to the diversity of history and society critical to achievement
- are substantially less likely to be familiar with the conventions and expectations of academic writing.

Why is it always the same students sliding down the same slope to failure?

Unsurprisingly, research suggests that extreme stress compromises our ability to regulate thought. Students facing extreme circumstances require very different kinds of interventions. We know from the analysis of performance tables that disadvantaged students are twice as likely to have a special educational needs statement, three times as likely to be excluded, etc. But the less acknowledged common characteristics are the greater likelihood of family and home turbulence, the smaller chance that they will make informed decisions on subject choices and the lack of cultural and social capital available to support them. In addition, Meaney (2002) and Blair (2011) found that environmental risks, like family turmoil and chaos, had a huge effect on children's cortisol levels. With the absence of buffers, our students are facing waves of emotion that will almost certainly capsize them. In *How Children Succeed*, Paul Tough summarizes this well when he highlights that children who grow up in more stressful environments

> generally find it harder to concentrate, harder to sit still, harder to rebound from disappointment, and harder to follow directions. This has to do with a particular set of cognitive skills located in the prefrontal cortex, known as executive functions. They have been compared to a team of traffic controllers overseeing the functions of the brain. Poverty itself does not compromise the executive functioning abilities of poor kids. It was the stress that goes along with it. (Tough, 2013: 17)

What does research suggest about minority cultural underachievement and more able students?

More able education is unavoidably fixed to cultural concepts of excellence and these ideas tend to reflect the society in which individuals live. What is prized in one culture may not be valued in another, and it is difficult to impose one belief system on a culture that may define talents very differently. A key task is to highlight the ways in which celebrating talents can lead to increased motivation in

(Continued)

(Continued)

other areas of learning, wider educational achievement and transferable skills. A further task is to work with community groups in identifying and celebrating culturally relevant and appropriate talents. Many reasons have been researched regarding the underachievement of highly able students from minority cultures in the USA.

It is only after we recognize potential that we can assess whether performance is below potential. Students whose talents and subsequent underachievement go unrecognized become hidden underachievers, and students who are not given adequate opportunities to begin to show or develop their talents often become involuntary underachievers. Minority students who do not believe in the achievement ideology, or who believe that glass ceilings and injustices will hinder their achievement, are not likely to work to their potential in school. This external locus of control attitude hinders minority students' achievements, as students who attribute their outcomes to external factors, such as discrimination, may put forth less effort than those who attribute outcomes to internal factors, such as effort and ability. In addition, Mickelson (1990) found that low teacher expectations for minority students may relate to a lack of teacher training in both multicultural and more able education and that such unprepared teachers are less likely to refer minority students for gifted education services. When students do not have access to appropriate education, they have difficulty reaching their potential, which may result in underachievement due to disinterest, frustration and lack of challenge.

Very able, disadvantaged underachieving students are highly conscious of the social constraints imposed on them by the environments in which they live, even if schools are substantially less aware. Ford and Harris (1990) and Ely (1996) argue that most minority students must simultaneously manipulate two cultures – one at home and the other at school – which may be quite diverse, and the value conflict set up may affect their sense of self-worth. The problem of gifted students who lack motivation to participate in school or to strive to excel academically may therefore reflect a mismatch between the child's motivational characteristics and the opportunities provided in the classroom.

Reis and McCoach (2000: 152–70) believe therefore that gifted students who are not challenged in school demonstrate both integrity and courage when they refuse to do the required work that is below them intellectually and are effectively 'dropping out with dignity'.

Some social-structural explanations for school failure argue that poor academic performance among bright disadvantaged students is a result of the social stratification and marginality experienced by socially and culturally distinct individuals in society at large. Inequalities in social and educational systems therefore lead many disadvantaged individuals in Ogbu's (1978) arguments to reject academic competition and to perceive adaptation to existing social structures as futile.

What is clear from the above research is that an able student's cultural background and frames of reference can force choices between the needs for achievement and affiliation. This is not only a 'minority' issue. Schools should know their pupils' heritage, cultures, histories, experiences and needs. The picture is complex and pupils often juggle numerous identities in their everyday lives, switching from one to the other as necessity dictates. It is vital that schools recognize and acknowledge these multiple identities and break the cycle of cultural stereotyping of pupils and their communities which can impact negatively on relationships, expectations and ultimately attainment. Claude Steele and Joshua Aronson pioneered 'stereotype threat' which shows that people's performance on many measures is automatically affected by their belief that they are doing something their 'group' is stereotypically good or bad at. They found that merely reminding people of a negative group stereotype worsens their performance. Stereotypes of inferiority are often imposed on poor white children. Able learners who live and/or attend schools in rural environments have also been recognized as a significant 'submerged' population whose needs are largely invisible and unconsidered and for whom negative community-led expectations can have a severe impact on their attainment (LG&T, 2008, available at www.londongt.org).

What are we meant to do for our most able students who face serious disadvantage every day of their lives?

One intervention is the simplest of all. It is to identify which children are likely to be suffering such stress and report it on to whichever pastoral system has been resourced to cope. The aim is to identify not only the more obvious aspects of stress but also the smaller chance that these children might have to make informed decisions on subject choices and the lack of cultural and social capital available to support them in this.

A second key is to look at the longer-term issues schools face. It is all too common to hear schools wondering aloud, for instance, why none of their most able students ever get into the top-ranked universities. When they are gently steered towards looking closely at their preparations for a university application, their interviewing schedules, the odd choices that their students might be making at key stages in their school career and the passivity and quietness of their students, they often realize that the data has not been illustrating a long-term discrimination against their school, but rather their own long-term failure to investigate what the data has been telling them about their own practices.

A third is not to fall prey to monitoring fatigue. The world is full of schemes for the most able that start with the best of intentions but become tired after one or two years, that tiredness being seen most often in a failure to continue to monitor the progress of set targets and to hit the alarm button when those targets are not met. Resilience and tenacity of purpose are not only crucial features of the success of the child, but of the success of the school too.

A fourth essential is to make programmes for the most able whole-school in terms of time as well as age. This is an area where the experience of some of the academically highest-achieving independent schools can be used to good effect. Some such schools found a three- or five-year repeating pattern in their under-achievers. The pupil in an early year in the school would not be achieving their potential, but individual subject and class teachers would not realize that the child was failing to achieve elsewhere in school, and were unwilling to report on it because as a high-quality professional they would first try and solve the problem on their own. When individual intervention failed, they blamed

(Continued)

(Continued)

themselves in part and did not wish to be seen by the Senior Leadership Team as having failed a child in their care. Typically, it could take half a school year for the problem to be recognized and passed on. Measures were then put in place, but come the next school year the record had been wiped clean, new staff were teaching the child and the whole process of intervention was started again from scratch. Moving into a new school year may be a rite of passage for the child, but it should be one for which they carry a ticket marked with a record of previous journeys.

A fifth strategy requires money to be spent on freeing up teachers to conduct triangulated interviews involving the students themselves, their parents and teachers. This can open up some fascinating areas. What are the perceived barriers to achievement, the broader concerns, students' views on what would help them most? What were parental experiences of school like? Inevitably, this widens out the debate and often leads directly into areas where 'soft' skills (that group together under the rubric of self-regulation) like optimism, resilience and social agility can be encouraged, as can ambition, confidence and aspiration. These are the real game changers that help students to deal with the inevitable stresses and rebuffs of their own lives.

Part 3

Countries

13

The PISA Tables, UK, Finland and South Korea

Key points

- The UK does not stand out in international terms regarding the performance of its gifted and talented children.
- The PISA league tables are of limited help in defining successful strategies for the most able.
- A study of what proportion of a country's school pupils gained places at a leading university would be a more effective indicator of how well a country is succeeding in realizing the potential of its most able than the PISA survey.
- Finland's successful education system has local elements to it that make it difficult to transport, and shows no interest in the most able as a distinct special needs group.
- The South Korean system is also largely non-transportable, and its high schools may demand too high a price in human and educational terms of their students.

In the 2009 PISA survey for the OECD, 7% of UK students had high literacy skills, as distinct from 13% in Finland and 17% in Shanghai; 10% of UK pupils had high mathematical skills (22% Finland, 50% Shanghai); and 11.4% high scientific skills (18.7% Finland, 24.3% Shanghai). Only UK independent schools were on a par with Shanghai. In the 2012 PISA survey, the UK hovered around the average proportion of its pupils ranked as 'top performers'. It had 12% in Maths, with a PISA average of 13%, 9% in Reading (average 8%) and 11% in Science (average 8%). These figures do not look too bad, until they are subjected to further interrogation. The 'average' figures can appear averagely bad when the top scores, such as Shanghai's 50% and Singapore's 40%, are taken into account (PISA, 2010).

Two other figures are of interest. The UK spends significantly more than the average on its schools, but has around half as many of its students on a very low score on the PISA index of social and economic background. Socially and economically disadvantaged pupils tend to do less well at school, and therefore the UK has only half the mountain to climb of many of its OECD counterparts.

However, it is arguable whether or not PISA should be brought into any effective evaluation of the UK's performance of its most able students. It is far from universally validated as an effective comparator of educational performance. Cynics argue that it is as influential as it is, not so much because it is accurate, but more because the media are desperate for any system that claims to be able to compare and contrast educational achievement across national, cultural, social and economic boundaries. Among the many criticisms made of it (and equally stoutly rebuffed by the PISA organization) are that its central statistical base is invalid; its tests of reading are not comparable as some languages, such as Finnish, are phonetic, whilst English is not; it measures only children who attend school, so that an industrialized country where it is illegal not to send a child to school suffers in comparison to those where large numbers of children do not even attend school; in East Asian countries, which do well generally, many pupils go to after-school crammers so their results are not just the outcome of school, and furthermore their cultures are more conducive to obedience and hard work; by no means all children sit the same PISA tests, so PISA is in effect seeking to compare apples and pears; some high-performing countries teach to the PISA tests; the tests themselves are insufficiently in tune with the differing national curriculums; it takes insufficient account of national and cultural foibles, such as that French students will not guess an answer so they do poorly in multiple-choice tests; some countries make students repeat years so in fact their 15-year-old groups include some 16-year-olds; and there is missing data in some years for large numbers of pupils for whom plausible values are substituted.

The debate over the validity of PISA is perhaps a different battle for a different book, but in fairness PISA's main interest is not in the most able and statistics relating to that group often have to be dug out of a morass of other figures. What can safely be said about the UK's performance in the PISA assessments is that it gives no evidence to suggest that the UK is doing a good job with its most able students. However, the real significance of PISA is often argued as not being country-specific but international. PISA is an international study which began in 2000. In its own words on its website, it 'aims to evaluate education systems worldwide by testing the skills and knowledge of 15–year-old students in participating countries/economies. Since the year 2000 over 70 countries and economies have participated in PISA' (www.oecd.org/pisa/).

Since its foundation, the PISA international league tables have become something of a Bible for various governments. The media headline a rise or fall in position and some countries at the top have received so much interest because of their high ranking that they have started to refuse visitors on grounds of what they refer to as 'educational tourism'. There is some cynicism towards PISA from experienced educational practitioners, who doubt the accuracy of its findings.

To suggest this doubt is educational heresy in the light of today's educational theology. Yet the rush of the world and its media to accept PISA as an absolute guide to educational standards across the world is surprising. A country such as the USA continually bemoans the fact that it can find no standardized measure that will allow it to compare educational standards of achievement on a like-for-like basis across the various states, yet the world seems to accept that PISA can do this across countries with wildly differing cultures. Nor is PISA's own account of its methodology, taken from its website (www.oecd.org/pisa/), reassuring:

Methods

All students take pencil-and-paper tests, with assessments lasting a total of two hours for each student. For the PISA 2009 assessment, some participating countries/economies have also opted for an assessment of the reading of electronic texts.

Test items are a mixture of multiple-choice items and questions requiring students to construct their own responses. The items are organized in groups based on a passage setting out a real-life situation ... A total of about seven hours of test items is covered, with different students taking different combinations of test items.

Students answer a background questionnaire, which takes 20–30 minutes to complete, providing information about themselves and their homes. School principals are given a 20-minute questionnaire about their schools.

It would be interesting to take this to a UK examination board and ask them if this satisfied their normal level of safeguarding and security. How does PISA guarantee the scrupulous invigilation that is the only guarantee against cheating? The time spent on the tests is short and must raise questions about just how much accuracy such a test can score in assessing anything like a range of core skills in maths, sciences, native and modern languages. Can the PISA tests guarantee to test students on what they have been taught in each respective country's national curriculum? How in particular do they test the achievement of G&T students who may have been skiing off-piste and whose true ability may be shown in non-standardized project work? It would also be interesting to know who checks the accuracy of the student background questionnaire and the questionnaire completed by principals. However, the most pressing need is for a rebuttal of the accusation that the PISA tests can be taught for, and results in the tests improved accordingly.

A more minor concern is that it is a feature of the PISA methodology that significant reductions in the number of 'points' scored are not always reflected in the numerical ranking achieved by a country. Between 2006 and 2009, Finland dropped 11 points in its score for reading but only dropped one place, from 2nd to 3rd. Korea dropped 17 points, but only moved to 2nd place from 1st. Yet Ireland, with a points reduction not hugely more than Korea's (24), dropped from 6th to 21st. Science declined significantly in Canada, whose 5-point reduction saw it drop from 3rd place to 8th, whereas Finland's 9-point reduction only dropped it from 1st to 2nd. Detailed statistical analysis of the 2012 PISA data has yet to be done, but one can assume that as the methodology does not appear to have changed similar disparities will exist.

Whatever doubts there may be, PISA has thrown a number of countries into prominence for their perceived success, and these countries' education systems have been hailed as icons of success as a result. An extract from the 2009 survey shows how PISA actively encourages the competitive ranking of countries on the basis of its material:

> Korea and Finland are the highest performing OECD countries, with mean scores of 539 and 536 points, respectively. However, the partner economy Shanghai-China outperforms them by a significant margin, with a mean score of 556. Top-performing countries or economies in reading literacy include Hong Kong-China (with a mean score of 533), Singapore (526), Canada (524), New Zealand (521), Japan (520) and Australia (515). The Netherlands (508), Belgium (506), Norway (503), Estonia (501), Switzerland (501), Poland (500), Iceland (500) and Liechtenstein (499) also perform above the OECD mean score of 494, while the United States, Sweden, Germany, Ireland, France, Denmark, the United Kingdom, Hungary, Portugal, and partner economy Chinese Taipei have scores close to the OECD mean. (2010: 6)

Where PISA can be helpful to the cause of the most able is in comments such as the following: 'Nurturing top performance and tackling low performance need not be mutually exclusive' (2012: 9). In most countries and economies, only a small proportion of students attains the highest levels and can be called top performers in mathematics, reading or science.

Even fewer are the academic all-rounders – those students who achieve proficiency Level 5 or higher in all three subjects. Nurturing excellence in mathematics, reading or science, or in all three domains, is crucial for a country's development as these students will be in the vanguard of a competitive, knowledge-based global economy.

Some high-performing countries in PISA 2012, like Estonia and Finland, also show small variations in student scores, proving that high performance is possible for all students. Equally important, since their first participation in PISA, France, Hong Kong-China, Italy, Japan, Korea, Luxembourg, Macao-China, Poland, Portugal and the Russian Federation have been able to increase their share of top performers in mathematics, reading or science, indicating that education systems can pursue and promote academic excellence whether they perform at or above the OECD average (e.g. Japan, Korea) or below the OECD average (e.g. Italy, Portugal, the Russian Federation).

PISA confirms that improving the performance of the most able need not be at the expense of the normally gifted, that the most able are frequently not all-rounders but show their ability in localized, specific areas, and comes close to suggesting that to define what proportion of a country's students come into the most able category is to create a self-fulfilling prophecy.

PISA has one weakness that is rarely, if ever, mentioned. It measures where children are at a certain age in their schooling. Yet the true success of education is measured by its outcomes. Schools are not an end in themselves but a stage in a journey to a different place, and whilst one can measure performance at any age in a child's school career, it could be agued that an altogether harsher but more telling judgement would be to survey what proportion of a country's secondary school children went on to attend a leading university. It is at least as interesting a statistic as that which tells us how many students qualify to be in PISA's Level 6 of achievement. If that survey were to include what proportion of a country's young people stay the course and graduate with a good degree, one is also learning about the wider success of a country's system in teaching to the emotional as well as the intellectual side of its pupils. It is interesting to note, for example, the extraordinarily low success rate at university of some of Russia's most able children who have been identified as among the most able (see below). The most common reason given for this is the sudden withdrawal of specialist support after pupils leave school. A survey such as the one proposed would, for example, throw interesting light on the Australian SHIP/IGNITE scheme. At ground level, observed as it was taking place, it was brilliantly impressive. Would it be as impressive if one plotted what happened in later life to those young people? The only scheme which has had such a scrutiny imposed on it, which has included elements designed to test how emotionally stable the products of the scheme are, as well as how academically successful, is that of the Robinson Center (see Chapter 6). No small amount of the credibility of that scheme has been established by the all-round success of its *alumni* in later life, as well as at the point of testing.

Finland

As a footnote to the point above, there is clear evidence that Finnish secondary school students are doing very well at the time when PISA measures their achievement. There is very little to show one way or the other whether these pupils who are in full bloom when PISA tests them go on to gather more strength or wilt and die.

One of the first conversations undertaken for this study was with a very senior figure in Finnish education, who was asked about Finland's teaching of gifted and talented children. He confessed that he did not know what was meant by 'gifted and talented'. If anything is to be learnt from Finland about G&T programmes, it comes from a study of how Finland educates the general mass of its pupils. If it is true that a rising tide lifts all ships, then there is no individual vessel marked 'Gifted and Talented' in Finland.

We can clearly learn some things from Finland. It has no national testing, no publication of results and no inspection, as we know it in the UK. All teachers have to have a Master's degree, only 13% of applications to teacher training are accepted and there are 16 candidates for every vacancy on teacher-training courses. Finland respects its teachers.

In other respects, Finland has unique or near-unique features that make it dangerous as a role model for other countries to emulate. It has a population of 5.4 million and is largely racially and ethnically homogenous. As PISA itself admits, the proportion of immigrant or non-native children in a country has a major impact on its performance: 'Across OECD countries, first-generation students – those who were born outside the country of assessment and who also have foreign-born parents – score, on average, 52 score points below students without an immigrant background' (2010: 10).

Finland is also typical of the Scandinavian countries in having blurred class differences, and in having a national culture that reflects what in the UK would be seen as middle class and in the USA as monied. Driving into many Finnish factories, it is impossible to distinguish easily the workers' cars from those of the company directors. It should be no surprise if the high ranking of a nation that is both small in its population, sits in a limited geographical area and is without significant racial or ethnic diversity provokes a sense of déjà vu. The same description might apply to South Korea and to Singapore, two other PISA stars. Their three common denominators – narrow boundaries, small population and cultural homogeneity – do not mean it is easy to have an effective education system, but they might well mean it is easier.

There have been concerns expressed about Finnish schools, not least of all by visitors unimpressed by such an apparently laidback system. It is far too early to suggest that the Finnish bubble has burst but there are storm clouds in the sky. A report cited in *The Times Educational Supplement* (27 May 2011) suggested a decline in learning and cognitive ability of 25% over six years among Finland's 15-year-olds.

Such reports will not dim the star of Finnish education but there appears to be very little academic research into the actual outcomes of the Finnish system, far less than exists, for example, in the case of the American system which seems to place itself, and be placed, under a perpetual spotlight. The internet is by no means always a reliable guide to anything, but a Google search can be informative in a variety of ways and much of the matter on Finland's education system is euphoric praise written by Americans who seem to be using the Finnish system as a way of damning their own education. Herein lies part of the tale of the Finnish success. Top world rankings appear to be being achieved without rigorous inspection or appraisal schemes, the publication of results or frequent testing of pupils – most Finnish students undergo only one national standardized test in their school careers. The Finnish National Curriculum is a suggestion, not a command. The result appears to be an education system that is a liberal's dream whilst producing the results so beloved of a conservative.

Is Finland's system too good to be true?

Probably not, but it is certainly so good that many people need it to be true. There is also a concern that results may be influenced by a prevailing culture that allows and expects teaching to be formal. There appears to be a widespread acceptance that because, outwardly, results between the very top students and the weakest are so close, Finland must by definition be doing a good job at both ends of the spectrum. Must it? Outstanding schools may still be doing a magnificent amount with 95% of the cohort, but failing those at the very top. Perhaps Finland is very different, but it is a matter of concern that Finland appears not to be willing to recognize the existence of the most able as a special needs category, as it clearly recognizes the least able. There is also a concern regarding the self-referential nature of the Finnish system. The pendulum in the UK has undoubtedly swung too much the other way in seeing teachers as a group not to be trusted. If the Finnish were failing to extend their most able pupils, who would issue the challenge to the establishment of teachers, administrators and politicians?

South Korea

The final stage of education in South Korea is high school, educating from age 15 onwards. Though not mandatory, 97% of South Korean students graduate from high school, the highest figure in the world. Though there are a variety of high schools, many of the specialist schools are ferociously difficult to get into; 30% of high schools are vocational.

There is a distinction between a good or effective education system and one that can act as a role model and be copied by other countries. Finland and South Korea may both have the former. It is very doubtful that they have the latter. South Korea has the population and geographical features listed above that make it difficult to replicate and transfer to a different culture. South Korea also has a culture of ferocious hard work among at least some of its pupils, a culture that is increasingly being challenged – 74% of Korean students in 2010 took some form of private, fee-paying after-school instruction – amid fears that the extra cost of this (an average of $2,600 per student per year) is actually serving to drive down the birth rate among families worried about the financial demands of parenthood. Police in Seoul actually carry out raids on *hagwons* (after-hours tutoring academies) to impose a 10.00pm curfew. Writing in *Time* magazine, Amanda Ripley stated:

> South Korea's hagwon crackdown is one part of a larger quest to tame the country's culture of educational masochism. At the national and local levels, politicians are changing school testing and university admissions policies to reduce student stress and reward softer qualities like creativity. 'One-size-fits-all, government-led uniform curriculums and an education system that is locked only onto the college-entrance examination are not acceptable,' President Lee Myung-bak vowed at his inauguration in 2008. (25 September 2011: 1)

Some sources report a glut of graduates in the labour market, and the government is certainly making noises about the value of vocational training and the need for creativity in the curriculum and from students. Academic success in South Korea comes at a price. It is produced in the main from schools that would be seen at best as crammers in Europe, at worst as sweat shops. It is often said that a prison only remains peaceful if the inmates agree for it to be so. South Korean high schools are not prisons but they could not operate unless South Korean students were willing to work all the hours God gave and to deny any need for sport, extra-curricular activity or even pastoral care as an integral part of education. It is a deal one suspects many students in Europe and America would not be willing to sign up to, and without that consent the South Korean system is an inert compound, even if it were deemed desirable in its catalyzed mode. As an ironic footnote, news reports cite Korean attempts to 'Americanize' South Korean schools, whilst some American schools seem determined to become more like their Asian counterparts.

One unexpected conclusion of this study is that educationalists the world over are obsessed with the idea that other countries somehow do it better. The truth is that most countries do parts of it well and nobody does it perfectly. It cannot be a bad thing to look at other countries and try to learn from what they do well, but perhaps the pendulum has swung too much in this direction. It might be a good idea to remember the character in Chaucer's *The Canterbury Tales* who was so busy looking at the heavens that he failed to see the cess pit at his feet. Different plants grow well in different climates. Different countries have different cultures. Extreme caution needs to be exercised in assuming that what works for a child brought up in one culture will work for a child brought up in another.

Questions for further thought

How do we embed habitual excellence?

'We are what we repeatedly do. Excellence, therefore, is not an act, but a habit.' (Aristotle)

The core element for embedding excellence into everyday lessons is that the resources and tasks are pitched to challenge the most able in the class based on an assumption that the most able students will be able to attain the top grades and can afford the time to go 'off-piste' as needed. It is critical that teachers have the time to embed content and concepts and get deep knowledge across and do not lower their own expectations of what their students can or will engage with.

Another prerequisite is that teachers are experts in their field and are on hand to respond intelligently to awkward or tangential questions and support students in how to learn from the specialized feedback given. Sometimes here the problem is psychological: the teacher fears they will not know the answer to a specialist question. Across the world there are brilliant and inspirational teachers who freely confess how much they don't know. Their response is simple honesty in the face of a question they can't answer, along the lines of 'I don't know the answer – but I'll find out and respond to you tomorrow'.

(Continued)

(Continued)

Also important is to insist on a default student 'persistence' in terms of work ethic, with a clear expectation regarding accuracy and precision in the use of high-level subject-specific language. The importance of language as a thought crystallizer was perfectly described by Alice who, on being admonished to think carefully before she spoke, indignantly commented, 'How can I know what I think till I see what I say?' It is there for a purpose in every subject area and that is to offer precision of explanation and thought. Simplification of these terms serves only to devalue the language and reduce the level of expertise that can be demonstrated by the student. The core characteristics that excellence demands from students are dedication and determination supported by teachers through rigorous and relentless reinforcement of scholarship. The reward is improved motivation through learning – students wanting to develop their subject knowledge, wanting to learn per se, rather than just to do well in exams.

What do top-performing students working at PISA level 6 have in common?

> In some countries and economies, such as Finland, Shanghai-China and Sweden, students master the skills needed to solve static, analytical problems similar to those that textbooks and exam sheets typically contain as well or better than 15-year-olds, on average, across OECD countries. But the same 15-year-olds are less successful when not all information that is needed to solve the problem is disclosed, and the information provided must be completed by interacting with the problem situation. A specific difficulty with items that require students to be open to novelty, tolerate doubt and uncertainty, and dare to use intuitions ('hunches and feelings') to initiate a solution suggests that opportunities to develop and exercise these traits, which are related to curiosity, perseverance and creativity, need to be prioritised. (PISA, 2012: 34)

It is made clear that Level 6 highly proficient problem solvers (2.5% of all OECD participants) can create complex, flexible, multi-step plans that they continually monitor during execution. Where necessary, they modify their strategies, taking all constraints into account, both explicit and implicit. The analysis shows that, in general, what differentiates high-performing systems, and particularly East Asian education systems, such as those in Hong Kong-China, Japan, South Korea, Macao-China, Shanghai-China, Singapore and Taiwan, from lower-performing ones, is their students' high level of proficiency in 'exploring and understanding' and 'representing and formulating' tasks. By focusing on the cognitive processes fundamental to problem solving, PISA is trying to uncover students who combine the mastery of a specific domain of knowledge with the ability to apply their unique skills flexibly, in a variety of contexts. By this measure, the deepest pools of top performers can be found in Singapore (25% of students), Korea (21%), Shanghai-China (18%) and Chinese Taipei (17%). On average across OECD countries, only 8% of students are top performers in both a core subject and in problem solving. It is fascinating and encouraging to see that the skills that are being assessed are to do with the ability to deal with ambiguity and uncertainty, and that the traits are related to curiosity and perseverance rather than simple recall and regurgitation.

14

Singapore and Hong Kong

Key points

- The Singaporean education system has cultural elements that make it difficult for western cultures to copy.
- In common with some other countries, Singaporean education fuses public and private provision.
- Singapore has one of the most detailed definitions of giftedness in the world, at the same time as declaring a commitment that provision for the most able will not detract from general provision.
- Singapore devolves considerable power to principals.
- Singapore has two of the most successful schools in the world.
- The Raffles Diploma summarizes the worldwide trend to broaden out from the simply academic what is achieved by the most able.
- The Hong Kong Academy for Gifted Children is an exemplary project.

Singapore

Singapore has one of the most widely admired schooling systems in the world, regularly coming in the top five world rankings for achievement in maths and sciences in particular. It has pioneered the highly acclaimed Singapore Maths teaching scheme and contains one of the most famous schools in the world, the Raffles Institution. It is similar to the Scandinavian countries, in that it is small (63 islands in a total of 272 square miles), with a small population to match and a comparatively small range of ethnicity (the population is 75% Chinese, 15% Malay Muslim and 5% Indian). Without detracting in any way from Singapore's remarkable 30-year achievement, it is worth repeating that small, wealthy and culturally homogenous countries find it easier to put educational revolutions into effect. South Korea is another obvious example.

What is not widely reported is the complexity of the general Singaporean system or that many of its results stem from independent schools, albeit ones charging relatively low fees and with an assumption that no child will be barred from an education commensurate with their ability on grounds of wealth. The situation is well summarized by one of the architects of the system:

> Prior to 1965, there … [were] … govt schools, church-aided schools, Chinese clan-assisted schools, etc. Between 1965 and 1985, a national system was created with the Ministry fully in charge, and the most important source of funding. All schools in Singapore charge some form of supplementary fees, set by the Ministry. Schools with wealthy alumni can rely on additional sources of income from parents. One of the functions of the School Advisory Committees is to help schools raise funds, largely for extra-curricular activities and special school projects.
>
> By the mid-eighties it was decided that the system had become too standardized and not sufficiently challenging for the very able, gifted and talented. A review led to the creation of independent schools. Raffles was the first, and there are currently nine of them. Another category of schools is called autonomous schools. What distinguishes independent, autonomous and other schools is not fees, but the degree of autonomy they are allowed in order to best maximize their resources for the benefit of their students. Admission to Raffles and other independent schools is solely by merit. The Government and the Raffles Institution have scholarship schemes to enable students and families to meet the fee requirements. There is no public disquiet that fees prohibit the talented but poor from applying to independent schools. So the term 'independent' has a different meaning in Singapore. (Personal correspondence with authors)

This extract points to a number of lessons for those interested in emulating Singapore's success. Monolithic, centralized systems do not work and countries should not be frightened of granting autonomy to schools. As the outstanding McKinsey report on how the most improved schools in the world keep getting better, clearly states:

> This is not to suggest that systems have no choice: they have a great deal of choice in how they implement interventions, in terms of the sequence, the emphasis, or the manner in which the system rolls out the interventions across its schools. It is here that the impact of history, culture, structure, and politics come fully into play, producing significant differences in the particulars of how systems manifest their reforms. (Barber et al., 2010a: 34)

As one Asian system leader says, looking back at his system's poor to fair journey, 'We did everything we could to make it as easy as possible for our teachers to teach'. However, when teachers achieve a higher level of skill, as is the case in good to great and great to excellent improvement journey stages, such tight central control becomes counterproductive to system improvement. Rather, school-level flexibility and teacher collaboration become the drivers of improvement because they lead to innovations in teaching and learning. The centre learns from these school-based innovations and then encourages their use in other schools across the system. Higher-skill teachers require flexibility and latitude in how they teach in order to engage in such innovation and to feel motivated and fulfilled as professionals.

Though there is no magic formula for improving school system performance, research points to a clear path that improving systems have undertaken at each stage in their journey – a path illuminated by signposts. A key element for 'Great to Excellent Interventions' is improving through peers and innovation by cultivating peer-led learning for teachers and principals and collaborative practice, decentralizing pedagogical rights to schools and teachers and a system-sponsored experimentation and innovation across schools.

The 'Thinking Schools, Learning Nation' initiative of 1997 gave teachers greater freedom and devolved more power to principals. Singapore acknowledges that the gifted and talented need to be recognized as having special needs. Needs-blind entry to high-achieving, selective schools is essential. Yet, at the same time, it is not deemed immoral to ask parents to make a means-tested contribution to the cost of their child's education and not immoral to ask them to raise funds for the icing on the cake.

The secondary education system in Singapore consists effectively of five groups of schools, feeding an academic or a vocational path to further education.

The first group consists of government or government-aided schools, autonomous schools with enhanced niche programming or independent schools with greater autonomy in their programmes and their operations. The two undeniably world-class schools in this group are the Raffles Institution – where the largest fee a local resident will pay is S$3,000 per month, though 90% of students have grades high enough to earn a discount and pay only S$100 per month – and the Hwa Chong Institution, a Chinese high school, where the maximum a local resident would have paid in 2011 is S$450 a month, with similar discounts available as at the Raffles Institution. In an ironic contrast, Eton College in the UK is frequently criticized for having produced so many leaders. In stark contrast, both the Raffles Institution and the Hwa Chong Institution headline their role as producer of future leaders and make this one of their major aims in their respective mission statements. Eton College almost has to apologize for having educated the current UK Prime Minister. The Raffles Institution will feel embarrassed if it has not produced the next equivalent.

The remaining four strands of secondary schooling are:

- specialized schools, described simply as being for 'students who can benefit from a more customized and practice-based curriculum'
- specialized independent schools, 'for students with talents in specific areas'
- privately funded schools, to 'provide more options'
- special education, 'for students with special needs'.

The Singaporean system is not for the faint-hearted. It is at times a bewildering fusion of public and private providers, and it unashamedly supports not only what in the west is seen as an elite group of gifted pupils but also elite schools to educate them. Western researchers often take a different line. One example that would be met with incredulity by many in authority in Singapore is:

> Increasingly, the focus is moving away from the categorization of some children as 'gifted' (with all others implicitly therefore in the 'not gifted' category) and toward an individual focus on individual differences in developmental trajectories, recognizing that pathways to high-level achievement are enormously diverse, domain specific, and incremental in nature. (Matthews, in Shavinina, 2009: 1366)

This extract summarizes what may have crippled gifted education in the west, namely a belief that to give to the most able is inevitably to take away from the majority and to stigmatize that majority as being without ability. The contrast between the intense nervousness shown by some primarily western academics to the very idea of gifted children and Singapore's wholesale acceptance of giftedness is stark. Of particular interest is the GEP (Gifted Education Programme) offered by the Singaporean Ministry of Education (SMoE), which begins at Primary 4, caters to the top 1% of the national cohort and envisages only three children in 100,000 being 'exceptionally gifted', though this figure accepts that 'the majority of gifted children are moderately gifted' (see Singapore Ministry of Education [SMoE] website at www.moe.gov.sg/).

The official SMoE website statement on the GEP programme is worth quoting in full, for all its length. Written for parents, it is perhaps the simplest, most jargon-free and clearest statement anywhere in the world of what constitutes giftedness:

- Who is an exceptionally gifted child?
- An exceptionally gifted child is one whose intellectual ability is significantly advanced. Some common characteristics of exceptionally gifted children include:

- Shows exceptional ability in a single domain but not necessarily in others.
- Is able to pursue passion in a single area of interest at an early age. This is done with minimum instruction and more often than not independently.
- Has an ability to relate to a broad range of ideas and synthesize commonalities among them.
- Does not compartmentalize knowledge and searches for patterns and/ or relationships between ideas.
- Has a high degree of ability to think abstractedly which develops early.
- Is able to reason in abstract terms at a very young age.
- Grasps concepts and sees relationships at an extraordinary speed.
- Is able to understand an abstract concept quickly and is able to demonstrate his/her understanding by explaining it in simple language or by using various examples.
- Displays a keen sense of security/Is highly inquisitive.
- Has an enquiring mind and is always seeking to acquire new knowledge or pick up a new skill.
- Will explore wide-ranging and special interests, frequently at great depth.
- Possesses an unusual capacity for memory.
- Is able to recall information and is observant even from a young age.
- Displays intense concentration when engaged in a task.
- Is able to concentrate on a single activity for a prolonged period of time, and can go on tirelessly, when his/her interest is engaged.
- Has a fascination with ideas and words.
- Is an avid reader since young.
- Uses an extensive vocabulary.
- Is able to use vocabulary that is above his age peers in both written and oral forms.
- Expresses himself/herself well.
- Is able to use figurative language and analogies to express feelings and ideas.
- Shows a sensitivity to the feelings of others.
- Has a high capacity for empathy and is able to understand and show sympathy for hurts that others have.
- Shows a strong sense of right and wrong.
- Shows sensitivity and reacts to things causing distress or injustice.
- Shows intolerance for vagueness/ambiguity.
- Has a need for extreme precision and would correct information or generalizations that are not precise.
- Shows a keen awareness of world issues.
- Shows an unusual interest in current affairs such as global warming and would attempt to find answers or solutions to the problem.

- Is acutely aware of his/her ability.
- Believes that he [sic] can excel in whatever he does and is not afraid to take up new challenges.
- If the child has knowledge and ability far beyond those of other children of the same age, it may be an indication that the child is exceptionally gifted.

Equally interesting as the definition and description of giftedness is the Ministry's preamble. It makes clear that the exceptionally gifted should be integrated within the Singaporean system and that their education should be 'well-rounded'. It makes clear its belief that the development of the exceptionally gifted must not be at the cost of the moral, social, physical and aesthetic aspects of the child's development. It is interesting that the above definition of giftedness contains far more moral issues – a sense of fair play, empathy, etc. – than any equivalent from around the world. The Singaporean definition of giftedness is more than purely academic. There is also an interesting footnote that programmes for the exceptionally gifted should not take away from existing resources. In other words, Singapore is determined not to pay for the exceptionally gifted at the expense of the normal achiever:

> In meeting the needs of the exceptionally gifted, MOE is guided by the following principles. First, these children should be in our Singapore school system. Second, they should receive a well-rounded education. Cognitive development should not be achieved at the expense of the development in the moral, social, physical and aesthetic domains. Third, the recommended interventions would be made within the constraints of existing resources.

To achieve its aims, Singapore uses virtually every accepted technique for catering to the gifted and is determined to offer flexible programmes adapted to each child, rather than imposing a single template. Enrichment is used to teach some topics in greater breadth and depth, and pupils are offered study material that allows them to take things at a self-directed pace. Internet resources are used to access high-level and advanced courses online. A classic mentor system is available, attaching a student to an advanced trainer in a given topic. Subjects studied can be accelerated without the pupil needing to leave their age cohort in other subjects. Again, the possibility exists for pupils to co-study, taking up a course in a second school or institution. Some children are allowed to enter Primary 1 a year early. 'Level skipping' (moving ahead of their age group, and known as 'grade skipping' in the USA) is permitted up to a maximum of five levels.

This flexibility in itself shows an interesting dichotomy. The government in Singapore is perhaps too easily dismissed with the tag 'authoritarian'. This is certainly a government with firm views as to what it thinks and which believes it has a mandate to demand civil obedience. Yet that same government has legislated for diversity and to allow schools to become 'independent', so as better to meet the hugely individual demands of pupils.

Water will find its own way downhill, often despite what humanity tries to do to stop it. Governments across the world are subject to changing fashions and trends, and frequently carry a massive load of cultural and historical baggage into their policies on education. One result is that educational policies sometimes tend to expend vast resources on pumping the water uphill. A sense from the Raffles Institution, and the Hwa Chong Institution, is that in terms of provision for gifted pupils these schools show what happens if you let the water flow downhill. Both schools are the product of a country that was founded as a trading entity, and which sees making an honest Singaporean dollar as a perfectly pragmatic and morally acceptable aim. One needs to emphasize the 'perfectly honest' element. Of course, Singapore is not perfect. It has poverty, deprivation and disadvantage, as does every country in the world. Yet the profits generated by Singapore plc have been fed back into society and the local population far more readily and quickly than in many post-war 'get-rich-quick' countries.

And the result of Singapore's historical development from a vital free port and trading centre, to a colonial dependency and thence to a free state? Largely, this can be summed up as an educational philosophy in which one's children are seen as a natural asset. One difference in the Singaporean philosophy is that an asset is defined not just in terms of intellectual ability, but also in terms of what the gifted pupil might offer his or her society in the future in terms of leadership.

Lessons to be learned from Singapore

The Singaporean system, therefore, despite its clear success, cannot be used simply as a template for western systems. It sprang from a very difficult culture. Some commentators believe that a significant portion of its success comes simply from the fact that Asian children work harder. There has been a tendency in certain quarters to see certain countries as having solved the problem of education for western countries. This is simplistic in the extreme. There are sufficient obvious differences between the two countries of Singapore and the UK to suggest that a simple copy of the Singaporean system would not transfer to the UK. Singapore supports the caning of its pupils, even, if the internet is to be believed, in public in front of a whole school. It is a country where drug dealing is punishable by death. Sex between males is illegal, though rarely if ever prosecuted. This is a very different culture and one in particular which would not recognize the west's obsession with elitism as a swear word and its confusion of the academic and the vocational paths.

That does not mean to say that countries cannot learn from it, and possibly from the Raffles Institution in particular. Singapore has a number of initiatives that the west might do well to emulate. It is keen on school clusters, for the effective sharing of successful teaching and learning practices. It has an excellent three-part career track for teachers, divided into Leadership, Teaching and Senior Specialist. Recruits into teaching are drawn from the top one-third of the graduate cohort, and teachers are expected to undertake 100 hours of professional development every year. Teachers are paid more than other civil servants. Singapore shows that whilst a rising tide may lift all ships, so does a plentiful supply of water from on high. It does not favour the publication of results, seeing this as negative and potentially humiliating in a manner that will damage rather than help a school. It fêtes its gifted and talented. It sees independent schools as having a central role to play in a national system. It does not insist on state education free at the point of supply to all parents, but allows for an element of parents paying what they can afford. It does not see as blasphemy parents raising money for their child's school, seeing it rather as a potential strength. It hails teaching as a highly regarded profession, rather than a trade.

The Raffles Diploma dates from 2010. It is the leaving certificate that all students who 'graduate' from the Raffles Institution are expected to earn. Rather than just a measure of academic achievement, the Raffles Diploma consists of five 'key development domains': Cognitive (combining exam qualifications and an enriched curriculum); Character and Leadership; Community and Citizenship; Sports and Health; and Arts and Aesthetics. The Diploma is granted in its basic form where students have to meet minimum criteria in all five areas, but is also granted with Merit and with Distinction.

The Diploma reflects a wider trend in the East to move away from the perceived force-feeding of knowledge into an environment that encourages a wide range of skills and attributes and encompasses the creativity that a number of the tiger economies perceive as missing from their educational provision. Whereas in the west 'breadth' is often interpreted as a student taking a mix of subjects across the arts and sciences, the Raffles Diploma encourages breadth, in both gifts and talents and across a range of activities, that recognizes the existence of several types of intelligence in addition to the purely academic. It does nothing to dilute academic rigour but adds creativity to it, as well as powers of leadership skills and a sense of social responsibility.

Buried in a pile of academic articles on the gifted and talented is a piece that throws a final light not just on Singaporean practice but on practice all over the world. As has been noted above, the Singaporean system is deeply rooted in the prevailing culture of Singapore itself and in Asian educational culture. Yet a 2006 study found more agreement than disagreement between teachers of the most able in Singapore and the USA:

> A total of 31 Singapore and 12 US secondary gifted class teachers were interviewed and/or surveyed. The study's results suggested that there were more similarities than differences between the two cultures about what an exemplary teacher signifies, what constitutes qualities of exemplary teachers, and what challenges exemplary teachers are facing in the two educational systems. Regardless of different cultural backgrounds, it is somewhat universal that an exemplary teacher embodies content expertise, flexible instructional repertoires, and passion for the discipline taught and for the students under his or her care. (VanTassel-Baska and Stambaugh, 2006: 38)

This reinforces the strong impression gained from the research for this text that the best ideas for how to teach the most able come from teachers.

Singapore also illustrates some of the simpler conclusions from this study. If education of the most able children is to be done well, first it is important to recognize that such children exist, second to be unembarrassed by their presence and third to recognize that sometimes they need to be treated and resourced in a different way to other children. It also helps if teachers are excited by the prospect of teaching highly able pupils, rather than fearful of it being seen as elitist and for that to count against them in their careers.

Hong Kong

The system of secondary education in Hong Kong changed from an essentially English model to a model much closer to standard Chinese practice when the former British colony was handed back to mainland China. As a system in transition, it cannot be used as a prime source of either information or good practice on the education of the most able, except in one key area.

The Hong Kong Academy for Gifted Education (HKAGE) is of particular interest, announced in 2006 and appointing its first chief executive in 2008. In many respects, it is what the UK should have been aiming for when it created its national academy. The term 'academy', implying as it does an actual school, is a misnomer. HKAGE is in fact a series of support services for gifted education, aimed at the students themselves, their parents and their teachers and schools, with a separate research arm.

The Academy describes what it will do for its students on its website (http://hkage.org), as follows:

> The target population will be Hong Kong's exceptionally gifted students, defined as those who consistently perform in the top 2% of the age-related ability range. Initially we will concentrate our resources on the 10–18 age range.

> We will provide challenging learning opportunities for gifted students to enable them to stretch their potential in a wide range of specialist areas, including leadership, creativity, personal-social competence. In due course the range and variety of these courses will be extended as the range of partners increases to include local universities, professional organizations, individuals and NGOs. All the courses will be available 'off site', though school venues will not be uncommon.

> Such programmes may include workshops, master classes, weekend courses, exchange programmes, mentoring, field trips, and the like in a wide variety of different domains.

It is too early to say whether or not the HKAGE has so far been a success. What can be said is that its design represents state-of-the-art thinking. It ticks all the boxes according to current wisdom. Its four-prong approach – students, parents, teachers and research – is the logical one, and it recognizes the crucial role of parents. It minimizes the amount of time a child is taken out of mainstream schooling and seeks to use the child's school as a partner in teaching the most able. School-based support, be it within the classroom or outside regular school hours, is the work of the Education Bureau, with the HKAGE acting as more of an off-site support on weekends or long holidays and partnering with universities or NGOs.

The Hong Kong Education Bureau itself runs a highly ambitious programme that aims to reach 100% of the region's learners in a genuinely inclusive way with a wide remit for accommodating learner diversity through three distinct levels of engagement. The gifted education policy of Hong Kong adopts a three-tier mode of implementation: Level 1 is 'whole-class' (school-based) support; Level 2 is pull-out support, again school-based; and Level 3 is off-site support (through the HKAGE, tertiary institutions, NGOs, etc.). Resolutely not tied to any one approach, it has utilized an adapt-and-adopt approach as appropriate to the context of the child in order to ensure fully personalized teaching and learning approaches. The Bureau uses wide consultative structures and strategies with open and responsive communication to engage with the full range of stakeholders from the government to academics and to the child and their parents. The primary strategy is the use of pilot programmes to trial approaches and strategies which, if successful, are then incorporated into online modules for further trialling to create transferability. At the same time, the strategy recognizes the value of the gifted child being attached to a mentor or organization outside the school system. It recognizes leadership, creativity and social and emotional development as key features which cannot be divorced from any plan to educate the most able. It deserves to be a worldwide success, but also stands as a rather sad reminder as to what the UK should have had.

Questions for further thought

What should teachers practically do to challenge and support the most able?

Often, more able students are not encouraged to explore subjects in more interesting, complex ways, sometimes because of the fear of the teachers that their students may actually be marked down in an exam if they come at a question from too unusual an angle. Bringing on the most able requires teachers to demonstrate flexibility, open-mindedness and a willingness to listen and learn equally as much as it requires exceptional subject knowledge. Yet taking risks has to be the hallmark of truly great teachers, and for that to work they need to have not just confidence in their own abilities but also the belief that their students will be able to survive and thrive in a more rarified, free-wheeling and demanding atmosphere than that which is normally found in classrooms. They must believe in how far and how fast such students can go if no limits are put on them, and understand that they can assist the roller-coaster ride, even if they themselves may need to leap off before the end.

How do we know what an appropriate level of challenge and progress might be?

Every student walks around with a picture of what is acceptable, what is good enough. Each time he works on something he looks at it and assesses it. Is this good enough? Do I feel comfortable handing this in? Does it meet my standards? Changing assessment at this level should be the most important assessment goal of every school. How do we get inside students' heads and turn up the knob that regulates quality and effort? (Berger, 2003: 103)

(Continued)

(Continued)

There are many potential gaps to understanding what the appropriate level of challenge might be for our learners in terms of the work we set and accept. To begin with, how do our students come to understand what is required of them? The first elements are inevitably their culture, home background and peer group. These set up powerful expectations. For some highly able students, they have become used to being the best in their first school – quite possibly without too much effort. This is a dangerous starting point, as they may well be the best in a very poor school. Automatically, their perception of what standards might apply has been corrupted. It is too easy to say that they should get used to producing what they are capable of. They won't know. None of us really do. We are all under-challenged underachievers. Our culture virtually demands it.

The second standards gap occurs between the exam board's perception of standards and the school or department's perception of standards. If a school sets up an expectation of what ought to be achieved by its students, it is highly likely to be working from a distorted perception of reality. Every school has its own ideas about what can be demanded of or expected from the students it is engaging with – effectively, its own success criteria. These may well be far below what could actually be possible, but how would we know? A school might unintentionally be constructing a glass ceiling of compliant underachievement based on a fear of making too many demands of and burning out its most able students.

Effectively, this is stealing from these students their chance to genuinely produce and understand what excellence might look like. It is unconsciously setting their sights well below what they might be able to achieve. Until we make the high-level, most challenging demands, we will never know if our students would have been capable of reaching the highest standards. To keep raising the bar is the only way of finding out how high athletes can jump. We have to stop setting limits on what our children do, and the most dangerous limit of all is the unconscious one that states, 'I can't ask a child to do that. I could never have gone beyond that level'. We need to share examples of the very best with our students and then at least we will know that we haven't prevented them from achieving genuine mastery.

What are the hallmarks of outstanding teaching for the more able?

There are several 'dimensions' that need to be understood and applied before teaching can be said to properly meet the needs of the more able. The effectiveness with which lessons are planned, resourced, structured and executed is critical, with particular emphasis on how this process is informed by high expectations.

Not everyone likes teaching the most able. You have to prepare lessons scrupulously, yet expect the pupils to blow your lesson plan out of the water and take the lesson where neither party has sailed before. And the big danger? Allowing yourself to set a limit on how far the pupil can go. It's an old story. If you walk into a class expecting all your students to get A* a surprising number of them will. Assume they're only going to get a C grade and it can become a self-fulfilling prophecy. The teacher–student interaction needs to be both trusting and demanding, with the dialogue that takes place in the lesson two-way and truth-seeking.

You know how important it is that they listen to you. Do you really know how important it is that you listen to them? Is your mindset that you will learn as much from them as they will learn from you? How teachers make effective use of assessment to understand learning needs and starting points will determine very quickly whether a student's prior expertise has been taken into account and whether adjustments to teaching and learning during lessons and over time have been duly put into place. How well do you know these people? Have you researched just how far they might actually go?

Ongoing feedback to pupils to guide them in the next steps in their learning will seek to ensure that the strengths and needs of pupils of all abilities are given appropriate support and challenge. The pace of learning must be well judged with no wasted time in lessons. This has often been misinterpreted to mean 'speed of delivery and coverage', which can become completely bewildering to even the most gifted child. What it needs to reflect is how pace is varied given the relative difficulty of the task, to ensure secured progress in learning and acquisition of the skills required for mastery of the subject. Teaching the most able isn't about saying the same old thing, only faster. It's certainly about not letting them get bored. Most of all, it's about putting them on the road to learning, and easing them gently from the baby or the passenger seat into the driving seat.

15

Australia

Key points

- The Adelaide-based SHIP scheme is a world-class programme for educating the most able within the context of a mixed-ability school.
- Successful schemes require a dedicated co-ordinator, the facility for relatively easy access into and out of the scheme and a flexible approach to planning.
- The scheme reinforces and supports teachers as well as pupils.

The SHIP programme

The Adelaide-based SHIP (Students of High Intellectual Potential) programme, now known as the IGNITE programme, is considered by many practitioners to be one of the most exciting and admirable schemes in the world.

A recent international survey dissected the SHIP programme as follows, listing its main elements as:

- curriculum compacting – following a pre-test, the curriculum is reduced to only those skills or content areas that the student has not already mastered, allowing students time to participate in acceleration or enrichment activities
- product flexibility over how work is presented; focus on addressing a real problem or concern and presenting to a 'real' audience
- learning environment – student-centred rather than teacher-centred; encouraging independence; open rather than closed; accepting rather than judgemental; abstract and complex rather than simple or concrete
- students negotiating their learning with individual contracts. (Freeman et al., 2010: 18)

This does not fully convey the excitement of the scheme, which in essence consists of taking the top 30% in ability of a year group of middle-school pupils and teaching them together for 80% of the curriculum. The SHIP class means very hard work indeed for those in it and is seen as being very rigorous. A number of pupils therefore express a strong desire *not* to be in the SHIP stream because of the perceived extra work involved. As detailed below, the fact that membership of the SHIP class is only one of the techniques used by schools to bring on the gifted and talented helps its social acceptability. It seems to be accepted that not all able children necessarily go into the SHIP class, and that pupils in general share much of the special teaching that is given the SHIP class. It helps, of course, that teachers move between the SHIP class and the mainstream as it means that the rest of the students do not lose a 'best' teacher due to the existence of the SHIP scheme.

How it works

Australian schools are non-selective. Schools in Adelaide probably have fewer seriously disadvantaged children than some of their comparable counterparts in Europe and the USA, and fewer children from families where English is not the first language. At the same time, there is a prestigious and long-established private school system based on the UK model in Adelaide, a clear first choice for many of the region's middle- and upper-middle-class professionals. The SHIP schools contain a genuine cross-section of the community and are local community schools. The scheme's success is not dependent on a privileged or elite entry.

Pupils suitable for the SHIP scheme are identified at age 13. Every possible tool is used for that identification. Formal strategies may include:

- psychologists' reports
- Standard Progressive Matrices
- the Slosson IQ test
- achievement tests, including Literacy and Numeracy tests.

Informal strategies may include:

- teacher observations and anecdotal notes
- cumulative school history
- interviews
- competition results, local and national
- nomination forms from parents, teachers or tutors
- nomination by the pupil.

SHIP is keen to recognize that giftedness and talent take many forms, and no one medium of selection can be rated above any others. It is also central to the whole concept of the scheme that giftedness may be seen in one particular area alone, rather than spread across a spectrum of talents and abilities. In other words, the truly able child may be able in only one area, field or discipline. When considering test results, the SHIP team look for any high mark, not necessarily a string of them – a technique sometimes known as looking for the 'outlier' or mark of high discrepancy. It is important to note that a single high mark, even among a sea of otherwise unexceptional marks, may often show a high correlation with subsequent outstanding academic achievement.

The programme is used only for the middle years, age 13–16. Students are either vertically accelerated through middle school, completing Years 8, 9 and 10 in two years, or opt for a companion programme that emphasizes subject acceleration and lateral extension, rather than grade-skipping. There is an unashamed focus on giftedness (= academic ability), particularly in maths and science. As stated above, the concept at the core of the scheme is for approximately a third of a year group to be taught separately for 80% of the curriculum, within the mainstream school.

One very clear feeling, on the part of those who administer and teach the scheme, is that both parents and child must want to be in it. This reinforces two of the strongest messages that came across consistently in the research for this book – parental involvement, support and co-operation is a vital element of success in any scheme for the most able, and the child has to own the scheme and want to be in it. Some critics of specialist provision for the most able see the focus on this as leading to inevitable discrimination against the less advantaged whose parents are beyond the pale. Infuriatingly, this negative response obscures the truth in many approaches to the most able, which is that 'their' techniques apply equally well to all children. A huge focus on parental involvement in schemes for the most able should not preclude greater parental involvement on the part of the normally gifted, but spur it on.

The commonest educational problem found in developed countries is urban or educational blight, where, for one reason or another, a significant number of children and families in effect opt out of the educational process, or seek to opt out, as a result of disadvantage, culture or simple failure to see what all the fuss is about. There are many admirable rescue schemes aimed at changing the culture and rescuing the child, such as the SEED School in Washington, DC, examined in a later chapter. Yet comparable schemes for the academically able do little or nothing to create the ability or the ambition, but rather harvest it or give it a natural outlet. The opportunity is there; the will is usually not there. Schemes for the most able are not the obvious medicine for social ills that schemes or schools for the disadvantaged are, and can suffer in terms of their glamour as a result.

The teachers

In a recent survey of the SHIP scheme, 70% of students said that the teacher was the most important single contributor to the success of the scheme. Teachers in the scheme clearly felt frustrated by external colleagues who failed to rise to the challenge of teaching the most able. 'We need to change the teachers' headsets' was one comment. Teachers outside the scheme were commonly described by those in it as 'very conservative', and it was felt by many of the SHIP staff that some educators were haunted by a fear that a collection of brighter students would show them up. It is an interesting observation that there are some, mainly male, teachers who feel a need to show that they are better than their pupils. A good teacher does not seek to be better than their pupils, but rejoices when their pupils become better than them. SHIP staff clearly felt that it was a weakness in the profession that staff feared having their ignorance revealed.

It was also emphasized that SHIP staff need a sense of humour. Perhaps the situation is not helped by the fact that there are no specific qualifications the SHIP staff can work for or to, and no obvious career path. Being a SHIP teacher does not seem to be a way-station on the path to becoming a head of department, deputy head or head.

One of the more interesting aspects of the scheme is how teachers are selected to join it. New teachers joining the scheme are selected by a panel of their peers, by a 'tap on the shoulder' process, rather than by any great weight given to an application. In effect, what seems to happen is that existing experienced SHIP teachers look at all staff joining the school and, on a basis of instinct and experience, choose those they think would best adapt to the demands of the scheme. This means that membership has a 'Man of the Match Award' feel to it, with promotion to the scheme being on the basis of peer-group approval rather than the whim of senior management. In any event, it seems to work in terms of the quality of teaching and learning.

However, it is clear that the organizational structure of the scheme and the lines of accountability are also very significant. The success of the scheme owes much to the fact that its inventor is overall Supervisor for the scheme. She is able to visit each member school for significant periods of time in each week, and chase and chivvy those responsible for delivering the scheme at the chalk face. It is a fault of many other schemes that the Gifted and Talented Co-ordinator is often responsible not only for the

Educational Special Needs pupils but also for a whole range of other duties. The 'I'm Gifted on Tuesday afternoons' approach is not a good one. The Gifted and Talented Co-ordinator needs to be a dedicated post and have a dedicated job description, though it can be a broad one which encompasses the teaching and learning agenda.

A rather depressing feature is that the clearly committed team who deliver SHIP are seriously worried that the imminent retirement of their founding co-ordinator might lead to the collapse of the scheme. State funding has already been withdrawn and the cost of the scheme – A$80,000 per annum – was being funded from the budget of individual member schools. This reinforces an impression, gleaned from other countries and schemes, that teaching programmes for the academically gifted are often not embedded or deep-rooted in the educational system as a whole, but loose temporary buildings that are likely to blow away at the first serious wind. The system in the UK has changed dramatically since the 19th century, when individuals such as Thomas Arnold at Rugby School and Edward Thring at Uppingham could essentially found a whole new system of schools. Education in the 21st century is run by governments and an educational establishment, not by individuals. Institutional inertia does not favour a programme for the minority, and there is a noticeable eccentricity and individuality to many of the pioneers and leaders of G&T programmes in the UK and abroad. Using the term as a compliment, there are quite a few 'loose cannons' among those who lead G&T schemes, and many lumbering men o' war in the state education fleet seem inclined to throw them overboard rather than harness their power.

The students

In terms of the general placing of the SHIP scheme, participating schools' commitment to the gifted and talented spreads out from the scheme itself, and indeed placement in the SHIP class is only one of the available strategies for differentiation cross-school. This also applies to feeder primary schools, and provides an excellent argument for linked primary/secondary schools and a seamless transfer. Available strategies include:

- early entry
- year-level acceleration
- subject acceleration
- working with a mentor
- enrichment/extension programmes, including working with the local high school

- individual pupil contracts
- Higher Order Thinking Strategies integrated into classroom programmes
- numerous competitions, local, national and international
- extra-curricular involvement.

This points to an issue some schools and colleges have difficulty with. A programme for the most able should not be a watertight tank, hermetically sealed against the outside world. The deserving student should still be able to enter such a scheme after initial selection, if only because no identification and selection scheme is perfect and children mature at different ages. The stratagems and teaching practices for the most able should be part of every teacher's armoury, and teachers should cross between the two groups of students, albeit with their cards marked as teachers trained to deal with the most able. It is sometimes assumed that the presence of the most able in mixed-ability classes pulls up the bottom students to the level of those at the top. This is a glass-half-full–glass-half-empty argument; it is just as easy to argue that the top students are pulled down and held back. The way for the fizz and bubble of the most able to cascade down to the normally gifted student is through the medium of a teacher who, by teaching the most able, has learnt new flexibility, open-mindedness and a willingness to listen to students.

Flexibility has to spread to principals, administrators and those who do the timetable. High ability can not only defy boundaries of race, colour, creed and advantage, it can, and frequently does, defy boundaries of age. Vertical groupings decided not by the age of pupils but by their ability make huge sense for the minority, though are often seen both as an administrative nightmare for those who regulate the majority and as something rather shockingly new and revolutionary. It used to be said that there is no more conservative group than children. There is. They are called school administrators, and are of the type that nearly destroyed an American scheme because it required a few children to take lunch early.

An Individual or Personalized Learning Plan or Programme forms a central pillar of the scheme. At the centre of these Learning Plans is a fairly ruthless assessment of the child's weaknesses as well as strengths. One child, Ruth (fictional name), was identified as a classic perfectionist – a common feature of able children. No piece of work was ever good enough to hand in, there was always much more to be done, and so on. After due deliberation and discussion with all teachers, and with Ruth herself, the school decided to act on its right to access pupils' files on the school computer system and take one of Ruth's drafts as a final piece of work and mark it as such. To a complete lack of surprise from her teachers, it was awarded top marks. It took counselling and much mentor time, but eventually Ruth was handing in assessments on schedule with the rest of the class. Perhaps such children need to be informed by Forster when he commented that 'A work of art is never finished. It is merely abandoned'.

Generally, Individual Learning Plans are quite probably one of the most abused techniques across the world. A worrying number are bland documents containing cut-and-paste phrases giving generic details of the course the class or the year were following, but not tailoring the profile of the pupil at all. Others are huge tomes created by teachers who have actually spent all their time just on the plan and none at all with the child. If it is to have any validity, the Personalized Learning Programme has to be just that: personalized, and it is essential to keep it flexible.

All the pupils in the SHIP class seem to share a strong sense of camaraderie. They are clearly receiving social reinforcement within their cohort. 'For the first time in school I'm with others who're like me', one pupil said, repeating a sentiment expressed very many times, as in, 'It's nice to be with kids who understand me'. In particular, pupils state their sense of relief at being in a group which understands their sense of humour (often a highly developed sense of irony), the absence of teasing as a result of their sometimes idiosyncratic tastes in music or film and acceptance of their 'quirkiness'. This does make it sound as if this class were a group of high-foreheaded freaks, but outwardly the class looks just like any other group of young adolescents, and initial conversations are such as might be had with any children of their age. Only after a while does the mask slip, and many of the young people confess to having felt not so much lonely as isolated before they came into the scheme. Nearly all cite boredom as a killer before their acceptance, and are full of praise for the way the scheme keeps this dreaded evil at bay. This echoes the feelings of many of the senior teachers, who cite boredom in lessons as the biggest threat to the achievement of their most able pupils. In fact, another notable feature of the scheme touches on these young people's ability *not* to become bored. Projects that last up to a year are accepted, even though the majority of children might well be expected to have run out of steam long before that. What is not commented on by the children or their teachers is the ferocious concentration they are clearly capable of. There were several moments in observed lessons when a juicy topic was introduced and the capacity of these children to focus was almost unsettling.

Other features of the scheme

The conversation of the teachers is almost as interesting as that of the students. One line bandied around is, 'Are grades Kryptonite to able students?' There is a feeling that 'grade chasing' is positively harmful to the most able, increasing stress on children who are already often self-driven, encouraging obsessive behaviour and the perfectionism cited above, and driving out wider reading and general enrichment. Staff are also scathing about critics of acceleration who damn it because one cannot accelerate the emotional maturity of students alongside their intellectual maturity. Their answer is that one does not have to: you can accelerate the intellectual without needing to touch the emotional.

The Renzulli concern to involve students in real-life projects is also a marked feature of the scheme, as is collaborative and group work. In one strategy, pupils are divided into groups of five or so and set specific design targets, such as a robot arm, a solar-powered magnetic latch and a greenhouse garden. Another project involves looking at how to stop Adelaide's outdoor municipal waste bins from rusting. SHIP projects frequently do not just ask students to design a product, but to sell it as well. There is an echo here of good practice such as in the Valley Park and Invicta schools in Maidstone, Kent, where students not only design and sell handbag designs to a top fashion designer, but also their own Christmas wrapping paper to and through a select high-profile retail outlet.

The SHIP class are expected to attend a camp on the beautiful Kangaroo Island. This is used for academic work, in that certain projects are based on it, but it is primarily an exercise in social bonding, despite the repeated assertion that 'This is not a camp. It is a study visit'. It emphasizes how crucial it is to manage the whole child in schemes for the most able, and not just the intellect of the child.

The scheme also shows that a powerful and effective programme for the gifted and talented can be run in a mainstream school without taking away from the quality of teaching and learning of the majority of students. It also shows that it can be done affordably and without either massive training costs for teachers or taking teachers out of mainstream teaching.

The emphasis on thinking skills and moral issues is exemplary. The former are at the heart of what one needs to teach able children, the latter an excellent way of stirring, exciting and stimulating discussion and thought. It is doubtful whether this programme, applicable to all students, would be in place were it not for the fact that the programme spreads out far and wide from the children in the SHIP class.

Good provision for the most able does not speed children through so they complete a course early. It speeds them through what they can do more easily than others so that they can do other things – often much more interesting and enriching things. Most education systems have a problem with 'other things'. Teaching, and teachers, are sometimes fixated on delivering a set quota of knowledge – the 'outcome' of education. Effective teaching for the most able is often more about process than outcome. The end result of a lesson is irrelevant. What matters is the development of thinking skills and intellectual curiosity. Very often, these can only be felt or experienced, unlike factual recall which can be measured. Good teaching for the most able therefore has two potentially fatal weaknesses for its success in a conventional educational environment. It can have no definite outcome, and the gain even an outstanding lesson has given a pupil often cannot be judged by performance in a test or marks in a mark book.

The SHIP scheme does not necessarily teach scientists more science or philosophers more philosophy. What it does do is equip young people with the drive to find out more and the thinking skills and confidence to make the most out of what they find.

Questions for further thought

Why should mindsets matter to the more able?

> After seven experiments with hundreds of children, we had some of the clearest findings I've ever seen: praising children's intelligence harms their motivation and it harms their performance. How can that be? Don't children love to be praised? Yes, children love praise. And they especially love to be praised for their intelligence and talent. It really does give them a boost, a special glow – but only for the moment. The minute they hit a snag, their confidence goes out the window and their motivation hits rock bottom. If success means they're smart, then failure means they're dumb. That's the fixed mindset. (Dweck, 2006: 170)

Individuals with a fixed mindset believe their talents and abilities cannot really be improved on. In the fixed mindset, it's not enough just to succeed. It's not enough just to look smart and talented. The fixed mindset is intolerant of change. The individual feels that they are either good at something or they aren't. People with fixed mindsets spend more time on preserving who they think they are than on improving themselves. They typically believe that they're born with a degree of talent and tend to view their abilities being challenged or tested very negatively as that carries the threat of failure which in turn may damage their self-esteem. If they fail, they would have to revise their self-image and they are heavily invested in preserving it. They are therefore inclined to guard against situations where they need to prove themselves.

In the same way that labelling a child as 'gifted' can have a devastating impact on the way they see themselves as learners, so Dweck's research discovered a single line of praise given to students had a remarkably negative power. In one experiment, praising children for their effort resulted in 90% of the students selecting harder tests in the following round choice. Of those praised for their intelligence, a majority chose the easier test. The so-called 'smart' kids took the less challenging way out. Calling a child gifted takes away the vital role of task commitment. Gifted can imply 'God given' which effectively means a student didn't and doesn't have to work hard at it. It also implies that if you find something hard then effectively you can't be that smart. Too many students think effort is only for the inept, a belief which either leads to imposter syndrome, where a child never really believes that they're clever and is waiting to be found out, or to a highly brittle self-image that is way too reliant on externally given accreditation. Recent research indicates that inflating students' self-esteem in and of itself has no positive effect on grades. One recent study (Baumeister et al., 2005) has in fact shown that inflating self-esteem can actually decrease grades.

   Not only does the relationship between self-esteem and academic results not show that high self-esteem contributes to high academic results, but repeatedly praising children for how intelligent they are has been shown to lower the scores on standardized test questions. This raises some fairly significant questions that both educators and parents need to address.

Why is getting it wrong so essential to getting it right?

Parents and teachers are key in the development of more 'flexible' mindsets where sustained effort over time is seen to be one of the key elements to outstanding achievement. Every word or action is a message that can either be judgemental or developmental. The problem here is that the majority of the time parents, teachers and coaches do what they think is best for the child, without realizing that by praising children for their talent, they may actually make those talents more fragile or even diminish them. Getting it wrong is the only way to truly start to get it right. But far too few academics, gurus or sporting superstars seem prepared to commit to paper how hard they had to work to get where they are, that they got things wrong and that they still find things difficult. An exception to this is American basketball star Michael Jordan who freely admits that he 'missed more than 9000 shots' in his career and lost almost 300 games. When he was trusted to make the game-winning shot, he missed 26 times. He concludes, 'I have failed over and over and over again in my life. And that is why I succeed'.

   This echoes Samuel Beckett's famous credo from *Worstward Ho*: 'All of old. Nothing else ever. Ever tried. Ever failed. No matter. Try again. Fail again. Fail better' (1983: n.p.). It is a core element of learning to play a musical instrument that, even from an early age, children learn that the overcoming of obstacles, practice and often exhausting persistence usually pay dividends. The capacity to resist the temptation to quit when the practice task looks like being beyond a learner's current ability level is critical to long-term achievement. Perseverance and diligence are cardinal Confucian learning virtues. Edison had 10,000 tries at making a light bulb before he had one that worked. Jack Dempsey commented that a champion was someone who got up off the floor when knocked down hard. Often, the attitude of pushing back as a response to failure is a critical dividing line between those who will make it and those who won't. On a wider level, willpower is often discovered through hardship, as Winston Churchill suggested in *Marlborough: His Life and Times* when he commented that 'the twinge of adversity, the spur of slights and taunts are needed to evoke that ruthless fixity of purpose and

(Continued)

(Continued)

tenacious mother wit without which great actions are seldom accomplished'. For many highly able children, the easy accomplishment they can feel when given tasks that are all too simple for them can be both a source of irritation and complacency. Critically, they get used to being praised and to easy success, both of which can damage their longer-term development as successful learners who thrive on challenge.

So what can support the more able in terms of their self-esteem?

High classroom challenge is partly to do with how we enable our students and ourselves to make useful mistakes, how we manage uncertainty and fear, create opportunities for risk taking and enable genuine engagement. Some students seem to be quite naturally mastery-oriented; they relish a challenge and pour effort into it. They have learned to thrive on difficulty. This leads to a high level of self-esteem, which they themselves seem to be in control of and can boost in constructive ways throughout their lives. As we have seen, self-esteem that has been promoted by external praise is highly fragile. Western culture has become steeped in the language and literature of self-esteem with more than 2,000 published books offering the attainment of self-esteem; educational programmes in schools designed to cultivate self-esteem continue to proliferate, and yet researchers such as Nick Emler (2001) strongly believe that 'there is absolutely no evidence that low self-esteem is particularly harmful ... It's not at all a cause of poor academic performance; people with low self-esteem seem to do just as well in life as people with high self-esteem. In fact, they may do better, because they often try harder'.

Teachers cannot 'give' their students self-esteem. Students need to be in charge of it themselves. It has to be earned. Research strongly suggests that one of the best things that teachers can do is to show students that their intellectual skills are things that can be cultivated, through hard work, reading and coping with obstacles. It would also help them if they believed that any award or performance reflects current skill levels and is not an indication of their overall worth or intelligence. Similarly, students need to understand that the confrontation of challenges is critical. Doing well on the simple tasks, where they may well be scoring top marks on a consistent basis, is pointless. Looking good when you aren't put into difficulty is too easy, and in fact doesn't equip you with the necessary skills when work actually gets hard. It is all too common to see highly able students hit a brick wall in later years of schooling and then begin to doubt their smartness and to pull back effort. What is far less common is to see students who can capitalize on setbacks. On a wider level, even the early pioneer of self-esteem, William James, made the point that self-esteem needs to be a true measurement of conduct and that accomplishment remains central to self-esteem, rather than self-esteem being something that can be inflated without substance. Now it seems as if self-esteem has to precede achievement, rather than being the result of it. A complicating factor for teachers is the pressure they come under from those parents who do not understand this, who believe all achievement springs from high self-esteem and who will consequently not allow their children to fail.

16

United States of America

Key points

- New York's Village East Gifted scheme is an exemplary private, pull-out programme for the most able.
- Charter schools offer variable standards and no special insight into provision for the most able.
- Some charter schools offer excellent provision but still fail to address entirely the needs of the most able.
- Schools for the most able attract the same animosity as UK grammar schools.
- In allowing the most able students to sit first-year university examinations, schools for the most able may be showing the way ahead to a new world where there is much more of a seamless gap between secondary and tertiary education.

Two areas of interest originating from the USA have already been looked at in this study – the Renzulli whole-school approach and the Robinson Center at the University of Washington in Seattle. Three other projects or schemes from the USA are of particular interest: the privately run Village East Gifted programme on Long Island; charter schools; and one particular 'public' (i.e. non-fee paying) school that markets itself as a specialist resource for the most able. These three have been chosen because they span a whole spectrum of provision, from a small, individually run and conceived bespoke service to an education programme designed to cope with massive urban disadvantage through to a form of selection on academic ability.

Village East Gifted

Of all the schemes examined in this book, the Village East Gifted scheme, based on Long Island, New York, is the most unusual. It is small, reaching out to perhaps 15 students at any one time, and is fee-paying, though clearly the fees are waived in hardship cases. Because it is run from the basement of a private home, it cannot advertise as a business and relies for its clientele on word of mouth. It caters for both genders and all ages, and is run by a former teacher and singer who was fired from her teaching post for being too 'different'. That fact alone gives her a special bond with her students, many of whom have come to her because their schools would like to fire them for being different.

The broad outline of the programme can be simply stated. It works by self-referral, from parents or from children, by those who feel that their potential is not being realized within the framework of school. Those accepted onto the course receive an exceptionally personalized programme. Common features are collaborative work, working against the clock, competitive exercises and challenging puzzles or tests that stretch, challenge and extend various cognitive skills. Previous recipients of the programme come back to act as mentors and classroom assistants to new members.

Further comment on the actual content of the Village East Gifted programme is limited by the fact that at the time of our visit it was on the verge of receiving private investment to allow it to expand, which meant that intellectual property rights were possibly about to pass to new proprietors whose permission to release core detail was not at that stage obtainable, through the fault of no one except those who devise US intellectual property law. What can be noted is that the wide range of children spoken to in the course of our visit – wide in terms of gender, age and background – had a number of things in common. Access to the Village East Gifted scheme had 'rescued' them, been their 'haven'. If one was to extrapolate a human story from these children, it would be that it is a particularly acute form of unhappiness and depression that afflicts very able children who cannot express their ability or have it recognized by the adult world. 'No one understands me!' is the cry of the adolescent across the world. Perhaps because it is so easy to dismiss the cry of those who are just undergoing a central part of the journey most humans make, we miss something important when the same words are used by the most able to describe something that is, at the same time, more true and more damaging than the general plaint.

Another notable feature is the entire absence from Village East Gifted of any mention of 'Regents' or any other test or examination. It illustrates both a need and a problem that is universal to provision for the most able. The need is to take the most able far and away from the set curriculum or testing regime and trust them to satisfy its demands easily and largely from within its own resources. The problem is that this approach, which is kindness itself to the most able, can be cruel beyond belief to those who are not so able and need large amounts of help to attain what for many might be life-enhancing pass grades.

Yet, the very best programmes for the most able recognize the need for these students to have whatever bit of paper is the accepted matriculation requirement of the country on the day, but are calm enough to see such certification not as the be-all and end-all of education but as a natural by-product, something that will fall out of the teaching and learning of the most able if conducted appropriately.

In an ideal world, alongside every KIPP NYC school (see below) there would be a Village East Gifted unit, offering after-hours and weekend enrichment. Outstanding schools such as KIPP NYC might rankle at the suggestion they could not entirely cope with their most able students. It is only when one sees what such specialist treatment can add to already able children that one's eyes are opened to just how much higher the able child can climb.

Charter schools

Projects or schemes looked at in this study fall into two categories. The first are those designed specifically to impact on gifted children. The second are those designed to improve the general lot of children, with a spin-off benefit for the most able. Interest in charter schools is based simply on whether or not they do a good job by the most able. However, to reach any conclusion on that, it is also necessary to look at them as a whole.

The first law allowing charter schools was passed in Minnesota in 1991; 41 states and the District of Columbia now have similar legislation. In 1995 there were only 100 charter schools. By April 2006, there were over 3,500 charter schools serving more than a million children. In 2009, there were 5,000 schools, and in December 2011 some 5,600 educating over two million children. Charter schools can close as well as start up and the closure rate runs at just over 12% of the total. Apart from their intrinsic interest, the model has gone overseas and been taken up by a number of countries – it has, for instance, heavily influenced the British City Academy and Free School movement.

Charter schools are publicly funded state schools often driven by local or interest groups and which are granted significant authority and autonomy in curriculum, governance and a wide range of other areas. The founding 'charter' is in effect a performance contract, stating the school's mission, programme and aims. Charter schools thus have greater freedom but trade this off against greater accountability. The charter is granted for a fixed term, usually 3–5 years, after which the body that granted the charter reviews the school and decides whether or not to renew it. Charter schools vary widely from state to state but things they can do include:

- lengthening the school day
- mixing grades
- requiring dress codes
- putting teachers on school boards
- offering boarding
- doubling up instruction in core subjects such as maths or reading.

The philosophy is pro-market and neoliberal, the assumption being that competition in public-sector schools will drive up standards and close bad schools. The schools themselves often seem driven by an evangelical fervour, and in their publicity make claims that they:

- increase opportunities for learning and access to quality education for all students
- create choice for parents and pupils in the public (state) sector
- provide a system of accountability for results and outcomes in public education
- encourage innovative teaching practices
- create new professional opportunities for teachers
- encourage community and parental involvement in public education
- spur on the improvement generally of public education.

There has been much debate about the success of charter schools. In response to claims such as the above, one major research study stated:

> We endorse every one of these goals wholeheartedly, and wish that charter schools were unquestionably reaching them. But too many of the facts we have documented in our research suggest that charter schools, on the whole, are falling short, at least as viewed through the eyes of the students and parents who are their customers … The assumption that charter schools are a cure for the ills of urban education flies in the face of the evidence. (Buckley & Schneider, 2007: 268)

Numerous surveys have produced evidence that over the whole gamut of educational sector results, parent and pupil satisfaction from charter schools is not notably better than that in public schools – 'for students from the same racial/ethnic backgrounds, reading and mathematics performance in charter schools did not differ from that in other public schools' (Buckley & Schneider, 2007: 272).

Yet the fact remains that a number of the charter schools visited were clearly, and by any standards, outstanding schools which had in no small measure used the freedom of the charter school system to achieve excellence, and which would in all probability not have achieved that excellence without the charter school model to adopt. This is one of the problems in judging large numbers of schools, where the mass of data can, at times, serve to disguise or hide individual brilliance.

There are undoubted weaknesses in the system. For example, the administrators of a charter school hold the school accountable but do not directly supervise it. This can lead to dysfunctional management. Furthermore, the absence in the USA of any standard method of declaring results allows for confusion and can make it difficult to compare like with like. Perhaps charter schools are an illustration of the Pareto Criterion, named after the Italian economist Vilfredo Pareto: 'a policy choice is to be preferred if it makes at least one person better off and no one worse off'. Two schools in particular, following a visit to them, suggest that rather more than one person is made better off by reason of their existence.

Case study: The SEED School, Washington, DC

The SEED School (SEED DC) is a remarkable success story. It received its Charter in 1997. All its students are Black or Hispanic; 72.7% rate as economically disadvantaged, with 76% eligible to receive free or reduced-price lunches; and 85% of students come from three of Washington's most disadvantaged wards. Given this entry, the figures cited by the school are extraordinary:

- In 2011, 60.4% of SEED DC students scored proficient or advanced in reading and 76.3% scored proficient or advanced in math on the DC CAS compared to students attending DC public schools who scored 48.2% in reading and 52.8% in maths.
- 91% of SEED DC students who enter the Ninth Grade graduate from high school.
- 94% of SEED DC graduates have been accepted at a four-year college.
- 94% of SEED DC alumni graduate from college at triple the rate of their peers. (see SEED's website at www.seedschooldc.org)

SEED DC has a number of interesting features. One is the fierce belief of its principal that every child is born a Mozart. Addressing visitors at one of the school's open days, he said, 'If you believe some kids are more gifted than others, this is not the school for you'. Later, he added, 'I don't believe people are born smart. Young people have control over their intellectual capacity'.

Every inch of the school reflects this philosophy. Basic messages are reinforced on every inch of wall space – 'Do What Is <u>E</u>xpected, Not What's <u>In</u>spected!' The 'Three Es' are also continually emphasized – 'Excellence. Effort. Exposure'. The latter is a blend of creativity and involvement in out-of-school experience. The pressure on students to reach high standards and to behave is relentless. The school is an extreme example of the belief that all children are born equally gifted. As such, it was to prove a most interesting test case as to whether or not that philosophy could sustain effective provision for the most able.

The boarding element

SEED DC makes the fullest possible use of the freedoms afforded it by Charter status. The primary difference from the mainstream is not its size – it has 327 pupils – but the fact that it is a weekly boarding school. This gives the school a capacity both to offset any negative elements in the pupils' home culture and to impose its own culture. As an example, there is a compulsory 40 minutes of reading after school each day. A house system (20+ pupils to each house) is used in the traditional manner, and boarding is handled sensitively, with two pupils apiece to a bedsit and no choice of roommate allowed. Another very interesting feature is the adoption of a diamond system, whereby girls and boys are educated separately in the middle school. All this and a clearly outstandingly committed teaching staff (one third of existing staff left in the early stages of the present principal's tenure) lead to a school that is extremely impressive by any standards.

Its one area of weakness, however, is its inability to give all that is needed to its most able students. It illustrates the truth revealed by the McKinsey report, 'How The World's Most Improved School Systems Keep Getting Better' (Barber et al., 2010a), that the techniques needed to create good schools are different from those needed to create world-class schools. The majority of students who come to SEED DC are two or three years behind their grade. To get these pupils to catch up requires a Herculean effort. The sheer hard grind of catch-up and the need to acquire missing core skills does not create an atmosphere where flights of fancy or gathering flowers by the wayside find it easy – or perhaps even desirable – to grow. A partial college acceptance list in 2012 listed 82 successes, by university or college rather than by name of student. It did not give the number of students accepted by each institution. Some well-known names appear – Brown, Cornell, Duke, Penn, Princeton and Stanford – but this is nevertheless a list in which the Ivy League is very much in a minority, in fact just over 7%. The whole school was possessed of a driving urge to set no limits on the achievement of its pupils, yet it was as if a place at an Ivy League university was seen as a luxury, something of a dessert to be served only after the main course. The problem for schools in challenging urban environments is that the main course can sometimes take a very long time to prepare. SEED DC cried out for there to be an out-of-school facility for its most gifted – a post-graduate course to run concurrently with the undergraduate course being run so well by the school. It is a dangerous fallacy not to recognize that the most gifted constitute a special needs group. When the admirable principal stated, 'I don't believe people are born smart', what he was saying was, 'I don't believe in dismissing anyone as stupid'. This is a common fallacy, in effect concluding that in admitting that some children are more able than others, one is also admitting that the remainder are not clever at all. Why it is morally unacceptable to condemn the less able, but not also morally unacceptable to deny the most able their rights? The easiest way, of course, is to deny that the most able exist at all.

SEED DC also raises another issue. Its system is expensive, and the school has a Director of Development, Individual and Major Gifts. Quality costs money. The enthusiasm with which SEED DC accepts that it has a responsibility to raise special funds as part of the price it pays for running a special school in a special way is one aspect of the charter school system that has not found its way over to the UK.

It is also worth noting that SEED DC places significant emphasis on extra-curricular activity, in terms of sport, the arts and internal and overseas visits. Children are not pure intellects, existing only from the shoulders up. Good schools, for the most able or not, encourage body and spirit, as well as mind.

KIPP Schools and NYC College Prep. School

KIPP ('Knowledge Is Power Program') Schools were among the first charter schools to be founded in the USA, originating in Houston in 1994. The current KIPP network serves 58,000 students in 162 schools in 20 states (plus Washington, DC) across the USA.

KIPP explains itself in its publicity brochures as follows (material is taken from the KIPP NYC website or their school's printed brochures):

Who We Are

KIPP, the Knowledge Is Power Program, is a national network of free, open-enrolment, college-preparatory public schools with a track record of preparing students in underserved communities for success in college and in life. There are currently 109 KIPP schools in 20 states and the District of Columbia serving more than 33,000 students.

What We Do

KIPP builds a partnership among parents, students, and teachers that puts learning first. By providing outstanding educators, more time in school learning, and a strong culture of achievement, KIPP is helping all students climb the mountain to and through college.

KIPP schools recruit 87% of their students from low-income families, and 95% are African American or Latino, yet more than 80% of KIPP alumni have gone on to college.

Case study: KIPP NYC College Prep. High School

KIPP (NYC) has a non-selective entry. Roughly equivalent to the overall figures for KIPP schools, 85% of parents are low-income, with their children qualifying for free or reduced-price meals; 95% are African American or Hispanic; and results are outstanding. The New York 'Regents' Exams are a city-wide set of what might be called matriculation exams, which are taken at the end of Grades 9–12, depending on the subject. Whatever debate there might be about the quality of these tests, they do provide across the New York region what is so lacking in assessment of charter schools nationwide, namely a general benchmark against which schools can be compared – 65% is deemed a minimum score. Currently, KIPP (NYC) students are scoring 89% 'passage rates' in Algebra (52% average for the district), 95% in Living Environment (53%), 96% in Global History (44%) and 100% in English (65%).

KIPP encourages pupils to take non-academic courses, but uses a number of the most attractive as unashamed rewards for academic success and 'character growth':

> If students pass all their classes with a 70 and Regents with a 75, they are not required to complete summer school at KIPP NYC College Prep. Instead they will have the chance to participate in some extraordinary summer opportunities.

These 'extraordinary summer opportunities' range from an experiment in International Living in Poland to a competitive, intensive four-week exposure to engineering at the Aspen Institute in Colorado. Music, dance and sport are emphasized. The message is gently enough stated but clear: this is what you get if you work hard and do well. It would be equally true to say that those who do *not* meet the required standards *will* be required to attend summer school. There is an iron fist here, albeit hidden in a kid glove.

Much of the philosophy and content of the KIPP (NYC) curriculum are neither revolutionary nor innovative, but are perhaps distinguished by so many approaches being concentrated in one place and time. KIPP schools share a core set of operating principles known as the 'Five Pillars': High Expectations, Choice and Commitment, More Time, Power to Lead, and Focus on Results, each one of which is looked at in more detail below:

- 'High Expectations' are *de rigeur* for any high-achieving school, the majority of whose intake are from poor, deprived or disadvantaged backgrounds. The expectation at both KIPP (NYC) and SEED (DC) is that the pupil will succeed.
- 'Choice and Commitment' are crucial to the school's success. From the outset, it is assumed that the student has chosen to attend the school, and that therefore total commitment to it is a given, not a choice. It is very clear that the KIPP (NYC) students take complete responsibility for their progress, and if things go wrong they see it as their responsibility and their fault, not as someone else's.
- 'More Time' is one of the more obvious reasons why KIPP (NYC) is so successful. Staff are expected to see their working day as lasting from 7.30am to 5.00pm, because extra time is made available to students and the working day is longer than in many schools for both staff and students. This applies to their Special Education Teacher Support Services (SETSS). Students are not pulled out of their core classes. Instead, extra teachers are laid on to better explain the material as it is being rolled out. Smaller maths and English classes are provided which take longer to cover the basic ground. Study skills classes are available as an extra to the core curriculum, along with extensive tutoring and counselling. A spin-off from the 'more time' philosophy is that there is a predominance of young staff, as those with children find it harder to work the necessary hours.
- 'Power to Lead' is an interesting element, echoing the emphasis found in an otherwise very different school, the Raffles Institution. The 'Power to Lead' motif and theme is a recognition of the importance

of leadership skills as a necessary talent to develop so as to make a contribution to the community or even just the team. Yet it also takes on a different meaning in a school where so many children come from disadvantaged backgrounds and home environments with low aspirations, low self-esteem and an atmosphere of defeated resignation. You do not have to accept someone else's agenda, the KIPP (NYC) emphasis on leadership seems to say. You are your own leader. You can set your own agenda. You can lead yourself out of no hope.

- 'Focus on Results' is exactly that. Plastered on the wall of a science laboratory, in unmissable letters bang over the whiteboard, is the statement, 'BIG GOAL. All of us will: Score an 85% or higher on the Living Environment Regents Exam 1'. This is very similar to the ubiquitous exhortations found at SEED DC. This pressure to achieve generates typical, albeit graphic, answers, as in this comment from a male student (9th Grade, 14 years old, middle-ability band): 'Sometimes you fool yourself it doesn't matter. With me it's when I get to use a new [computer] game for the first time. Then the school tells me the math matters more, and it kinda helps me get off my butt and do the math.' Another pupil (female, 9th Grade, top-ability band) commented: 'It's like a private school. They push you and you always have to think, but they help you as well.'

KIPP (NYC) also has some clever tricks to embed aspiration. This is a new school, with no alumni as yet who have graduated from college or university. In the Elementary section of the school, classes are named after leading universities and numbered by the year in which the pupils will graduate. There are continual affirmative messages displayed on walls, often quotations from famous people. These are mixed with more basic messages, such as, 'You must speak and write in complete sentences'.

It is very noticeable that in every lesson attended there is some attempt at enrichment. Students facing an inevitably fact-laden revision session are tempted with future gems the class might discuss or write on. Under various subject headings, classes discuss the worship of celebrity. Another class discusses whether a woman with five children is responsible for her own poverty. Should she go to college and thus reduce her poverty? Should the government pay towards the care of her children to allow this to happen? Great emphasis is placed on communication skills and group work. KIPP (NYC) has a buzz to it that is tangible.

The key to any success KIPP (NYC) has with the most able lies in the extra time it is willing to allocate to students, and in its seeing matriculation and, above all, results not as an end in themselves, but rather as a gateway to higher and more successful achievement. Yet, despite this splendid school's obvious success, in our observation there was one thing lacking. Top-tier candidates lacked the bounce and cheerfulness in class of those in other schools who spend significant time with other children of equal ability. There is some indefinable quality that seems to accrue to able children who have ample time to socialize and work with young people of equal ability. KIPP (NYC) students are keen, eager, determined and hard-working – a tremendous advertisement for the school. The only criticism that could be levelled at it is the same for all mixed-ability schools. The intensity and drive necessary to bring schools recruiting from disadvantaged backgrounds up to scratch are inevitable, but occasionally exhausting and draining. Schools or classes composed entirely of able children can be surprisingly relaxed. Contrary to the popular conception that high-ability classes are driven power houses, ironically teaching all able children can lead to a significantly more relaxed atmosphere, perhaps because the teachers themselves feel more relaxed and less driven to squeeze the last drop of results out of pupils.

The public school as private school

The last case study here is of a New York school – 'NEST+m' – that is no longer a member of any national organization or group, but which represents a phenomenon that is replicated worldwide, namely the state or 'public' school (the latter in the US rather than the UK definition of 'public') that achieves results that are as good as or better than fee-paying schools. Such schools are sometimes unashamedly selective, as with the UK grammar schools, or in the case of sixth form colleges *de facto* selective because their students need to have reached a certain standard in their public examination results to be able to pursue academic post-16 goals. Whatever their declared entry policy, such schools can become the victim of their own success in terms of ensuring the widest possible access to the school. Success breeds success and when outstanding results are produced, the aspirational middle classes gravitate towards it.

We were introduced to this particular case-study school as a 'Magnet' school, though both the school and MSA (Magnet Schools of America) now deny any link. Magnet schools were so named because the driving force behind their foundation was to create schools that were so good that they would act as a magnet and draw pupils in from a wide enough catchment area so as to ensure diversity. Indeed, early funding for the Magnet schools (there are 3,400 of them) often came from funds set aside to increase diversity within schools, rather than with any academic aim. In terms of the school below, the magnetic attraction it exerts seems to have little to do with diversity and much more to do with parents and children who are highly academically aspirational. It is a common feature of many countries worldwide that where choice exists, aspirational parents will seek to colonize schools that are centres of academic excellence, the simplest method of all being to live in a house in the school's catchment area. The problem with such colonization is twofold. Such schools can simply attract the academically aspirational, whereas the challenge facing many countries is to create the aspiration in the first place. In other words, such schools, in terms of their parents and pupils, can end up preaching to the already converted. Second, and however good a job such schools do for the most able, they can run headlong into the access and diversity agenda, and in so doing arouse passionate objections to their very existence.

NEST+m is also of interest because it is at the extreme end of the spectrum from another public provider, the KIPP schools. Whilst these focus entirely on a disadvantaged, non-selective entry, the case study school equally unashamedly defines itself as being not only for the gifted and talented, but with a further specialization in those committed to STEM subjects. However, it demands to be studied in a book of this nature most of all because it is an unashamed specialist in the teaching of the gifted and talented. It proclaims itself as such on its website and in all its publicity material.

Case study: NEST+m

NEST+m stands for 'New Explorations into Science, Technology and Math'. Situated in New York, NEST+m is a public school but unashamedly for the gifted and talented. It is the only such school in New York that offers a seamless education from Kindergarten through to 12th Grade, with what is, in effect, three separate schools sharing the same building and united by a common philosophy. That philosophy, as summed up on its website, could be issued by any number of schools worldwide for the gifted and talented:

> NEST+m is committed to providing not just an outstanding academic education for all our students, but to creating programs that support their growth as scholars, artists and citizens of the world. We aim to teach outstanding communication skills, whether through one of the five world languages that we offer, the required computer courses, our workshop model of reading and writing, or an expanded vocabulary in physics. We encourage students to make a difference to those around them, in their community, their city, and the world, by performing community service and we nurture their hearts and minds by providing a welcoming place for self-expression through music, art, writing, drama, and science. (http://nestmk12.net/about-nestm)

NEST+m has around 1,600 students apply for entrance to 9th Grade (13–14-year-olds). Of these, some 800 are 'ranked' (deemed worthy of a place), 420 offers are made and the expectation is that 170 will accept places. The fall-off is because the school is competing with large specialized schools, mostly specializing in science. The size of these other schools – two have over 3,000 students, one over 5,000 – means they can offer a significantly greater variety of courses than is possible at NEST+m. At 6th Grade, there are 1,000 applicants for 80 places. In the lower Grades, NYC testing suggests the entry is in the top 1% of academic ability. The school's teaching serves two masters. All students sit the ubiquitous Regents, but most will combine this with APs (Advanced Programs), which are much more demanding and more akin to entry-level college courses. This, incidentally, was also a pattern at KIPP NYC. A key feature of the NEST+m approach is the personalization of a student's course. As well as a choice of APs, there is acceleration (up to four years or more and highlighted as crucial to the school's success by the principal and staff), compaction and students sent out to take college-level courses.

In many respects, NEST+m is a gifted child's heaven. It uses, positively and well, every single technique known to bring on the gifted and talented. Staff and students are passionate and committed, and the students are self-evidently and self-confessedly stretched but happy and fulfilled. The school has confidence in the ability of its pupils that is a hallmark of all schools which gather together and separate out the most able, that confidence showing itself in an atmosphere that is at one and the same time competitive but relaxed. NEST+m accepts one of the basic truths about educating the most able, namely that the children drive the staff as much as the other way round.

Yet, if NEST+m is Heaven, it also has its Hell. What New York has created in this world-class school is an even more selective version of the English grammar school. And, just as did the English grammar school, it has trodden on significant sensitivities. Success breeds success, but also jealousy. No one at KIPP NYC was willing to say a rude word about NEST+m. Outstanding schools are as confident as their pupils; they are happy to be judged on their merits and do not need to condemn other schools' success in order to boost their own. Yet clearly there are institutions and individuals who are not like this, and much of the hostility that was and is shown towards grammar schools in the UK is replicated in New York.

Such schools are frequently brilliant but the divisions they cause can be punitive. It is also clearly untrue that merely being selective guarantees that a school does well by the most able children. A number of UK grammar schools had or have negative value-added scores. It is not widely recognized that bright children can encourage bad teaching. Their ability to teach themselves and still get the grades can cover for bad delivery in the classroom. The most able can have a pragmatic streak – 'OK, it's not fun, but it will get us the grade and there's always the chance the next lesson will be good'. Selective schools are not a universal panacea. Where they are brilliant, it is because passionate, committed and knowledgeable staff act as a catalyst to students' ability. Where they also profit is in their ability to mix like with like. Put a large enough group of able children together, give them powerful leadership and they reach critical mass, or what an economist would call the take-off into self-sustained growth.

It is interesting to note that NEST+m has schemes to allow students to take credits for university courses and a very strong insistence on its pupils undertaking significant community service, the latter being a development already noted at Singapore's Raffles Institution. It is clear that the specialist, academically selective school has moved on from the dry, single-minded and atonal hothouses of the past. Such schools as still exist recognize that their pupils need to be not just good academics but also good citizens. Perhaps even more significant is the development whereby students still at school can take significant elements of a first-year university course. This is part of the blurring of the difference between school and university that has leapt on apace in the past decade, driven in no small measure by the increasing cost of a university education and the huge saving to a student of having to spend one less year as an undergraduate. There is a strong case for arguing that the creation of a much more seamless join between secondary and tertiary education is going to be a major feature of the years ahead for the most able. Cynically, history tends to suggest that initiatives for the most able have been driven more by economic than academic factors in the first instance, and there is a compelling economic argument for students shortening their time at university where they and their schools can cover course content within the school environment. Interestingly, there is also a compelling educational argument. Allowing students to move beyond Baccalaureate, International Baccalaureate, A level or other national qualification usually taken at 18+ and on to university-level material removes what for some of the most able young people is a wholly artificial crash barrier. It exchanges having them go as far as society and the educational strictures of the day will allow with letting them go as far and as fast as they can, and as such is intensely liberating. It is, of course, a lesser version of the Robinson Center (see chapter 6), but by being less extreme and even dramatic it becomes all the more easy to do within the conventionally conservative and risk-averse environment of secondary education.

Questions for further thought

If spoon feeding works, why do more?

There are clear comparisons here with a number of UK schools serving disadvantaged urban areas. In a country where the 'C' grade at GCSE is viewed as the main goal for a school to be deemed to have reached its target, it is impossible to avoid making this not the half-way point on a journey, but the destination. A caveat is needed here. It is easy – too easy – to ridicule 'teaching to the floor grade', but those who criticize it often do so unreasonably. For many students, this grade is a sign that they have achieved their potential, and to teach to it is simply to set an achievable and valuable target for students. It might not qualify a student for Oxbridge or the Ivy League, but only very few pupils need to qualify for such universities. The problem comes with the fact that for those very few students worthy of the A* many of the techniques needed to teach the 'C' grade are simply living death. 'Layer-cake' teaching, frequent repetition and rigid adherence to the core curriculum spell disengagement for the most able on an industrial scale, and that is one of the biggest threats to achievement for those pupils. It needs to be accepted that very often bringing on the most able is a separate job. To use an analogy, the blend of fuel used for racing is tuned for the demands of different circuits – or even different weather conditions. More potent fuels give noticeably more power but that needs to be balanced against the danger of engine wear. The culture within so many schools has become obsessed with protection, scaffolding and spoon feeding. Put simply, the lack of ignition is a far more serious problem in schools than the risk of burning out. As a result, students who are fed a controlled low-grade fuel are less likely to feel the sense of flow that comes from real engagement, and they are less likely to acquire the work habits and enquiry skills that they will require to get them through university.

Do the teaching and learning styles that most help the normally gifted have a damaging effect on the most able?

There has been a worldwide backlash against the 'pressure cooker', highly selective hothouse variant of school and a move towards the comprehensive, mixed-ability school. Perhaps we have spent too much time worrying about the type of school we send our children to, and too little time on recognizing that within the all-embracing school different children have varying needs and have to be taught in different ways. Csikszentmihalyi et al. (1990) point out that there are two motivational states that interfere with learning. One is anxiety; the other is boredom. Anxiety occurs when teachers expect too much, boredom when they expect too little. The greatest destroyer of able children is boredom, but if these children need to run, the probability is that at least two-thirds of a cohort need to be able to walk. It might not be an easy or comfortable concept, but in the light of schools in the USA which are doing an outstanding job in raising the aspirations and achievement of disadvantaged children but doing little or nothing for their most able, it is a concept we need to scrutinize ruthlessly. Many educators argue that children from disadvantaged homes remain poor and illiterate because they lack

(Continued)

(Continued)

the accumulative advantage of cultural capital and core background knowledge. They argue that students need to follow a slow pattern of accretion with coherent, cumulative factual knowledge. The Michael Barber/McKinsey report (2010a) suggested that it required two separate approaches to raise a school from weak to good and from good to outstanding. Should it surprise us if the same were true of the teaching style applied to the children who fill the schools?

Can we do too much for the children in our care?

Seligman's concept (1991) of learned optimism is an interesting idea. Students who succeed at university are not necessarily those who excel academically but are often those who possess other gifts or skills such as persistence and resilience that help them to cope with the floods of pressure that would otherwise capsize them. Classic texts on education such as Plato's *Republic* and Locke's *Some Thoughts Concerning Education* emphasize that character development and virtue are far more important educational goals than mere acquisition of knowledge. At the same time, those writers are quite explicit in setting forth the breadth of knowledge children need to acquire. The world has come a long way from the days when teaching was didactic, strictly authoritarian and not infrequently punitive and violent towards its consumers. We are all now inclined to be nice towards children as our fail-safe setting and long may that continue, yet some of the outstanding schools dealing with largely disadvantaged children in the USA adopt a straightforward 'tough love' philosophy. You get the rewards in terms of trips and extra-curricular activities if you do the work and gain the results. The vast majority of teachers like children and are prepared to work their socks off to get the best for them, but do we need to re-examine our attitude towards sanctions? Can we, by trying too hard, make it *our* responsibility if they succeed or fail, rather than *their* responsibility? Do we let our children *own* their education and its outcomes or do we merely rent them occasional space? Child development theories often focus on tools of the mind such as self-regulation, with the stated intention to help children learn different kinds of skill such as controlling their emotions by avoiding distraction and staying focused by organizing their thoughts. Many commentators on early years education now point out how important it is for very young children to learn that there are consequences for every action, rather than being hothoused (the so-called RugRat Race). Are we letting our older children learn this, and what role, if any, do sanctions have to play in that learning scenario?

Do we have enough rewards on offer in our various schemes?

Do we need to look at how we use rewards in our teaching, as well as how we use sanctions? It is easy for adults to see the benefits for someone in a scheme for the most able: improved results, better interview technique, improved chances of a place at a top university, a better (i.e. more highly paid) job, yet these are a long way away for many children in terms of time, and even further away in terms of their own experience: more work, more demands, more pressure; less time socializing, on the internet or simply hanging out; the image of a geek, nerd, anorak or whatever is the new word for a child whose value structure mimics that of people much older. Granted, the schools visited in the USA were not running specifically for the most able, but what many of them did was make sure that success in the classroom was fun, by virtue of what it earned in the shape of activities and opportunities outside of it. For students with an intrinsic desire to learn and a strong internal locus of control, rewards may be redundant. Indeed, some argue about the possible threats to intrinsic motivation that may result from the use of extrinsic rewards. For others, the teacher's recognition and approval support their motivation to achieve. Some able students can become so disengaged and unmotivated in school that they have little inclination to give of their best, even in formal test settings. Sadly, the increase of high-stakes testing has resulted in an undue focus on test performance rather than on the quality of learning that it is supposed to assess. Is performance on a test in an academic domain wholly meaningful if it is improved when rewards are made available? It's a very simple question we need to ask ourselves of any scheme we mount for the most able: what's in it for them?

Part 4

Future Directions

17

Core Issues

Key points

- Able children benefit from being educated with each other. Selective schools can be an effective way of meeting this need, but the design of such schools should differ radically from that of the old grammar school.
- An alternative way to give more able students a fairer deal is the creation of a genuinely separate stream for the most able in non-selective schools.
- In both cases, the crucial ingredients for success are the capacity for able children to spend significant time with children of similar ability and, as importantly, for them to be taught by trained, specialist and committed teachers.
- The existence of selective schools need not preclude or take away effective and successful education from the rest of the pupil cohort.
- Broadening the aims of education for the most able has ironically made it less popular by making it less affordable.
- Too much of the best provision for the most able in the world depends on the commitment and energy of individual teachers.
- Able children are an invaluable national asset but often do not get a fair educational deal.
- Outside of a crisis, education for the most able is seen as a luxury and is under threat worldwide.

Education for the most able is in crisis across the world. Increasingly, what used to be the dominant force in such education – systems which favour special, highly selective schools – is being challenged. The challenge can be political and financial, as in Russia, or ideological, as in the UK. Such schools tend nowadays to be seen as elitist and catering only for a privileged minority, as well as failing to meet the needs of the lower end of the ability and achievement spectrum. This is at the heart of a quite bitter dispute over the merits of comprehensive schools being carried out in Germany and Northern Ireland. The latter is a re-run of the battle still being fought in the UK. Politicians who admit that the Northern Ireland education system does badly by the lower end of the pupil spectrum are increasingly arguing that it does not make sense to start improving a system with excellent achievement at the top but weak achievement at the bottom by doing away with the top.

There are two key provisions that unite all and any effective schemes for the most able. Such young people must be allowed to spend at least a significant amount and perhaps a majority of time with children of similar ability and they must be taught by trained, specialist and highly committed teachers. Provide these two elements and the vehicle which delivers them becomes less important than the people. As for delivery vehicles, not to put teachers first is akin to developing a marvellous new medicine that can only be given by injection, before one has invented the syringe with which to do it.

Indeed, part of the problem with education for the most able is that, as a cause, it is often associated with specialist, selective schools. These schools are strange objects, which appear to deny the laws of physics in that they can be looked at by two people who clearly see totally different things. One person sees a wonderful engine of social mobility which ignores class by focusing on meritocratic entry, whilst the other sees exam factories that grossly favour middle-class children at the expense and to the exclusion of the rest.

This is a debate that will be carried on in several books to come. It is easy to be an opponent of grammar schools. In the UK, grammar schools carried the seeds of their own destruction in that they seemingly condemned two thirds of children to bad, low-aspiration schools, and labelled those children unjustly and indefensibly as failures. Opposition is not weakened internationally by schools such as the South Korean high schools which are little more than crammer 'sweat shops', illustrating a Darwinian theory of the survival of the toughest rather than any acceptable educational doctrine, or indeed some of the German *Gymnasiums* and their stripped-bare efficient provision.

Yet it is also increasingly clear that selective schools might possibly be the most effective and certainly the simplest way to educate the most able children. This must come with two major provisos. The first is that selective schools in the UK at least need to be radically different from the old grammar schools. The second proviso is that an acceptable alternative is the creation of a truly separate stream for the most able in a non-selective school.

The first reason for seeing selective schools as an effective answer to the needs of the most able is the oldest. Schools such as the Raffles Institution and New York's NEST+m school, and the Village East Gifted Scheme, are pure antidotes to the sweatshop/exam factory image and show just how good specialist schooling for the most able can be. Such schools may ignore 70% or more of the school populace who cannot attend them but they work like a dream for those who do. There are incalculable benefits brought to children by their being educated like-with-like, and the failure of otherwise outstanding all-ability schools to rise above the 'we must all achieve a minimum mark' philosophy and soar into the realm of 'you can achieve at a level we haven't even dreamt of' is a sad reminder that some schools become the fire under the pot, whilst others have the ability to take the lid off.

The second reason for seeing selective schools as the preferred option for the most able is based on many years of research suggesting a very unpalatable fact that may well be politically impossible to do anything about, or even say out loud. That is that a significant proportion of teachers either cannot or will not accept that the most able are truly different children with substantially different needs, who as a result need to be taught in a different way. Some teachers are resolute to the point of dogma that children must not be divided on the basis of their ability. Other teachers cannot seem to adapt their teaching to the free-wheeling roller-coaster ride that the most able require. Given this, it might well make sense to concentrate such teachers as can do it, enjoy it and believe passionately in it together in relevant institutions so that they can share their expertise and enthusiasm.

But what about those not privileged or able enough to attend such places? How can selective schools be justified if their price is to pin the label of second or third class on to so many children?

It is simply wrong to assume that to create a selective school automatically means the creation of sump schools. There are numerous schools which achieve huge success despite competition with selective schools. In the final chapter in this book, there is a proposal that a later age of transfer, and free, non-examined entry into the early years of the grammar school would solve at least some of the problems implicit in a grammar school system. The new, unashamedly vocational university technology colleges also help make selective schools a realistic political and cultural possibility, by producing a coherent and viable alternative. Selective schools can lead to the remaining schools being 'bad schools' but they need not do so.

However, selective schools are clearly not the only way to organize a fair deal for able children. Most countries which have a form of effective provision for their most able do not use academically selective schools. An outstanding example of a scheme-within-a-scheme is the Australian SHIP programme, which threatens nobody and helps all pupils. If a fair deal for the most able is to be provided without specialist schools, then it is necessary to offer highly specialist provision within non-selective schools, along the lines of the SHIP scheme but extended in terms of the academic years it covers and dovetailed into university education.

Difficulties faced

Neither specialist schools nor in-school schemes will protect countries or systems from attack for their G&T programmes or stop attacks on those programmes. In a recession, provision for the most able is often the first thing to go, on the fallacious grounds that intelligence will always win through, though as with any other talent or skill it needs both encouragement and training. Cash provision for the most able is usually linked to a crisis, as in a negative report, a disastrous slide down the ubiquitous PISA tables or a failure to produce enough scientists or mathematicians.

Teaching the most able has also suffered because it has traditionally focused on purely academic intelligence, and perhaps tended to neglect both social and emotional development and the fostering of creativity, civic responsibility and leadership skills. The gold standard for the new vision of the most able that includes these other dimensions is the outstanding Singaporean Raffles Diploma, but the move towards a much wider (and healthier) definition of what and how the most able should be taught unfortunately makes it harder to deliver, in terms of time, money and the skills set of teachers. The traditional grammar school, *Lycée* or *Gymnasium* education could be comparatively cheap and cheerful, requiring little more than a graduate teacher to turn up for lessons and lecture the willing students. As ever, increasing standards and a diversity of provision that recognizes sport, creativity and social awareness brings increasing cost.

That is not all. In at least two instances, the commitment of teachers to schemes for helping the most able is abused, in the sense that there is no central funding offered, but rather schools scrimp and save from their other budgets to subsidize the provision. The central authority does not feel its unwillingness to fund the schemes stops it from basking in the glory reflected from them. Too much of the best provision for the most able in the world depends on the commitment and energy of individuals and is not institutionalized in any manner that guarantees its continuation beyond the career of the individual.

Most of all, the cause of the most able lacks a champion, a flagship organization or an individual to fight for it. The academics in the field are few in number, are quite inward-looking and spend far too much time on the issue of how to determine ability, fighting ideological wars and proving how elitist they are not. Many are self-referential, in the manner of academics the world over, and lack experience in teaching or indeed of children. Professor Joe Renzulli is one of the few to have crossed international boundaries and spoken directly to teachers, but even he is a prophet not always known in his own time. Charities such as NAGC (National Association for Gifted Children) fight manfully for gifted children but inevitably lack the bite and clout of a government agency. Heads of schools that specialize in able children are a beleaguered minority, and very few educational or political careers are made by nailing one's flag to the good ship 'Most Able'.

At the heart of the ills affecting the issue of teaching the most able is a rising tide very different from that which lifts all ships. It is the rising tide of an unthinking egalitarianism which has taken the priceless doctrine of equal opportunity and turned it into an ideology that states that all children must only have the same opportunity. It is an ideology that thinks the way to improve educational systems that do not achieve high standards at the lower end is to dismantle the schools that succeed at the top.

The importance of specialist provision

So why should education systems provide specialist provision for their most able pupils? Advocates of such provision tend to place in the vanguard of their army the argument that high ability is a special need just like any other, and the job of any self-respecting educational system is to realize the needs of every child. Arguments such as this are the flavour of the decade, but there are many others. Among the most potent, but also one of the least-often stated, is a variation of the rising tide argument. The qualities that make a good and successful teacher of the most able are respect for pupils as intellectual equals, a high level of subject knowledge, commitment to Individual or Personalized Learning Programmes, flexibility and willingness to follow the flow and perhaps even the capacity to take risks. Such teaching is of benefit to every pupil in a school and is the perfect antidote to the 'C-grade-or-bust' philosophy that bedevils English schools in particular.

In western culture, obsessed as it sometimes is with a definition of the teacher as a social worker, it is also sometimes seen as distasteful to see the economic value of the gifted child, a value not lost on some other cultures. At a time when increasingly the earnings of western societies depend on a knowledge economy rather than a manufacturing economy, the potential for knowledge has never been more important economically. It is a rich ore mined most easily from the most able.

It is also a common mistake to see this mining and refining of knowledge as something that can be started at age 18. It cannot. Indeed, it can have been driven out sometimes by the time the child starts school at age 5.

A second misconception is that academically selective education is limited to the production of those skilled in the sciences. Just to take one small sector of the arts, two of the most celebrated theatre directors in the UK, Sir Nick Hytner and Sir Trevor Nunn, attended grammar schools, one private and one state, as did Sir David Frost (state) who was as influential in the media as Hytner and Nunn have been in the theatre. The most able have a powerful cultural value that is frequently of economic value as well.

There is a final point which, it could be argued, is the most significant one to arise as a result of the research that went into this text. We can (and do) argue endlessly about types of school for and methods of teaching the most able. The fact is that a single teacher stuck in the bush teaching a class of 50 under a tree with the nearest computer a hundred miles away can make a significant difference to the educational development of an able child, if the will is there.

If the will is there. In too many schools, it is not. Too many people simply do not care enough about educating our most able children, to the lasting detriment of those children and the society of which they are a member.

The most able pupils in our schools are our most valuable natural resource. We ignore them or take them for granted at our and society's peril.

18

A Proposal for the UK

Key points

- There is a viable and affordable scheme utilizing worldwide best practice that would place the UK as a world leader in educating the most able.
- There is a second, more radical and more expensive scheme that would transform UK education for all pupils.

It would be perfectly possible for the UK to be a world leader in the education of the most able, if it willed it so. Some of the steps needed to make it so are not expensive.

At the lower end of expense, education of the most able lacks a champion, as it does in most of the world. Such a champion must have guaranteed access to the corridors of power, which means, in effect, full access to the Prime Minister, to the various Ministers of Education and, crucially, to the senior civil servants and the decision-making process in the Department of Education, or whatever the name of the day is for it. Successive governments have appointed a Czar for just about everything else; it must also make a senior appointment of someone who is able to lobby at the highest levels of government, education and commerce for the interests of G&T children in the UK. The post needs to differ in one crucial area from other Czars. This Czar needs teeth, and the only teeth likely to work are a degree of control over the inspection process. This would require each school in the country to have a programme for the gifted and talented, and for this to be separately assessed rather than simply absorbed into a general report. It would require inspectors to be trained in this specialist field, and for assessment to be based on actual eyeball-to-eyeball experience of the programme on offer, rather than the current fashion for virtual inspection measured by ticks in a box based on paper submissions, rather than sight of actual lessons. However, inspection of G&T provision need not take place at the same time as a regular inspection, in the same manner as inspection of boarding provision can take place separately.

An interesting variation on a conventional inspection regime would be to make it mandatory for schools who claimed to offer a programme for the gifted and talented to request and satisfy the needs of inspection before they were allowed to claim to offer it. That way, a school that did not rate highly the teaching of the most able would at least have to declare that as a fact, and justify it to their consumers if need be. It would also stop the nonsense of some schools which believe that pinning a label to a teacher of 'Head/Director of Gifted and Talented' is the same as having a viable programme.

However, it is not top-down legislation that will create a world-class system. Teachers are the beginning, middle and end of any successful programme. Any institution offering teacher training needs to be mandated to offer courses in teaching the most able, preferably such courses being compulsory for all trainee teachers. After all, every teacher in the world will face gifted and talented children in their classes. A clear career path needs to be carved out for teachers specializing in the field. A major 'official' internet forum should be set up on which all teachers with an interest in teaching the most able can talk, discuss and exchange good practice, with the British Council and the Foreign Office enrolled to make this forum international and free at the point of access at the earliest possible opportunity. It is not difficult to imagine that some of the leading educational publishers in the world might wish to sponsor such a site. The skeleton of an excellent system already exists in the University of Warwick's IGGY (International Gateway for Gifted Youth) scheme and the London Gifted and Talented site.

The hidden army of post-graduates must be utilized to run morning or afternoon master classes for the gifted and talented. Universities should be encouraged to offer subject-refresher courses, where teachers can acquaint themselves with the latest developments in their academic subject, and more links offered to bridge the Grand Canyon gap that has opened up between our schools and our universities. As one example, more teachers should be encouraged to complete Master's degrees or PhDs in their academic subject, rather than in 'Education' or 'Management', and more places made available. Schools should be urged to form clusters and pool their resources for teaching the most able, including encouraging teachers from cluster schools to meet regularly. An overall post of co-ordinator for each cluster needs to be established.

Instead of treating academically selective schools as leading figures in the existence and creation of educational apartheid, such schools – maintained and private – should be encouraged to throw their doors open and invite teachers in mixed-ability schools to observe lessons where the whole class counts as gifted and talented, and teachers have evolved styles and techniques to cope accordingly.

As for schools, setting and streaming need to be stood down from the naughty corner and become standard in maths, the sciences and modern languages. It also needs to be recognized that it is never too early to start. The UK should import the New Zealand concept of 'One-Day School' but apply it to primary years rather than secondary. If this is then fed into an application of the Australian SHIP scheme in secondary years, the UK would indeed be up and running in its provision for the most able. A key feature of the 'One-Day School' system and the SHIP scheme is that they need cost little extra money if schools realize that the most able can speed through the curriculum in less time and so free up teacher time that can be spent on such schemes.

If there is one lesson to be learned from international experience, apart from the all-importance of the teacher, it is the need to involve parents in any successful scheme for the most able. Such partnerships have three strands. First, it has been shown that parents can play an effective role in the identification of the most able. Second, parental support for the child in a scheme is essential. Third, there is an extent to which parents need to be educated, be it the highly aspirational parents who need to be told to hold off every now and again and let their child have some fun, or the family who have never had one of their own go to university to be gently reminded that their child will need a quiet room to do homework in, where the TV is not playing. It would not require a genius to devise a CPGC (Consortium for Parents of Gifted Children) programme for parents of the most able children in the UK that took the best of the Hungarian Genius Program and the work of a charity such as the NAGC.

A notch-up in terms of expense would be the formation of a new NAGTY, based on the Hong Kong Academy, the existence of which would greatly help the CPGC and Internet Gateway proposed above. Some sense would need to be knocked into the concept before its launch, instead of the lack of it being used to knock it to pieces in its early years, as happened with NAGTY. The UK would have to decide just who constituted the most able, with the top 15% of the cohort the best bet, based on international practice. Its four arms would aim to provide resources and support for children, their parents and teachers, and commission and publish research. The latter would be quasi-commercial, provided free to UK maintained schools but at a charge to overseas customers.

The radical option

All the above could be achieved at relatively little cost. It is doubtful that we shall find a government with both the money and the will to mount the radical change that is needed to give the UK a world-class education for all its children, not just the most able. It is not a viable part of any such change simply to bring back grammar schools across the UK on the old lines. Too much water has flown under the bridge, and too much blood spilt into it, for us just to put the clock back. The 11–18 grammar school system has been all but demolished once already, and to bring it back would be to declare the outbreak of full-scale war all over again, a war that the long-suffering UK educational system cannot afford, financially or emotionally.

Yet there is a radical change to our system that could allow a form of the grammar school to return. Under this system, the major age of choice and transfer for a child would be at age 14. This is far more sensible than age 11, which in any event we know produces a serious dip in school performance among many children. At 14, the child is also much more in a position to exercise some personal choice as to the path they follow. Following a new School Graduation Certificate taken at age 14 and guaranteeing basic literacy, numeracy and technological skills, a child would need to pass this to move on to the next phase – the choice being between the 'grammar' school and the university technical school on the lines proposed by Lord Kenneth Baker, the latter offering primarily a vocational route into employment at either age 16 or 18, with the 'grammar' schools preparing for university. At all times, the footpaths between the academic and the vocational streams would be kept open, so that no child was imprisoned in either.

A key element in sanitizing the selective school would be that no child was denied a place in the first year of the 'grammar' school, but had to reach minimum agreed standards at the end of each year before being allowed to move on, with the chance to re-sit the year offered for as long as it was wished. If this approach is adopted, no child is denied access to such a school, so entry depends far less on social and economic background or the quality of a child's previous teaching. Each child has access to the teachers, resources and aspirational culture of the school, again regardless of background. Promotion through the system depends on the child's motivation and hard work, and is never barred to them while they wish to continue. In this system, the child who fails – and yes, we do need to reinvent the 'f' word – does so because it becomes clear they have chosen the wrong pathway for them, not because they were born into the wrong family or postcode. Use of compaction and acceleration in the 'grammar' school would lead either to early entry to university at age 16, in a model based on the University of Washington in Seattle's Robinson Center, or to students taking first-year degree modules in their final year of school. Such a scheme does not exclude any of the less costly proposals listed earlier.

English education bears a passing resemblance to an ancient Soyuz Space Station which has had module after module after module added to it over the years, but nothing ever removed. We have grammar schools, 11–16 comprehensive schools, 11–18 comprehensive schools, city academies, free schools, university technical schools, middle schools, sixth form colleges and colleges of further education that serve at least some children of school age. We have single-sex and co-educational schools, state boarding schools and 7% of the nation's children in independent schools. A radical reorganization of the structure of English education might, through simplification, benefit far more than only the most able.

19

The Future: Creativity, Critical Thinking and Mindfulness

Key points

- Narrow definitions of giftedness are increasingly unfashionable around the world and the trend is towards broader educational experiences.
- Critical thinking and thinking skills in general are now seen as an essential companion to traditional subject disciplines.
- Life coaching and mindfulness are similarly coming to be seen as part of and integral to good education for the most able, rather than as an extra or a bonus.

There are three trends in the world which, though largely separate at present, might come together to form a new future for a new philosophy to underpin the education of the most able.

The first is the worldwide rejection of the narrow definition of giftedness that is based on a traditional academic intelligence, and a realization that such intelligence can benefit and be enhanced by the application of other skills. Though there is a moral element in this trend, it is also pragmatic. It reflects the fact that skills and knowledge traditionally acquired through a fast-lane, hard-driving and selective academic education are not always those that guarantee success in a modern world dominated by technological and other changes and challenges. Creativity, flair and imagination are now in demand economically, as well as artistically and culturally. The inventor of the new machine is seen as more valuable than its mere manufacturer. We have seen how Singapore has sought to broaden both its definition and its treatment of the most able children, and a similar tide is lapping even at the shores of the South Korean high school. The creative classroom is described by one teacher as:

one in which thinking is valued far more than memory, one in which the child expects to make a contribution that is valued and respected ... The teacher is the facilitator, not the only authority with the right answer ... The non-creative classroom by comparison is one in which the teacher is authoritarian, rigid, dominated by time, insensitive to students' emotional needs, unwilling to give of themselves, preoccupied with discipline and the giving of information. (Gilbert & George, 2011: 40–1)

In such a classroom, it is argued, the new knowledge will be formed.

The second trend is the growth in popularity of critical thinking as a discipline taught at schools. This can be seen as merely one aspect of growing interest in cognitive skills, as opposed to the acquisition of hard knowledge. It undoubtedly owes much to the fact that nowadays even a young child is only a few clicks away from acquiring a mass of knowledge that 30 years ago would have required a reader's ticket to one of the world's great libraries. Acquiring knowledge, and even remembering it, has become correspondingly less important than processing knowledge once acquired. The growth in interest in cognitive skills has been boosted by research into the various types of intelligence and how they work. In other words, current fashion is less concerned with what you know and far more concerned with how you use it. This is not so new an idea as some of its proponents claim. Critical thinking is a transferable skill that can cross and harvest all academic disciplines.

A third trend is the growing interest in something that can take many forms but is best described as mindfulness or life coaching. This can be expressed as the increasing focus by some schools on the pursuit of 'happiness' or 'well-being', and has aroused the scorn of some right-wing commentators who do not believe that happiness is something that can be taught but is something acquired through hard work and decent moral values. This particular aspect of the debate is not helpful, as it obscures something actually of great importance, not least of all for our most able pupils. Quite a large number of books have been written on or around this issue, among them *Subliminal: The Revolution of the New Unconscious and What It Teaches Us About Ourselves* by Leonard Mlodinow (2012), and Joseph Lehrer's (2012) *Imagine: How Creativity Works*. These works and others point out that the smartphone, emails, texting and constant access to news and the media create 'noise' that gives people no rest and take out any time for contemplation and thought, the result being a massive loss of creativity. It has long been suggested that the key importance of sleep is the dreaming it allows, with it being dream and not sleep deprivation that drives people mad, and that in terms of pure energy output the brain is as active asleep as it is awake. The recognition that the human brain needs 'down time' has spread to awareness of the importance of sleep but not of the need for the brain to be offline in its waking mode, symbolized by such simple pleasures as taking a long walk or even a long bath without the phone perched on the side. Mindfulness asks students to 'live in the now'. It allows them to banish the fear of how many Facebook friends they might have lost in the last hour or of a forthcoming exam. It banishes the white noise of a modern, technological lifestyle. Wikipedia defines mindfulness in part in the following terms:

> The current research does suggest that mindfulness practices are useful in the treatment of pain, stress, anxiety, depressive relapse, disordered eating, and addiction, among others. Mindfulness has been investigated for its potential benefit for individuals who do not experience these disorders, as well, with positive results. Mindfulness practice improves the immune system and alters activation symmetries in the prefrontal cortex, a change previously associated with an increase in positive affect and a faster recovery from a negative experience. (see http://en.wikipedia.org/wiki/Mindfulness)

Its relevance to the most able lies in its ability to communicate acceptance and hence to reduce to productive levels the very able child's restless search for perfection. Mindfulness is one technique that can soften the relentless, driving specialist school by a broadened curriculum and approach that recognizes the damage done to creativity by modern lifestyles. A variation of mindfulness, which also links to creativity, is sometimes referred to as 'Spiritual Intelligence', or 'SQ', described as:

> an essential component of a holistic approach to life and work [which] finds expression in creativity and all forms of the arts. Antonio Damasio (1994), a neurologist who has studied the links between cognitive and emotional intelligence, believes that spirituality is the 'glue' that holds together our conscious intellect and our intelligent action. (Gilbert & George, 2011: 109)

It is perhaps no accident that some of the best schemes for the most able in the world favour projects chosen wholly or in part by the student. The capacity these give the student to work on their own and to follow their own interests is a form of academic isolation that does not carry the same social skills penalty as a love affair with the screen, yet goes some way to turning down or even switching off the noise that blocks creativity. Emphasis on critical thinking and cognitive skills is also nowhere more marked than in schemes for the most able, suggesting that here too this sector of the school populace is sensitive and responding to the challenge of contemporary life, just as it has responded to changing values and needs to make creativity a prime skill. If we need to justify that change, we only need to remind ourselves that global warming is unlikely to be solved by a traditional application of old knowledge, but rather by a critical thinking and creativity that create new answers.

It is sometimes said that genuinely new teaching only arrives as the third of three phases. First, old knowledge is taught the old way. Second, old knowledge is taught the new way. Third, new knowledge is taught in a new way. It is possible that the third phase, as well as the most exciting future direction for education of the most able, lies in its development of creativity, critical thinking and mindfulness. Not only do schemes based on these three areas offer much for the realization of the talent of the most able: in this instance, the most able have acted as an early warning system, like the flickering candle flame in the coal mine, pointing out early some basic evolutionary needs that will soon percolate down to all children, not just the most able. If this happens, we might at least be able to put to rest the Chinese saying that we always educate our children to meet the world we lived in, not the world they live in. How ironic if the Cinderella of teaching, the most able, should point to the crucial importance of new skills and actually lead the way to major changes in the manner in which we approach the education of all children, whose future will present them with challenges undreamed of 50 years ago.

Bibliography

We have restricted listings to articles and books that we have either quoted from or found useful, and also largely to material written this century.

Articles, abstracts and reports

These are listed by author or, where no author is credited, by sponsor/ agency or, failing both, by title.

Angoff, W.H. (1988) 'The Nature–Nurture Debate, Aptitudes and Group Differences', *American Psychologist*, 43, 713–20.

Bahar, M.F. (2010) 'A Reflection: The Japanese Approach to Gifted and Talented Students', 22 December. Available at: http://fathil.blogspot.co.uk/2010/12/reflection-japanese-approach-to-gifted.html

Bailey, R., Pearce, G., Winstanley, C., Sutherland, M., Smith, C., Stack, N., et al. (2008) 'A Systematic Review of Interventions Aimed at Improving the Educational Achievement of Pupils Identified as Gifted and Talented.' Research Evidence in Education Library. London: EPPI-Centre, Social Science Research Unit, Institute of Education, University of London.

Barber, M., Chijioke, C. and Moursed, M. (2010a) *How the World's Most Improved School Systems Keep Getting Better*. London: McKinsey & Co.

Barber, M., Whelan, F. and Clark, M. (2010b) *Capturing the Leadership Premium: How the World's Top Schools are Building Leadership Capacity for the Future*. London: McKinsey & Co.

Baumeister, R.F., Campbell, J.D., Krueger, J.I. and Vohs, K.D. (2005) 'Exploding the Self-Esteem Myth', *Scientific American*, 292 (1): 84–91.

Beckett, S. (1983) *Worstward Ho!* Novella. Available at: http://www.samuel-beckett.net/w_ho.htm

Blair, C. (2011) 'Salivary Cortisol Mediates Effects of Poverty and Parenting on Executive Functions in Early Childhood', *Child Development*, 82 (6): 1970–84.

Brooks, J. (2010) 'The Challenge of Secondary Transfer: A G&T Perspective', June, Research paper held in possession of the co-authors.

Churchill, W. (1933) '*Marlborough : His Life and Times*'. London: Harrap.

Claxton, G. (2006) 'Expanding the Capacity to Learn: A new end for education?'. Opening Keynote address, British Educational Research Association Annual Conference, 6 September 2006.

Council of Europe (1994) *Recommendation No. 1248 on Education for Gifted Children.* Strasbourg: Council of Europe.

Csermely, P. (2011) 'The Hungarian Talent Support Program – and its European Dimensions', *Hungarian Review*, II (5), 2 September. Available at: http://hungarianreview. com/article/the_hungarian_talent_support_program_-_and_its_european_dimensions

'Curriculum Provision for Exceptionally Able Students' (2010) Report of a CIDREE Collaborative Project (Consortium of Institutions for Development and Research in Education in Europe), March.

D'Alessio, S. (ed.) (2009) 'Gifted Learners: A Survey of Educational Policy and Provision.' European Agency for Development in Special Needs Education. Available at: http:// europa.eu.int/comm/dgs/education_culture/index_en.htm

Department for Children, Schools and Families (DCSF) (2008) 'What Works in Improving the Educational Achievement of Gifted and Talented Pupils: A Systematic Review of Literature'. Research Brief DCSF-EPPI-04–08, September. School of Education, Roehampton University; Scottish Network for Able Pupils; Faculty of Education, University of Glasgow; West Dunbartonshire Council; London Gifted and Talented; EPPI-Centre.

Department for Children, Schools and Families (DCSF)/ACL Consulting (2009) 'National Academy for Gifted and Talented Youth: Evaluation.' Research Report DCSF-RW078.

Department for Education and Science (DES) (2010) *Curriculum Provision for Exceptionally Able Students.* CIDREE.

Department for Education and Skills (DfES) (2007) 'The Characteristics of High Attainers', National Statistics Bulletin, Statistics of Education, June.

Ely, R.D. (1996) 'Making Differences Matter: A New Paradigm for Managing Diversity', *Harvard Business Review*, Sept–Oct: 79–80.

Eriksson, G. (2014) 'Lessons from the Best: How Top Scoring Countries Meet the Needs of their Gifted Students', UCF ADAGE/FLAG Professional Development, 15 March.

Ford, D.Y. and Harris, J.J. (1990) 'On Discovering the Hidden Treasure of Gifted and Talented African-American Students', *Roeper Review*, 13 (1): 27–32.

Freeman, J., Raffan, J. and Warwick, I. (2010) *Worldwide Provision to Develop Gifts and Talents: An International Survey.* Reading: CfBT Educational Trust.

Gagné, F. (1999) 'My Convictions about the Nature of Abilities, Gifts, and Talents', *Journal for the Education of the Gifted*, 22, 109–36.

Gifted Phoenix (2011) 'Are Leonardo Schools a Good Model of Gifted Education?'. Blog, 'giftedphoenix', 6 February.

Grossenbacher, S. and Vogelli, U. (n.d.) *Support Measures for Gifted and Talented Children in Switzerland.* Aarau: SCCRE.

Heller, K.A. and Ziegler, A. (1996) 'Gender Differences in Mathematics and Natural Sciences: Can Attributional Retraining Improve the Performance of Gifted Females?', *Gifted Child Quarterly*, 41, 200–10.

Jarvis, J.M. and Henderson, L. (2011) 'Defining a Coordinated Approach to Gifted Education.' Paper presented at the Malaysia–Australia Gifted Education Forum in Kuala Lumpur, June.

Jessrdio, D. (2011) 'Righting the Balance: Where "Excellence in Schools" Outcomes is Found.' Unpublished paper.

Koshy, V., Mitchell, C. and Williams, M. (2006) 'Nurturing Gifted and Talented Children at Key Stage 1: A Report of Action Research Projects.' Department for Education and Skills, Research Brief No. RB741, May.

Kulik, J.A. (1992) *An Analysis of the Research on Ability Grouping: Historical and Contemporary Perspectives*. Storrs, CT: The National Research Center on the Gifted and Talented, University of Connecticut.

Lambert, M. (2006) 'Evaluation of "Advanced Learning Centres" for Gifted and Talented Pupils.' Department for Education and Skills, Research Brief No. RB742.

Lehmann, R.L. (2002) 'Differentiating the Curriculum: What Difference Does it Make?' Paper prepared for AERA Annual Meeting, University of Minnesota.

Martin, L.T., Burns, R.M. and Schonlau, M. (2010) 'Mental Disorders among Gifted and Non-Gifted Youth: A Selected Review of the Epidemiologic Literature', *Gifted Child Quarterly*, 54, 31–41.

Meaney, M.J. (2002) 'Maternal Care, Gene Expression, and the Transmission of Individual Differences in Stress Reactivity across Generations', *Annual Review of Neuroscience*, 24: 1161–92.

Mickelson, R. (1990) 'The Attitude–Achievement Paradox among Black Adolescents', *JSTOR: Sociology of Education*, 53 (1): 44–61.

Miraca, U.M.G. and Van Vliet, H.E. (n.d.) *Radical Acceleration of Highly Gifted Children: An Annotated Bibliography of International Research on Highly Gifted Young People who Graduate from High School Three or More Years Early*. Sydney: Gifted Education Research, Resource and Information Centre, University of New South Wales.

Neihart, M., Reiss, S.M., Robinson, N.M. and Moon, S.M. (eds) (2002) *The Social and Emotional Development of Gifted Children*. Texas: Prufrock Press.

Noble, K.D. and Childers, S.A. (forthcoming) 'Swimming in Deep Waters: Twenty Years of Research about Early University Entrance at the University of Washington', in L. Shavinina (ed.) *International Handbook of Gifted Education*. Seattle, WA: Halbert and Nancy Robinson Center for Young Scholars, University of Washington.

Office for Standards in Education (Ofsted) (2003) *The Education of Six Year Olds in England, Denmark and Finland: An International Comparative Study*. London: Ofsted.

Office for Standards in Education (Ofsted) (2009) *Gifted and Talented Children in Schools, Aged 15–18*. Report no. 090132, December. Manchester: Ofsted.

Office for Standards in Education (Ofsted) (2013) *The Most Able Students: Are They Doing as Well as they Should in our Non-Selective Secondary Schools?* London: Ofsted.

PISA (2010) *PISA 2009 Results: Executive Summary*. Paris: OECD. Available at: www.oecd.org/pisa/pisaproducts/46619703.pdf

PISA (2012) *Results in Focus: What 15-year-olds Know and What They Can Do with What They Know.* Paris: OECD. Available at: www.oecd.org/pisa/keyfindings/pisa-2012-results-overview.pdf

Reay, D. (2004) 'Education and Cultural Capital: The Implications of Changing Trends in Education Policies', *Cultural Trends*, 13 (2): 73–86.

Reis, S.M. and McCoach, D.B. (2000) 'The Underachievement of Gifted Students: What do we know and where do we go?', *Gifted Child Quarterly*, 44: 158–70.

Renzulli, J.S., Smith, L.H. and Reiss, S.M. (1982) 'Curriculum Compacting: An Essential Strategy for Working with Gifted Students', *The Elementary School Journal*, 82 (3), Special Issue: Gifted Education, January, pp. 185–94.

Riggall, A. (ed.) (2010) 'Young, Gifted and Talented: Journeys through Australia, China, South Africa and the United States of America.' CfBT Education Trust.

Sahlgren, G.H. (2010) 'Schooling for Money: Swedish Education Reform and the Role of the Profit Motive.' Web publication, IEA.

Slavin, R. (1990) 'Achievement Effects of Ability Grouping in Secondary Schools: A Best-Evidence Synthesis', *Review of Educational Research*, 60 (3): 471–99.

Smithers, A. and Robinson, P. (2012) *Educating the Highly Able.* Report, July. London: Sutton Trust.

Stollers, P. and McPhee, A.D. (2002) 'Some Perspectives on Musical Gift and Musical Intelligence', *British Journal of Music Education*, 19 (1) 89–102.

Sutton Trust (2008) *Wasted Talent? Attrition Rates of High-Achieving Pupils Between School and University.* Report, June. London: Sutton Trust.

World Council for Gifted and Talented Children (Various) *Gifted and Talented International (GTI).* A peer-reviewed journal, published twice a year.

World Council for Gifted and Talented Children (Various) *Yearbook of the World Council for Gifted and Talented Children.* New York: Trillium Press.

Yanqing, Z. (n.d.) 'Theory and Study about the Development of the Good Personality Qualities of Gifted and Talented Children.' Unpublished, undated paper presented to authors. No. 8 Middle School, Beijing.

Yun Dai, D. and Sternberg, R.J. (eds) (2004) *Motivation, Emotion, and Cognition: Integrative Perspectives on Intellectual Functioning and Development.* Hillsdale, NJ: Lawrence Erlbaum Associates.

Zagorsky, J.L. (2007) 'Do You Have to be Smart to be Rich? The Impact of IQ on Wealth, Income and Financial Distress', *Intelligence*, 35, 489–501.

Books

Ambrose, D. and Cross, T. (eds) (2009) *Morality, Ethics and Gifted Minds.* New York: Springer.

Ambrose, D., Sternberg, R.J. and Sriraman, B. (eds) (2012) *Confronting Dogmatism in Gifted Education.* New York: Routledge.

Baines, E., Adey, P. and Dillon, J. (eds) (2012) *Bad Education: Debunking Myths in Education – Grouping Pupils by Ability.* Oxford: Oxford University Press.

Balchin, T., Hymer, B. and Matthews, D.J. (eds) (2009) *The Routledge International Companion to Gifted Education.* London: Routledge.

Banks, A.J. and McGee Banks, C.A. (eds) (2010) *Multicultural Education: Issues and Perspectives.* New York: John Wiley.

Bauby, J.D. (2008) *The Diving Bell and the Butterfly.* London: Harper Perennial.

Beckett, S. (2006) *Waiting for Godot.* London: Faber & Faber.

Berger, R. (2003) *An Ethic of Excellence.* London: Heinemann Educational Books.

Brouillette, L. (2002) *Charter Schools: Lessons in School Reform.* Mahwah, NJ: Lawrence Erlbaum.

Buckley, J. and Schneider, M. (2007) *Charter Schools: Hope or Hype?* Princeton, NJ: Princeton University Press.

Clarke, C. and Callow, R. (1998) *Educating Able Children.* London: David Fulton.

Claxton, G. (2002) *Building Learning Power: Helping Young People Become Better Learners.* Bristol: TLO.

Claxton, G. and Lucas, B. (2010) *New Kinds of Smart: How the Science of Learnable Intelligence is Changing Education.* Expanding Education Horizons series. Maidenhead/New York: Open University Press/McGraw Hill.

Colangelo, N. and Davis, G.A. (eds) (2003) *Handbook of Gifted Education*, 3rd edition. Boston/New York: Allyn and Bacon.

Csikszentmihalyi, M. (1990) *Flow*: *The Psychology of Optimal Experiences*. New York: Harper and Row.

Davis, G., Rimm, A. and Sylvia, B. (2004) *Education of the Gifted and Talented*, 5th edition. Boston/New York: Pearson.

Dixon, F., Moon, A. and Sydney, M. (eds) (2006) *The Handbook of Secondary Gifted Education.* Waco, TX: Prufrock Press.

Dweck, C. (2006) *Mindset: The New Psychology of Success.* New York: Random House.

Emler, N. (2001) *Esteem: The Costs and Causes of Low Self Worth.* York: York Publishing Services.

Ericsson, K.A. (1996) *The Road to Excellence: The Acquisition of Expert Performance in the Arts and Sciences, Sports and Games.* New York: Lawrence Erlbaum.

Eyre, D. (1997) *Able Children in Ordinary Schools.* London: David Fulton.

Finn, C.E., Manno, B.V. and Vanoureck, G. (2001) *Charter Schools in Action: Renewing Public Education.* Princeton, NJ: Princeton University Press.

Flynn, J.R. (2007) *What is Intelligence?* Cambridge: Cambridge University Press.

Freeman, J. (1996) *Highly Able Boys and Girls.* London: DfEE/NACE.

Freeman, J. (1998) *Educating the Very Able: Current International Research*. London: The Stationery Office.

Freeman, J. (2010) *Gifted Lives: What Happens When Gifted Children Grow Up*. Abingdon: Routledge.

Friedman, R. and Rogers, K.B. (eds) (1998) *Talent in Context: Historical and Social Perspectives on Giftedness*. Washington, DC: American Psychological Association.

Gallagher, J.J. (1985) *Teaching The Gifted Child*, 3rd edition. Boston/London: Allyn & Bacon.

Gardner, H. (1983) *Frames of Mind: The Theory of Multiple Intelligences*. New York: Basic Books. [Fontana Press, London, 1993.]

Gardner, H. (1999a) *Intelligence Reframed: Multiple Intelligences for the 21st Century*. New York: Basic Books.

Gardner, H. (1999b) *The Disciplined Mind: Beyond Facts and Standardised Texts – The K-12 Education That Every Child Deserves*. New York: Simon and Schuster/Penguin Putnam.

Geake, J.G. (2009) *The Brain at School: Applications of Neuroscience in the Classroom*. London: McGraw Hill.

Gilbert, I. and George, D. (eds) (2011) *Young, Gifted and Bored*. Camarthen: Crown House Publishing.

Gladwell, M. (2009) *Outliers: The Story of Success*. London: Little, Brown and Co.

Goodhew, G. (2009) *Meeting the Needs of Gifted and Talented Students*. London/New York: Continuum Press.

Gross, M.U.M. (2004) *Exceptionally Gifted Children*, 2nd edition. London: Routledge Falmer.

Handy, C. (1994) *The Empty Raincoat: Making Sense of the Future*. London: Random House.

Hart, B. and Risley, T. (2003) *Meaningful Differences in the Everyday Experience of Young American Children*. Baltimore, MD: Brookes Publishing.

Heller, K.A., Monks, F.J., Sternberg, R.J. and Subotnik, R.F. (eds) (2000) *International Handbook of Giftedness and Talent*, 2nd edition. Amsterdam/Oxford: Elsevier.

Herrnstein, R.J. and Murray, C. (1994) *The Bell Curve: Intelligence and Class Structure in American Life*. New York: Free Press.

Horowitz, F., Subotnik, R. and Matthews, D. (eds) (2009) *The Development of Giftedness and Talent across the Lifespan*. Washington, DC: American Psychological Association.

Hughes, T. (2008) *Tom Brown's Schooldays*. Oxford's World Classics. Oxford/New York: Oxford University Press.

Hunt, N. and Marshall, K. (2002) *Exceptional Children and Youth*, 3rd edition. Boston/New York: Houghton Mifflin Co.

Karnes, F.A. and Bean, S.M. (2005) *Methods and Materials for Teaching the Gifted*, 2nd edition. Waco, TX: Prufrock Press.

Lehrer, J. (2012) *Imagine: How Creativity Works.* Edinburgh: Canongate Books.

Lucas, B. and Claxton, G. (201) *New Kinds of Smart.* Maidenhead: Open University Press.

Mlodinow, L. (2012) *Subliminal: The Revolution of the New Unconscious and What It Teaches Us About Ourselves.* London: Penguin.

Monks, F.J. and Pfluger, R. (2005) *Gifted Education in 21 European Countries: Inventory and Perspective.* Germany: BMBF.

Montgomery, D. (ed.) (2009) *Able, Gifted and Talented Underachievers.* Chichester: Wiley-Blackwell.

Nathan, J. (1999) *Charter Schools: Creating Hope and Opportunity for American Education.* San Francisco: Jossey-Bass.

Oakes, J. and Goodland, J. (2012) *Keeping Track: How Schools Structure Inequality.* Yale, CT: Yale University Press.

Ogbu, J. (1978) *Minority Education and Caste: The American Educational System in Cross-Cultural Perspective.* New York: Academic Press.

Otto, B. (2006) *Language Development in Early Childhood.* London: Pearson.

Owens, R.E., Jr. (2012) *Language Development: An Introduction.* Boston: Pearson, pp. 130–5.

Perrett, Y. and Wills, L. (2011) *Journeys in Gifted Education by Some Who Have Made their Mark.* Abingdon: NACE.

Pfeiffer, S.I. (ed.) (2008) *Handbook of Giftedness in Children: Psychoeducational Theory, Research and Best Practices.* New York: Springer.

Polyzoi, E. and Klassen, C. F. (eds) (2009) *Reaching Gifted and Talented Children: Global Initiatives.* The World Council for Gifted and Talented Children (Raporteurs report). world.gifted.org.

Riordan, J. (ed.) (1988) *Soviet Education: The Gifted and the Handicapped.* London: Routledge.

Robinson, A., Shore, B.S. and Enersen, D.L. (2007) *Best Practices in Gifted Education.* Waco, TX: Prufrock Press.

Seligman, M. (1991) *Learned Optimism.* New York: A. A. Knopf.

Shavinina, L.V. (ed.) (2009) *International Handbook on Giftedness.* New York: Springer.

Sontag, C. (2009) *The (Almost) Forgotten 5% Rising Interest in the World's Top Performing Students.* Regensburg: Department for School Research, School Development and Evaluation, University of Regensburg, Germany.

Sternberg, R.J. and Davidson, J.H. (eds) (2005) *Conceptions of Giftedness.* Cambridge: Cambridge University Press.

Sutton Trust (2011) *'Degrees of Success: University Chances by Individual Schools'.* London: Sutton Trust.

Sutton Trust (n.d.) *The Impact of the Sutton Trust's Summer Schools : A Summary.* London: Sutton Trust.

Taylor, R.L. (2000) *Assessment of Exceptional Students: Educational and Psychological Procedures,* 5th edition. Boston/London: Allyn & Bacon.

Templeton National Report on Education (2004) *A Nation Deceived.*

Thompson, R. and Thompson, A. (2012) *'Gifted! The Story of a Teenage Genius'.* London: Creative Space.

Tough, P. (2013) *How Children Succeed: Grit, Curiosity and the Hidden Power of Character.* Boston/New York: Mariner Books.

VanTassel-Baska, J.L. and Stambaugh, T. (2006) *Comprehensive Curriculum for Gifted Learners,* 3rd edition. Boston, MA: Pearson.

Vygotsky, L.S. (1978) *Mind in Society: The Development of Higher Psychological Processes.* Cambridge, MA: MIT Press.

Wallace, B. and Eriksson, G. (eds) (2006) *Diversity in Gifted Education: International Perspectives on Global Issues.* London: Routledge.

Winner, E. (1996) *Gifted Children: Myths and Realities.* New York: Basic Books.

Winstanley, C. (2004) *Too Clever by Half: A Fair Deal for Gifted Children.* Stoke-on-Trent: Trentham.

Index